REVOLUTIONARIES

REVOLUTIONARIES

CONTEMPORARY ESSAYS

E. J. HOBSBAWM

WEIDENFELD AND NICOLSON
London

ISBN 0 297 76549 3

Made and printed in Great Britain by The Garden City Press Limited, Letchworth, Hertfordshire SG6 1JS

CONTENTS

PREFACE vii

I COMMUNISTS

1 Problems of Communist History 3
2 Radicalism and Revolution in Britain 11
3 French Communism 16
4 Intellectuals and Communism 25
5 The Dark Years of Italian Communism 31
6 Confronting Defeat: The German Communist Party 43

II ANARCHISTS

7 Bolshevism and the Anarchists 57
8 The Spanish Background 71
9 Reflections on Anarchism 82

III MARXISM

10 Karl Marx and the British Labour Movement 95
11 The Dialogue on Marxism 109
12 Lenin and the 'Aristocracy of Labour' 121
13 Revisionism 130
14 The Principle of Hope 136
15 The Structure of Capital 142
16 Karl Korsch 153

IV SOLDIERS AND GUERRILLAS

17 Vietnam and the Dynamics of Guerrilla War 163
18 Civilians versus Military in Twentieth-Century Politics 177
19 Coup d'État 192

V INSURRECTIONARIES AND REVOLUTION

20 Hannah Arendt on Revolution 201
21 The Rules of Violence 209

22 Revolution and Sex 216
23 Cities and Insurrections 220
24 May 1968 234
25 Intellectuals and the Class Struggle 245

INDEX 267

PREFACE

This book consists of essays on a number of related subjects. The first part deals with the history of communism and communist parties, mainly in the period of the Communist International. The second part deals with anarchism, a movement in which interest has revived of late, the third part with various aspects of the international debate on Marx and marxism, which has been lively since the middle 1950s. It contains some footnotes to Marx and Lenin, but consists chiefly of comments on some rediscovered old and some new marxist writers, and on the debates to which they have given rise. Finally a number of topics are considered which can be loosely grouped under the heading of 'violent politics' – revolution, insurrection, guerrillas, coups d'état and such like.

Writers choose some subjects and have others chosen for them. The great majority of those in this volume have been chosen for me, partly by those who invited me to give various lectures but mainly by editors who commissioned them in the form of book-review essays. No doubt they thought that a marxist of the 'old left' ought to know something about the subject-matter of the books they sent me and might be interested in expressing his views about them. The second assumption is evidently correct, but the first cannot be made without substantial qualifications. Over the years I have acquired some knowledge both of marxist ideas and of the history of recent revolutions and revolutionary movements but, speaking as a historian, these are not fields in which I would claim professional expertise. Much of what I know comes from the authors reviewed here. Little is based on first-hand research. The most I can claim is to have kept my eyes open during the past decades as a modest participant, or what the anthropologists call a 'participant observer', to have listened to friends in numerous countries who know a great deal more than I, and to have had at least a tourist's view of some of the activities with which these essays deal.

Still, first-hand observation ought to count for something. If the results of reflecting upon it can be communicated, it may perhaps help those who have not lived through the era which formed my generation – the period during which the hopes and fears of revolutionaries were inseparable from the fortunes of the Russian revolution – to understand an important part of twentieth-century history. That is why I have tried to be as lucid as possible about the movements of that era. As for the more recent episodes discussed here, I have done my best to write about them realistically though not dispassionately. It is improbable that the lessons which may be drawn from such an analysis will be learned, but the least a historian can do is to provide material for education.

The object of these essays is not to add to an already vast literature of polemic and counter-polemic, accusation and justification. It is not even certain whether the questions which haunt middle-aged and elderly men and women who gave themselves – and others – to their cause, will strike their less committed contemporaries or their younger successors as equally important. Their object is to assist clarification and understanding. What the author's views are on the polemical issues discussed, should be clear. However, it would be a pity if interest in these papers were confined only to those who agree with them.

The dates of writing of the essays have been indicated. Three have not been published before (nos 5, 18 and 25). A small part of the first appeared as a review in the *Times Literary Supplement*, the others were given respectively as lectures in Montreal and London. The rest of the chapters first appeared in English in the *Times Literary Supplement*, the *New York Review of Books*, the New York *Nation*, *New Society*, *New Statesman*, *New Left Review*, *Marxism Today*, *The Spokesman*, *Monthly Review*, *History and Theory* and *Architectural Design*. Chapter 7 appeared in *Anarchici e Anarchia nel Mondo Contemporaneo* (Fondazione Luigi Einaudi, Turin, 1971). Minor changes have been made in almost all, but some have been more or less extensively rewritten. My thanks are due to the publishers for permission to reprint.

E.J.HOBSBAWM

I
COMMUNISTS

I

PROBLEMS OF COMMUNIST HISTORY

We are today at the end of that historical epoch in the development of socialism which began with the collapse of the Second International in 1914 and the victory of the bolsheviks in October 1917. This is therefore a suitable time to survey the history of the communist parties which were the characteristic and dominant forms of the revolutionary movement in this era. The task is difficult because communist party historiography has special complications, but also for wider reasons.

Each communist party was the child of the marriage of two ill-assorted partners, a national left and the October revolution. That marriage was based both on love and convenience. For anyone whose political memories go back no farther than Khruschev's denunciation of Stalin, or the Sino-Soviet split, it is almost impossible to conceive what the October revolution meant to those who are now middle-aged and old. It was the first proletarian revolution, the first regime in history to set about the construction of the socialist order, the proof both of the profundity of the contradictions of capitalism, which produced wars and slumps, and of the possibility – the *certainty* – that socialist revolution would succeed. It was the beginning of world revolution. It was the beginning of the new world. Only the naïve believed that Russia was the workers' paradise, but even among the sophisticated it enjoyed the general indulgence which the left of the 1960s now gives only to revolutionary regimes in some small countries, such as Cuba and Vietnam. At the same time the decision of revolutionaries in other countries to adopt the bolshevik model of organization, to subordinate themselves to a bolshevik international (i.e. eventually to the CPSU and Stalin), was due not only to natural enthusiasm, but also to the evident failure of all alternative forms of organization, strategy and tactics. Social democracy and anarcho-syndicalism had failed, while Lenin had succeeded. It seemed sensible to follow the recipe of success.

The element of rational calculation increasingly prevailed, after the ebbing of what had, in the years after 1917, looked like the tide of global revolution. It is, of course, almost impossible to separate it in practice from the passionate and total loyalty which individual communists felt to their cause, which was equated with their party, which in turn meant loyalty to the Communist International and the USSR (i.e. Stalin). Still, whatever their private feelings, it soon became clear that separation from the communist party, whether by expulsion or secession, meant an end to effective revolutionary activity. Bolshevism in the Comintern period did not produce schisms and heresies of practical importance, except in a few remote countries of small global significance, such as Ceylon. Those who left the party were forgotten or ineffective, unless they rejoined the 'reformists' or went into some overtly 'bourgeois' group, in which case they were no longer of interest to revolutionaries, or unless they wrote books which might or might not become influential on the left some thirty years later. The real history of Trotskyism as a political trend in the international communist movement is posthumous. The strongest among such exiled marxists worked quietly in isolation until times changed, the weakest broke under the strain and turned passionately anti-communist, to supply the CIA culture of the 1950s with several militants, the average retreated into the hard shell of sectarianism. The communist movement was not effectively split. Still, it paid a price for its cohesion: a substantial, sometimes an enormous, turnover of members. The joke about the largest party being that of the ex-communists has a basis in fact.

The discovery that communists had little choice about their loyalty to Stalin and the USSR was first made – though perhaps only at the highest levels of the parties – in the middle 1920s. Clear-sighted and unusually strong-minded communist leaders like Palmiro Togliatti soon realized that they could not, *in the interest of their national movement*, afford to oppose whoever came out on top in the CPSU, and tried to explain this to those less in touch with the Moscow scene, such as Gramsci. (Of course even a total willingness to go along with Stalin was no guarantee of political, or for residents of the USSR physical, survival in the 1930s.) Under the circumstances loyalty to Moscow ceased to depend on approval of the Moscow line, but became an operational necessity. That most communists also tried to rationalize this by proving to themselves that Moscow was right at all times is another matter, though it is relevant to the argument, because it confirmed the clear-headed minority in the belief that they would never be able to take their parties with them against Moscow. A British communist who attended the meeting of the leadership in September 1939 which was told that the war was not, after all, supposed to be a people's anti-fascist war but just an imperialist one, recalls saying to himself: 'That's it. There's nothing to be done. An imperialist war it is.' He was right at the time. Nobody bucked Moscow successfully until Tito carried his party against Stalin in 1948 – to Stalin's and a lot of other party leaders' surprise. Still, he was by then not only a leader of a party but also of a nation and a state.

There was, of course, another factor involved: internationalism. Today, when the international communist movement has largely ceased to exist as such, it is hard to recapture the immense strength which its members drew from the consciousness of being soldiers in a single international army, operating, with whatever tactical multiformity and flexibility, a single grand strategy of world revolution. Hence the impossibility of any fundamental or long-term conflict between the interest of a national movement and the International, which was the *real* party, of which the national units were no more than disciplined sections. That strength was based both on realistic argument and moral conviction. What convinced in Lenin was not so much his socio-economic analysis – after all, at a pinch something like his theory of imperialism can be derived from earlier marxist writings – but his palpable genius for organizing a revolutionary party and mastering the tactics and strategy of making revolution. At the same time the Comintern was intended to, and very largely did, give the movement immunity against the terrible collapse of its ideals.

Communists, it was agreed, would never behave like international social democracy in 1914, abandoning its flag to follow the banners of nationalism, into mutual massacre. And, it must be said, they did not. There is something heroic about the British and French CPs in September 1939. Nationalism, political calculation, even common sense, pulled one way, yet they unhesitatingly chose to put the interests of the international movement first. As it happens, they were tragically and absurdly wrong. But their error, or rather that of the Soviet line of the moment, and the politically absurd assumption in Moscow that a given international situation implied the same reactions by very differently situated parties, should not lead us to ridicule the spirit of their action. This is how the socialists of Europe should have acted in 1914 and did not: carrying out the decisions of their International. This is how the communists did act when another world war broke out. It was not their fault that the International should have told them to do something else.

The problem of those who write the history of communist parties is therefore unusually difficult. They must recapture the unique and, among secular movements, unprecedented *temper* of bolshevism, equally remote from the liberalism of most historians and the permissive and self-indulgent activism of most contemporary ultras. There is no understanding it without a grasp of that sense of total devotion which made the party in Auschwitz make its members pay their dues in cigarettes (inconceivably precious and almost impossible to obtain in an extermination camp), which made the cadres accept the order not merely to kill Germans in occupied Paris, but first to acquire, individually, the arms to do so, and which made it virtually unthinkable for them to refuse to return to Moscow even to certain imprisonment or death. There is no understanding either the achievements or the perversions of bolshevism without this, and both have been monumental; and certainly no understanding of the extraordinary success of communism as a system of education for political work.

But the historians must also separate the national elements within communist parties from the international, including those currents within national movements which carried out the international line not because they had to, but because they were in genuine agreement with it. They must separate the genuinely international elements in Comintern policy from those which reflected only the state interests of the USSR or the tactical or other preoccupations of Soviet internal politics. In both national and international policies they must distinguish between those based on knowledge, ignorance or hunch, on marxist analysis (good or bad), on local tradition, the imitation of suitable or unsuitable foreign examples, or sheer trial and error, tactical insight or ideological formula. They must, above all, make up their minds which policies were successful and sensible and which were neither, resisting the temptation to dismiss the Comintern *en bloc* as a failure or a Russian puppet-show.

These problems are particularly difficult for the historian of the British CP because, except for a few brief periods, they appear to be so unimportant in this country. The party was both entirely loyal to Moscow, entirely unwilling to involve itself in Russian or international controversies, and an unquestioned chip off the native working-class block. Its path was not littered with lost or expelled leaders, heresies and deviations. Admittedly it enjoyed the advantage of smallness, which meant that the International did not expect the spectacular results which put such a strain on, say, the German party, and of operating in a country which, even on the most cursory inspection, was unlike most of Europe and the other continents. Being the child, not of a political split in social-democracy, but of the unification of the various groups of the extreme left, which had always operated to some extent outside the Labour Party, it could not be plausibly regarded as an alternative mass party to Labour, at least an immediate alternative. Hence it was left free – indeed it was generally encouraged – to pursue the tasks to which militant British left-wingers would have devoted themselves anyway, and because they were communists, to do so with unusual self-abnegation and efficiency. Indeed initially Lenin was chiefly concerned to discourage the sectarianism and hostility to Labour, to which the native ultra-left was spontaneously drawn. The periods when the international line went against the grain of the national left-wing strategy and tactics (as in 1928–34 and 1939–41) stand out as anomalies in the history of British communism, just because there was so obviously – as there was not in all other countries – such a strategy. So long as there was no realistic prospect of revolution, there was only one TUC and the Labour Party was the only – and still growing – party likely to win the support of the politically conscious workers on a national scale, in practice there was only one realistically conceivable road of socialist advance. The disarray of the left today (inside and outside the Labour Party) is due largely to the fact that these things can no longer be taken for granted and that there are no generally accepted alternative strategies.

Nevertheless, this apparent simplicity of the British communists' situation conceals a number of questions. In the first place, what exactly did the International expect of the British, other than that they should turn themselves into a proper communist party, and – from a not entirely certain date – that they should assist the communist movements in the empire? What precisely was the role of Britain in its general strategy and how did it change? This is by no means clear from the existing historical literature, which is admittedly not of high quality, with rare exceptions.

In the second place, why was the impact of the CP in the 1920s so modest, even by unexacting standards? Its membership was tiny and fluctuating, its successes the reflection partly of the radical and militant mood of the labour movement, partly of the fact that communists still operated largely within the Labour Party or at least with its local support. Not until the 1930s did the CP become, in spite of its modest but growing membership, its electoral weakness and the systematic hostility of the Labour leadership, the effective national left.

Thirdly, what was the base of communist support? Why did it fail, again before the 1930s, to attract any significant body of support among intellectuals, and rapidly shed most of the relatively few it attracted (mostly from the ex-Fabian and guild socialist left)? What was the nature of its unusually strong influence – though not necessarily membership – in Scotland and Wales? What happened in the 1930s to turn the party into what it had not previously been, a body of factory militants?

And of course, there are all the questions which will inevitably be asked about the rightness or wrongness of the party's changing line, and more fundamentally, of this particular type of organization in the context of interwar and post-1945 Britain.

James Klugmann[1] has not seriously tackled any of them. This extremely able and lucid man is clearly capable of writing a satisfactory history of the communist party, and where he feels unconstrained, he does so. Thus he provides the best and clearest account of the formation of the party at present available. Unfortunately he is paralyzed by the impossibility of being both a good historian and a loyal functionary. The only way yet discovered to write a public 'official' history of any organization is

[1] James Klugmann, *History of the Communist Party of Great Britain: Formation and Early Years*, London, 1966.

to hand the material over to one or more professional historians who are sufficiently in sympathy not to do a hatchet job, sufficiently uninvolved not to mind opening cupboards for fear of possible skeletons, and who can, if the worst come to the worst, be officially disavowed. That is, essentially, what the British government did with the official history of the second world war, and the result has been that Webster and Frankland were able to produce a history of the air war which destroys many familiar myths and treads on many service and political toes, but is both scholarly and useful – not least to anyone who wishes to judge or plan strategy. The Italian CP is the only one which has so far chosen this sensible, but to most politicians almost unthinkable, course. Paolo Spriano has therefore been able to write a debatable, but serious and scholarly work.[2] James Klugmann has been able to do neither. He has merely used his considerable gifts to avoid writing a disreputable one.

In doing so he has, I am afraid, wasted much of his time. What, after all, is the use of spending ten years on the sources – including those in Moscow – when the *only* precise references to contemporary unpublished CP sources – give or take one or two – appear to number seven and the *only* references even to printed Communist International sources (including Inprecorr) number less than a dozen in a volume of 370 pages. The rest are substantially references to the published reports, pamphlets and especially periodicals of the CP in this period. In 1921–2 the Presidium of the Comintern discussed Britain thirteen times – more often than any country other than the French, Italian, Hungarian and German parties. One would not have known it from Klugmann's book, whose index lacks all reference to Zinoviev (except in connection with the forged letter bearing his name), Borodin, Petrovsky-Bennet, or, for that matter, so purely British a field of party activity as the Labour Research Department.

An adequate history of the CP cannot be written by systematically avoiding or fudging genuinely controversial issues and matter likely to be regarded as indiscreet or bad public relations within the organization. It cannot even be offset by describing and documenting, more fully than ever before, the activities of the militants. It is interesting to have 160 or so pages on the party's work from 1920 to

[2] Paolo Spriano, *Storia del Partito Comunista Italiano*, vol. 1, *Da Bordiga a Gramsci*, Turin, 1967.

1923, but the basic fact about this period is that recorded in Zinoviev's report to the Fourth World Congress at the end of 1922, namely that 'In no other country, perhaps, does the communist movement make such slow progress', and this fact is not really faced. Even the popular contemporary explanation that this was due to mass unemployment is not seriously discussed. In brief, Klugmann has done some justice to the devoted and often forgotten militants who served the British working class as best they knew how. He has written a textbook for their successors in party schools, with all the clarity and ability which have made his high reputation as a teacher in such courses. He has provided a fair amount of new information, some of which will only be recognized by those very expert at deciphering careful formulations, and little of which – on important matters – is documented. But he has neither written a satisfactory history of the CP nor of the role of the CP in British politics.

(1969)

2

RADICALISM AND REVOLUTION IN BRITAIN

The learned study of communist movements, an academic industry with a large but on the whole disappointing output, has generally been practised by members of two schools, the sectarian and the witch-hunting. They have tended to overlap, thanks to the tendency of many ex-communists to progress from disagreement to total rejection. Broadly speaking, the sectarian historians have been revolutionaries, or at least left-wingers, mostly dissident communists. (The contribution of communist parties to their own history has been muffled and until recent years negligible.) The main purpose of their enquiry has been to discover why communist parties failed to make revolutions, or produced such disconcerting results when they did. Their main occupational weakness has been an inability to stand at a sufficient distance from the polemics and schisms within the movement.

The witch-hunting scholars, whose orthodoxy was not fully formulated until the years of the cold war, saw communist parties as sinister, compulsive, potentially omnipresent bodies, half religion and half plot, which could not be rationally explained because there was no sensible reason for wishing to overthrow the pluralist-liberal society. Consequently they had to be analyzed in terms of the social psychology of deviant individuals and a conspiracy theory of history. The main occupational weakness of this school is that it has little to contribute to its subject. Its basic stereotype is rather like the Victorian one of 'the trades union', and it therefore illuminates those who hold it more than communism.

Mr Newton's rather ambitiously named *The Sociology of British Communism*[1] demonstrates, to the satisfaction of anyone ready to be

[1] Kenneth Newton, *The Sociology of British Communism*, London, 1969.

convinced, that the witch-hunting school has no visible bearing on the British Communist Party. This CP does not consist, and has never consisted to any substantial extent, of deviants or alienated minorities. In so far as its social composition can be discovered – and Mr Newton has collated what information is available – it consists primarily of skilled and semi-skilled workers, largely engineers, builders and miners, and of school teachers who come largely from the same family backgrounds. As in the case of so-called 'traditional radicalism', it is 'not supported by uprooted or unattached individuals, but on the contrary by individuals who are closely connected with their community and its radicalism'. It does not consist of 'authoritarian personalities' similar to fascists, and indeed the conventional myth that the two 'extremes' interchange easily has little basis in fact.

Its activities did not and do not conform to the sociologist's pattern of 'mass movement' ('direct and activistic modes of response' in which 'the focus of attention was remote from personal experience and everyday life'). Whatever the ultimate aims of the party, its militants, in the unions or the unemployed movements between the wars, were passionately concerned with practical matters such as improving the condition of the workers here and now. There is not even evidence that the CP is any more oligarchic than other British parties, that its members pay less attention to inner-party democracy, or have a notably different attitude to their leaders.

In brief, Mr Newton establishes at some length what everyone who has actual experience of British communists knows. They are, sociologically speaking, much what one would expect an activist working-class elite to be, sharing notably 'the persistent attempt at self-improvement through self-education' which is familiar to any student of the cadre of working-class leadership at all periods of British history. They are the kinds of people who have provided labour movements with leadership and a cutting edge at most times. Mr Newton implies that they are in this very like the Labour Party activists, and that the chief reason for the unusual smallness of the British CP is that (until recently) the Labour Party expressed the views of most politically conscious British workers quite satisfactorily. In this he is almost certainly right, though there has always been a working-class left which found it inadequate. This ultra-left is the subject of Mr Kendall's book.

The real question is whether it has constituted or constitutes a 'revolutionary' movement. In so far as the CP is concerned, what is at issue is not its subjective commitment to a fundamental social change, but the nature of the society in which it pursued and pursues its objectives, and the political context of its activities. For the young ultras of 1969, whose idea of revolution is, if not actually to stand on a barricade, then at least to make the same sort of noise as though standing on one, it is plainly not revolutionary and has long ceased to be so. But the question is more serious than that. How far can any party be functionally revolutionary in a country in which a classical revolution is simply not on the agenda, and which lacks even a living tradition of past revolution?

Walter Kendall's enquiry into the left of 1900–21 raises this question in an acute form.[2] The author himself sometimes appears to get lost in the intricacies of sectarian history and spends too much time on the argument that the CP grew not out of the past of the British radical left but out of the international requirements of the Russian bolsheviks. This argument can be briefly dismissed. If anything is clear about the period 1917–21 it is (*a*) that the ultra-left passionately identified itself with the bolsheviks, (*b*) that it consisted of squabbling small groups, (*c*) that most of them wanted nothing more than to become the Communist Party, whatever the Russians wanted, and (*d*) that the natural and sensible course for the Russians was to see that a single unified party emerged. In fact, what happened was pretty much what might have been expected. The largest and most lasting of the independent marxist organizations of the British left, the British Socialist Party, became the main nucleus of the CP, absorbing politically important but numerically small groups of other left-wingers. The Russians used their prestige to knock some of the extreme anti-political sectarianism out of it, though the process of turning it into a 'bolshevik' party did not seriously begin until after Mr Kendall's book ends.

But how far was this radical left revolutionary? How far could it be revolutionary? It is evident from Kendall's very full and scholarly account that only a tiny fraction of the smallish pre-1914 radical left consisted of revolutionaries in the Russian or Irish sense:

[2] Walter Kendall, *The Revolutionary Movement in Britain 1900–21*, London, 1969.

mostly in Scotland, the East End of London (with its Russian connections) and perhaps south Wales. These few score, or at best few hundred, militants played a disproportionately large part in the years 1911–20, when the British labour movement, probably for the first time since the Chartists, showed signs of genuinely rejecting 'the system', including 'politics', the Labour Party and the trade union leadership. To say that it was revolutionary would be misleading.

The immediate reason for failure was that the British left had neither a sense of power nor organizations capable of thinking in terms of power. The rebels merely faced the more modest choice of either capturing the traditional mass organizations of labour from the reformist leadership or refusing to have any truck with them. But the one course, though more fruitful in the long term, lowered the temperature of militancy in the immediate crisis; the other maintained it at the sacrifice of effectiveness.

The south Wales miners – their union was essentially the produce of rank-and-file rebellion – chose the first, with the result that after the great 1915 strike there was no widespread unofficial movement in the pits which could link up with that in industry. But the miners held together, were radicalized *en bloc* (the South Wales Federation even thought of affiliating to the Comintern at one point), elected A.J. Cook in 1924 and pushed the whole of labour into the General Strike – at a time when this had ceased to have much political significance. As Kendall notes rightly, their success 'staved off radical action during the war only to cause it to break out once the war was over'.

The shop stewards, on the other hand, by their very grass roots syndicalism, their distrust of any politics and officialdom, wasted their efforts and produced – as Kendall also points out – a mere supplement to official trade unionism. They expressed rather than led a genuine revolt, though unable to give it effectiveness or even permanence. Hence their movement melted away, leaving behind only a few score valuable recruits to the new CP. 'In 1918', wrote Gallacher, 'we had marched through Glasgow a hundred thousand strong. On 1 May 1924 I led a demonstration through the streets. A hundred was our full muster.'

The trouble about the revolutionary left in stable industrial societies is not that its opportunities never come, but that the normal conditions in which it must operate prevent it from developing the movements likely to seize the rare moments when they are called upon to behave as revolutionaries. The discouraging conclusion to be drawn from Mr Kendall's book is that there is no simple way out of this dilemma ; it is built into the situation. A self-sealing sectarianism is no solution. Nor is a reaction of simple rebellious rejection of all politics and 'bureaucracy'. Being a revolutionary in countries such as ours just happens to be difficult. There is no reason to believe that it will be less difficult in future than it has been in the past.

(1969)

3
FRENCH COMMUNISM

The history of communism in the developed economies of the west has been the history of revolutionary parties in countries without insurrectionary prospects. Such countries may be, and at various times in our century have been, involved in revolutionary activities arising out of the international contradictions of capitalism (e.g. Nazi occupation), or reflecting the glow of fires elsewhere (e.g. in eastern Europe), but their own political roads have not led, or ever looked like leading for more than a fleeting moment, towards the barricades. Neither the two world wars nor the intervening great slump, seriously shook the social basis of any regime between the Pyrenees, the southern border of the Alps, and the North Cape: and it is not easy to imagine more massive blows hitting such a region in the relatively short period of half a century. In eastern Europe – to take the nearest example – the situation has been very different. Here we have in the same period at least four and perhaps five cases of endogenous social revolutions (Russia, Yugoslavia, Albania, Greece,[1] perhaps Bulgaria), not counting temporary but serious upheavals.

Spontaneously or deliberately, the labour movements of the west have had to adapt themselves to this situation, and in doing so they have always run the grave risk of adapting themselves to a permanent and subordinate existence within capitalism. In the period up to 1914 this predicament was to some extent obscured by the refusal of bourgeois regimes to admit them formally or completely into their system of political and economic relations, by the miserable conditions of existence in which most workers lived and the self-contained social universe of an outlaw proletariat, and by the strength of the revolutionary traditions – mainly marxist, but also anarchist – which had formed most labour movements and still

[1] Successful, that is, but for British military intervention and Soviet diplomatic abstention.

powerfully imbued them. In the generation after 1917 it was also partially obscured by the collapse of capitalism into mutual massacre, slump and barbarism, and more specifically by the bolshevik revolution, which was (correctly) seen as the herald of world revolution. In our generation it has emerged with much greater clarity, because of a combination of three factors: the remarkable and unprecedented economic prosperity of the 'west' (including the bulk of its working classes), the disintegration of the Third International – whether in its formal or its informal versions – and the remoteness – both geographical, social and political – of the post-1945 phase of the world revolution from the problems of the developed western countries.[2]

The period before 1914 has passed into history. The Second International collapsed totally, and beyond any chance of revival, and so did the part-rival, part-complementary movement of anarchizing revolutionary trade unionism ('syndicalism'). If we study that period at all for any reason other than academic curiosity, it is simply to help to explain what happened later, and perhaps to seek some clues about the operation of what was then usual, but is now rare, namely single national socialist movements organizationally united but ideologically pluralist. The period of the Third International is still with us, at least in the form of the permanent schism between communist and social-democratic parties, neither of whose patterns of behaviour or traditions can be understood without constant reference to the October revolution. Hence the importance of studies like Annie Kriegel's massive *Origins of French Communism, 1914–20*.[3]

The French Communist Party is in many respects unique. It is one of the few mass communist parties in the 'advanced' economies of the west, and, with the exception of the Italian CP (which operates in a country that came late and incompletely into the 'advanced' sector of the world economy), the only one to have become the majority party within its labour movement. At first sight this poses no great problem. France is the classical country of

[2] I do not say that it ought to be remote; merely that, as a matter of observable fact, the Chinese revolution and the revolutions of national liberation have not impregnated the socialist and communist movements of the west in anything like the same extent that the October revolution did.

[3] A. Kriegel, *Aux Origines du Communisme Français, 1914–20* (2 vols), Paris and The Hague, 1964.

west European revolution, and if the traditions of 1789–94, 1830, 1848 and 1871 will not attract a nation to revolutionary parties, nothing will. Yet on second thoughts the rise of the CP is rather more puzzling. The classical traditions of French revolutionism – even that of the working class – were not marxist and even less leninist, but Jacobin, Blanquist and Proudhonist. The socialist movement of before 1914 was already a German graft on the French tree, and one which took only incompletely in politics and even less in the trade unions. Guesdism, the nearest thing to social democratic orthodoxy, though still some way from it, remained a regional or minority phenomenon. The French CP marked a much more radical 'bolshevization' or russification of the native movement, and one for which there was little foundation in it. Yet this time the graft took. The French Communist Party became and has remained not merely the mass party of most French workers, the main force on the French left, but also a classically 'bolshevik' party. This poses the major problem of its history. Mrs Kriegel does not set out to answer it directly – her two volumes end with the Congress of Tours which founded the party – but she does answer it indirectly, as it were, by a process of eliminating alternative possibilities. The history of the years she has taken as her subject did not complete this elimination. Indeed, one of the main points of her argument is, that the subsequent development of the CP was by no means readily predictable in 1920. Nevertheless, war and post-war cleared a very large area of historically accumulated, but obsolete or impracticable politics.

The impact of the war and the Russian revolution must be traced by parallel enquiries into the evolution of the working class and the loosely organized and sometimes unrepresentative minority which made up the French labour movement. The distinction is important, because the very fragility, instability or narrowness of the French movement may, as she argues, have made the appeal of revolutionary parties after the war greater than in countries in which the labour movement was more representative of the masses. Mrs Kriegel's book tells us comparatively little about this evolution, though it clearly passed through four major phases: a solid reversion to nationalism in 1914, a rapidly growing war weariness from the end of 1916, culminating in the abortive strikes and army mutinies of the spring of 1917, a relapse into inactivity after their failure (but one combined with an increasing influx of workers into labour organizations), and after the end of the war, a rapid and cumulative radicalization, which almost certainly ran *ahead* of the formal labour organizations. Its chief carriers were the demobilized soldiers – the rhythm of gradual demobilization maintained the momentum of radicalization – and the industries (metals and railways) which combined a record of wartime importance with the return of ex-servicemen to their old occupations. Nevertheless, until the end of the war the deep-seated nationalism which is the oldest and strongest tradition of the French left, kept the masses remote from a revolution (including the Russian revolution) which seemed to imply a German victory. Compared with Britain, for instance, the movement of sympathy for the soviets in 1917, was strikingly weak. Only after the armistice had eliminated the choice between patriotism and revolution, could the political radicalization of the French workers proceed unhampered. And when it did, it was dissipated by the failure of their labour movement.

For the labour movement the years from 1914 to 1920 were a succession of defeats, and of historically decisive defeats. 1914 meant the total failure of all sections and all formulae of the earlier movement – both socialist and syndicalist. From early 1915 a modest pacifist-internationalist (but not revolutionary) opposition emerged, though – significantly enough – not on the foundation of the prewar radical left. It failed in 1917, and slowly a revolutionary pro-bolshevik left emerged after the armistice, though – again significantly – it was only very partly based on the pacifist-internationalist 'Zimmerwald' current of 1915–17, many of whose leaders refused to join it. There was at this stage no split in the French labour movement, or at any rate no more divergence than there had always been in it, since the formula of loose unity had been devised in the early 1900s; nor was there a serious prospect of a permanent split. On the contrary, in 1918–19 both the Socialist Party and the General Confederation of Labour appeared once again to have found a basis for unity in a shift to the left – but not the bolshevik left – which criticized but did not disavow the nationalist and class-collaborationist excesses of 1914. Unlike Germany, the war had not split the party. Unlike Britain, the leaders of class collaboration in 1914 (such as Arthur Henderson) did not carry a united party with them into opposition to the war and into a moderate socialism. But like Austria, the former pacifist minority became a majority, without dividing the party.

Of course in the heady atmosphere of world revolution all sections of the movement except the tiny and discredited extreme nationalist right, looked forward to 'revolution' and 'socialism', though it is a moot point whether the battles fought in 1919–20 actually had it as their object. Whatever their object, they all failed. The small ultra-left who dreamed of a western-style proletarian revolution based on 'councils' and equally hostile to Parliament, parties and trade unions, failed in the strikes of the spring of 1919, for it never reached the masses.[4] The solution of libertarian or decentralized communism was eliminated. The political socialists had always put their money on elected socialist governments, and drafted an ambitious programme of what such a government would do. They failed in the autumn of 1919, because the political shift of the electorate to the socialists was disappointingly small; only about 14 per cent, much smaller than in other countries. But for the half-heartedness of the reformist leadership, it would, as Mrs Kriegel proves convincingly, have been considerably more, but even so, an electoral majority was never in sight and thus saved the leadership of the party the probable demonstration that they would have done nothing with it. At all events the reformist road was temporarily barred.

Last, and most seriously, the revolutionary syndicalists – perhaps the strongest purely proletarian tradition of revolution in France – tried and failed in 1920, with the collapse of the great railway strike. The traditional myth of French labour, the revolutionary general strike, was dead. So, more significantly, was revolutionary syndicalism as a serious trend in the French movement.

It was in these circumstances – and only in these circumstances – that the bulk of the French socialist party was prepared to follow Moscow, and even then it did so only with tacit qualifications – 'unreservedly, but without inopportune clarifications', as Mrs Kriegel puts it. It required the reflux of the majority of socialists into the old party shortly after and the elimination of the original CP leadership some years later, to lay the foundation for a real bolshevik party. This is doubtless true, but one may still doubt whether the permanent emergence of a mass CP was as 'accidental' as she suggests.

[4] Mrs Kriegel rightly points out that there was a genuine revolutionary alternative to bolshevism, and one which sought to combine socialism and liberal or libertarian values; but also that its failure, under whatever label it was organized, was total. In fact, it was simply a political non-starter.

In the first place the bankruptcy of the earlier currents and formulae of French socialism was irreversible. What is more, the traditional pride in France as the 'classical' country of European revolution, and French revolutions as international style-setters, which had kept the French movement largely immune to marxism, was broken. The French had failed – lamentably, and for the first time in an era of European revolution – whereas the bolsheviks had succeeded. In any future French extreme left Lenin had to supplement the failing vigour of Robespierre, Blanqui or Proudhon. The way for a transformation of French revolutionaries was, for the first time, open. But in the epoch of the Third International such a transformation excluded any maintenance of the prewar formulae of socialist unity. A communist left would be bolshevik or it would not exist at all.

In the second place, as Mrs Kriegel rightly observes, the entire social basis of the pre-1914 French labour movement disappeared. The war brought the French economy for the first time into the twentieth century, that is to say it made impossible (or marginal) not only the unstable minority trade unionism of pre-industrial craftsmen, which had been the foundation of revolutionary syndicalism, but also the illusion of an outlaw working class, linked to the capitalist system by nothing except hatred and the hope of its total overthrow. One way or another both the reformism and the revolutionism of before 1914 had to change, to be re-defined or more precisely defined. In this sense also, the road back to 1914 was barred.

But this very change in the French economy and the relationship between employers, workers and the state, raised problems which neither the socialists nor the communists faced, or even fully recognized, and in this failure lies much of the tragedy of western socialism. Léon Blum's Socialist Party became neither the ideal Fabian party approaching socialism via elections and piecemeal reforms, nor even a simple reformist party within capitalism. It degenerated into something like the Radical Party of the Third Republic, and indeed took over its political role in the Fourth: a guarantor of social and economic immobilism, sweetened by ministerial office for its leaders. The Communist Party remained the party of international proletarian revolution and, increasingly, of effective labour organization. Bolshevization made it almost certainly into the most effective revolutionary organization in French history. But inevitably, since the world revolution turned out to be simply the Russian revolution, the hope of its extension lay in the USSR, and would remain located there so long as the USSR 'continued to see herself as the advancing revolution'.[5] And since there was no revolutionary situation or perspective in France 'the PCF necessarily became the seat of all the contradictions and antinomies of pre-1914 French revolutionary socialism: reformist in its daily practice, though revolutionary; patriotic though internationalist'. And, as she correctly observes, it discovered a pseudo-solution for them 'by turning itself into a sort of imaginary global society, on the model of the soviet Russian universe'; and, we may add, by increasingly retiring from effective participation in politics. Only one thing has firmly divided it from becoming a reincarnation of socialism. Unlike it, in the crucial crises which made a choice between nationalism and internationalism mandatory, it has opted for internationalism (in the only available form, loyalty to the October revolution as embodied in the USSR).

Was there – is there – no way out of this dilemma of the revolutionary party in a non-revolutionary environment ? To ask this question is not to deny the correctness of the international course prescribed for the communist movement by Lenin, whose towering political genius emerges from Mrs Kriegel's book as from all other serious studies of his activity. There was, after all, a revolutionary situation in half the world in 1917–21, though this does not mean, and Lenin never supposed it to mean, that soviet republics were on the agenda in London and Paris. Hindsight may show that the developed countries of capitalism – even Germany – remained fundamentally unshaken, but it was correct, not to mention natural, for political generalship at the time to see Europe – or at any rate central Europe – as a battlefield on which victory was possible and not as a territory to be promptly evacuated. Furthermore, not to have divided the labour movement, even if this had been possible, would have solved nothing. The record of movements which remained substantially united, like the British and the Austrian,

[5] Under the conditions of stalinism this implied a total identification with all the actions of the CPSU, for any hesitation meant expulsion and the loss of contact with the reality of world revolution; but Mrs Kriegel may perhaps be defending her own past when she argues that 'any attempt to establish any distinction between the soviet state and . . . the French CP, would have been radically absurd in theory as well as in practice'.

shows that the interwar failures cannot be blamed simply on the socialist-communist schism. Lastly, the creation of effective revolutionary parties, which was the great achievement of the Comintern, had striking positive results, as was proved in the 1930s and 1940s, and especially in the resistance movements against fascism, which owed far more to the communist parties than these were willing to claim at the time or their enemies to admit subsequently.

This is not to accept the Comintern uncritically. Gross mistakes of political appreciation were made, which the military rigidity of its organization passed on to the communist parties. Its inevitable domination by the CPSU had extremely bad consequences, and eventually wrecked it. But those who think that the international labour movement, especially in western Europe, should never have taken the road it did in 1917–21 are merely expressing a wish that history ought to have been different from what it was. What is more, they overlook the positive achievements, however qualified, which make the period of the Third International so much less discouraging for the socialist than that of the Second. They are easy enough to overlook, particularly in the present era of reaction against stalinism and of international communist schism, and at a time when the Comintern clearly no longer provides a useful model for international socialist organization. However, the historian's business is not praise and blame, but analysis.

Curiously enough, such analysis would reveal that the fundamental problem of the revolutionary party in a non-revolutionary environment was not neglected in the Comintern. Indeed, it adumbrated one possible solution for it, and the extreme sensitiveness of anti-revolutionaries on this point suggests, that it was by no means an impracticable one: the 'popular front' and – until it was turned into a mere cover for the CP after 1946, or until the CP was driven out of it in the same period – the national anti-fascist fronts of resistance and liberation. At the time the character and possibilities of such movements and governments were obscured by a number of historical irrelevancies: by the reluctance of communist parties to admit that such fronts were steps towards socialism, or by their insistence that they would only be so if they became assimilated to the CP; by the briefness of their careers and the exceptional circumstances in which they often operated; and by various other factors. However, so far this phase of communist thinking has been the only one in which the specific problems of achieving socialism in the advanced countries of the west have been realistically considered at all on an international scale. It is worth remembering that it was initiated by the French Communist Party. Whether, or how far, the experiences of the 1930s and 1940s remain relevant, is a matter for discussion. In any case they fall outside the scope of Mrs Kriegel's book.

(1965)

4
INTELLECTUALS AND COMMUNISM

The love affair between intellectuals and marxism which is so characteristic of our age developed relatively late in western Europe, though in Russia itself it began in Marx's own lifetime. Before 1914 the marxist intellectual was a rare bird west of Vienna, though at one point in the early 1890s it looked as though he would become a permanent and plentiful species. This was partly because in some countries (such as Germany) there were not many left-wing intellectuals of any kind while in others (such as France) older pre-marxist ideologies of the left predominated, but mainly because the bourgeois society to which the intellectual – satisfied or dissident – belonged was still a going concern. The characteristic left-wing intellectual of Edwardian Britain was a liberal-radical, of Dreyfusard France a revolutionary of 1789, but one almost certainly destined for an honoured place in the state as a teacher. It was not until the first world war and the 1929 slump broke these old traditions and certainties that the intellectuals turned directly to Marx in large numbers. They did so via Lenin. The history of marxism among intellectuals in the west is therefore largely the history of their relationship with the communist parties which replaced social democracy as the chief representatives of marxism.

In recent years these relations have been the subject of a vast literature, mainly the work of ex-communists, dissident marxists and American scholars, and chiefly consisting of autobiographies or annotated who's whos of prominent intellectuals who joined, and mostly left, various communist parties. David Caute's *Communism and the French Intellectuals*[1] is one of the more satisfactory specimens of the second type, for it accepts – indeed it argues strongly – that the

[1] David Caute, *Communism and the French Intellectuals*, London, 1969.

reasons which led intellectuals into communist parties and kept them there were often both rational and compelling, and controverts the characteristic 1950s view that such parties could attract only the deviant, the psychologically aberrant, or the seeker after some secular religion, the 'opium of the intellectuals'. The greater part of his book therefore deals not so much with communism and the intellectuals as with the intellectuals and communism.

The relations of intellectuals and communist parties have been turbulent, though perhaps less so than the literature would suggest, for the prominent and articulate, with whom it mainly deals, are not necessarily a representative sample of the average and the inarticulate. In countries like France and Italy, where the party has long been and remains the major force of the left, it is likely that political behaviour (e.g. voting) is much stabler than the turnover of party membership – always rather large – would indicate. We know this to be so among workers. Unfortunately the difficulties of finding a workable sociological definition of 'intellectuals' have so far deprived us of reliable statistics about them, though the few we have suggest that it applies to them also. Thus party membership at the École Normale Supérieure dropped from 25 per cent after the war to 5 per cent in 1956, but the communists obtained 21 per cent of the votes at the Cité Universitaire in 1951 and 26 per cent in 1956.

Still, whatever the general trend of political sympathy among intellectuals, there can be no doubt of the stormy path of those who actually joined communist parties. This is normally ascribed to the increasing conversion of these parties, following the Soviet lead, into rigidly dogmatic bodies allowing no deviation from an orthodoxy that finished by covering every conceivable aspect of human thought, thus leaving very little scope for the activity from which intellectuals take their names. What is more, unlike the Roman Catholic Church, which preferred to keep its orthodoxy unchanged, communism changed it frequently, profoundly, and unexpectedly in the course of day-by-day politics. The ever-modified *Great Soviet Encyclopedia* was merely the extreme example of a process which inevitably imposed great and often intolerable tensions on communist intellectuals. The unpleasant aspects of life in the USSR also, it is argued, alienated many of them.

This is only part of the truth. Much of the intellectuals' difficulty arose from the nature of modern mass politics, the communist party being merely the most logical – and in France the first – expression of a general twentieth-century trend. The active adherent of a modern mass party, like the modern MP, abdicates his judgment in practice, whatever his theoretical reservations or whatever the nominal provision for harmless dissent. Or rather, modern political choice is not a constant process of selecting men or measures, but a single or infrequent choice between packages, in which we buy the disagreeable part of the contents because there is no other way of getting the rest, and in any case because there is no other way to be politically effective. This applies to all parties, though non-communist ones have hitherto generally made things easier for their intellectual adherents by refraining from formal commitments on such subjects as genetics or the composition of symphonies.

As Mr Caute sensibly points out: the French intellectual, in accepting broadly the Third or Fourth Republics has had to do so despite Versailles, the domestic policy of the Bloc National, Morocco, Syria, Indo-China, the regime of Chiappe, unemployment, parliamentary corruption, the abandonment of republican Spain, Munich, McCarthyism, Suez, Algeria.

Similarly the communist intellectual, in opting for the USSR and his party, did so because on balance the good on his side seemed to outweigh the bad. Not the least of Mr Caute's merits is to show how, for example in the 1930s, not only hard-shell party militants but sympathizers consciously refrained from criticism of Soviet purges or Spanish republican misdeeds in the interests of the greater cause of anti-fascism. Communists did not often discuss this choice in public. It could be quite explicit in the case of non-members who deliberately opted for the communist side, or against the common adversary, such as Sartre. It may be that not only the proverbial gallic logic but also the background of Roman Catholicism (shared, in different ways, alike by believers and unbelievers) made the idea of adhering to a comprehensive party with mental reservations more readily acceptable in France than in the Britain of a hundred religions and but a single sauce.

Still, all allowances made, the way of the party intellectual was hard, and most of the actively committed ones had a breaking-point, even those who joined the party in the stalinist period and largely because of its stalinism, i.e. because they welcomed the construction of a totally devoted, disciplined, realistic, anti-romantic army of revolution. Even this Brechtian generation, which deliberately trained itself to approve the harshest decisions in the war for human liberation, was likely – like Brecht himself – to arrive at the point where it questioned not so much the sacrifices as their usefulness and justification. Unthinking militants might escape into the self-delusion of the faithful, to whom every directive or line was 'correct' and to be defended as such because it came from the party which was by definition 'correct'. Intelligent ones, though capable of much self-delusion, were more likely to retreat into the posture of the advocate or civil servant whose private opinions are irrelevant to his brief, or the policeman who breaks the law the better to maintain it. It was an attitude which grew easily out of the hard-headed party approach to politics, but one which produced a breed of professional bruisers of intellectual debate.

Mr Caute is understandably hard on these intellectual apparatchiks, ready at a moment's notice to find the tone of sincerity for the potential ally or to blackguard him as an 'intellectuel-flic', but never to pursue the truth. The French version of them is indeed an especially disagreeable one, and the book is largely dominated by the author's disgust with them. One can hardly fail to sympathize with him. Aragon's gifts as a writer are towering, but irrelevant to one's feelings about his intellectual gutter-journalism, and there are plenty of others whose personal talents command no respect. Nor can they be excused because gutter-journalism is an old habit among committed French intellectuals of other political tendencies also. Yet two important questions should not be obscured by this distaste.

The first is about the object of the exercise. If it was to gain support for the party among intellectuals, as Mr Caute assumes, then the public activities in the 1950s of MM Stil, Kanapa, Wurmser, *et al.* were quite the worst way of setting about it, because they merely isolated the party among them ; and intelligent party men knew this. The truth is rather that two motives conflicted: that of extending the influence of the party and that of barricading a large but isolated movement, a private world within the world of France, against assaults and infiltrations from outside. In periods of political expansion, such as those of Popular Front and Resistance, the two aims were not mutually exclusive; in periods of political stagnation they were. What is interesting is that in such periods the French party chose (as the Italian never quite did) the second aim, which was essentially to persuade the comrades that they did not need to listen to the outsiders who were all class enemies and liars. This required both a constant barrage of reassurance and an adequate supply of orthodox culture for internal consumption, and Mr Caute has not perhaps paid enough attention to this attempt at systematic cultural autarchy, though he has noted some of its symptoms. It implied the attempt to make the party artist or writer economically independent of the outside world. It also implied that at such times Aragon's outside reputation, like Belloc's for prewar English Catholics, was valuable as an asset within the movement, rather than as a means of converting outsiders.

The second question is the crucial one of how communist policy can be changed. Here again the Roman Catholic parallel (of which French communists were more aware than Mr Caute allows) is relevant. Those who have changed party orientation have not been men with a record of criticism and dissidence, but of unquestioned stalinist loyalty, from Khruschev and Mikoyan to Tito, Gomulka and Togliatti. The reason is not merely that such men in the 1920s and 1930s thought stalinism preferable to its communist alternatives, or even that from the 1930s criticism tended to shorten life among those domiciled in the USSR. It is also that the communist who cut himself off from the party – and this was long the almost automatic consequence of dissidence – lost all possibility of influencing it. In countries like France, where the party increasingly *was* the socialist movement, leaving it meant political impotence or treason to socialism; and for communist intellectuals the possibilities of settling down as successful academic or cultural figures was no compensation. The fate of those who left or were expelled was anti-communism or political oblivion except among the readers of little magazines. Conversely, loyalty left at least the possibility of influence. Since the 1960s, when Mr Caute's book ends, it has become clear that even hard-core intellectual functionaries like Aragon and Garaudy were more anxious than he allows to initiate policy changes. Nor ought their arguments or their hesitant initiatives to be judged by the standards of liberal discussion, any more than the behaviour of the reforming prelates before and during the Vatican Council.

However, to see the problem of communism and the French intellectuals chiefly as one of the relations between party and intellectuals, whether from the party's or the individual intellectual's point of view, is to touch it only at the margin. For at bottom the issue is one of the general character of French politics, of the secular divisions within French society, including those between intellectuals and the rest. It may be argued that party policy in general and in intellectual matters could have been more effective, particularly in certain periods such as the 1920s and the 1950s. But such arguments can, if they are to have value, be based only on the recognition of the limits imposed on the party by a situation over which it had little control.

We cannot, for instance, make sense of the 'dilemma' of the communist intellectual in a proletarian party unless we recognize that the causes which have mobilized French intellectuals most fully have, since 1870, rarely been popular ones. One of the genuine difficulties of the Communist Party during the Algerian war, as of the Dreyfusard socialist leaders in the 1890s, was the fact that their rank and file was largely out of sympathy with Dreyfus or the FLN. Why this was so requires analysis. So, more generally, does the failure of the entire French left since 1870 – and perhaps since before 1848 – to achieve political hegemony in the nation which it created during the great Revolution. Between the wars governments of the left (1924, 1936–8) were as rare in Jacobin France as in conservative Britain, though in the middle 1930s it did look for a moment as though the left might resume its long-lost leadership. One of the crucial differences between the French and the Italian Communist Parties is that the Italian Resistance, like the Yugoslav, was a national movement led by the left, whereas the French Resistance was merely the honourable rebellion of a section of Frenchmen. The problem of breaking out of minority opposition into national hegemony was not only a communist one.

Aragon's *La Semaine Sainte*, underrated in Britain and unmentioned by Mr Caute, is essentially the novel of such secular divisions among Frenchmen – even among those who 'ought' to be on the same side. This is probably one reason why French critics of all parties, whose political nerve it touches, have overrated it. The aim of the French left has always been to become a movement of both workers and intellectuals at the head of the nation. The problem of the Communist Party has arisen largely from the extreme difficulty of achieving this ancient Jacobin object in the mid-twentieth century.

(1964)

5
THE DARK YEARS OF ITALIAN COMMUNISM

The Italian Communist Party is the great success story in the history of communism in the western world, or that part of the world in which such parties are not in power. The fortunes of the various CPs have fluctuated, but in the course of the half century or so since most of the European ones were founded few have substantially improved their international ranking order or (what is much the same thing) transformed the character of their political influence in their native country. There have been some rare cases of 'promotion' from a lower to a higher division of the political league, as, presumably, the Spanish CP which was relatively insignificant until the Spanish Civil War,[1] and some obvious cases of relegation such as the CP in Western Germany, which never recovered from the blows received under Hitler. But by and large, though their strength and influence have fluctuated, most of the communist parties at least of capitalist Europe have never played in their countries' political First Divisions, even when they emerged at the end of the last war with the prestige of their unparalleled record in the resistance. On the other hand some of them, such as the French and the Finnish, have always been major political forces, even at the worst points of their careers. How far this is true of the world as a whole is more difficult to assess, but need not concern us here.

The Italian CP is one of the rare examples of unquestioned 'promotion'. Before fascism it was never more than a minority party within what was admittedly a rather left-wing socialist

[1] The illegality under which several CPs have operated for most of their history, and a number still do, makes the assessment of their political strength and influence somewhat speculative.

movement: somewhat over a third at the Congress of Livorno (1921). As the dust of the split settled down it became rapidly clear that it represented a comparatively modest minority, whatever the revolutionary sympathies and possibilities of the rest of the socialist movement. In 1921 it polled less than a fifth of the socialist vote, in 1924, despite the socialist decline, the proportion was still almost three to one against it. Its own percentage of the popular vote never reached 5 per cent. Since the war it has emerged increasingly as the major force within the left, as the effective 'opposition' in a *de facto* two-party structure of politics, and, what is more, it has gained strength steadily and almost without interruption.[2]

What changes this has implied in its revolutionary role and perspective is a question that may be hotly debated. However, there can be no doubt that the party has been incomparably more important in national politics since the war than it ever was before, and that it has not only maintained but strengthened its position for a generation.

Those who write history by extrapolation may be tempted to project this rising curve of communist influence backwards, but this is to miss the point. What is really interesting about the history of the Italian CP is the startling contrast between its extreme weakness for most of the fascist period and its astonishing expansion during and after the Resistance; or alternatively between the remarkable continuity of an unusually able party leadership, whose quality was internationally recognized, and the enormous difference between the party which was regarded by the Comintern as notoriously feeble and disappointing, and that which, in 1947, was one of the only two non-governmental parties to be invited to join the Cominform.

How great that difference was can now be established from Paolo Spriano's *Storia del Partito Comunista Italiano*, written with full access to the archives of state and CP, but not to those of the

[2] Percentage of communist vote in elections for Chamber of Deputies:

1946	18·9
1948	31·0 (joint list with socialists)
1953	22·6
1958	22·7
1963	25·3
1968	26·9

The 1948 elections almost certainly marked a temporary decline.

Communist International, which are only slowly being made available to extremely official researchers.[3] In May 1934, shortly before the reorientation of international communist policy, the Italian party had, according to the Comintern, 2,400 members in all, less than the British CP at its lowest point in this period. The bulk of its leading cadres was in jail, the apparently inevitable destination of relays of brave and devoted militants sent into Italy during the past seven years. Its activities in the country were minimal. The fascist regime was sufficiently self-confident to include several hundred communist prisoners in the amnesty with which Mussolini celebrated the tenth anniversary of the March on Rome.

This catastrophic situation could no doubt be blamed to some extent on the lunacies of Comintern policy during the notorious so-called 'Third Period' (1927–34), when the communist movement in Europe was reduced to its lowest ebb. They are sufficiently well known: the obligation to see social democracy as the *main* enemy ('social-fascism') and the left wing of social democracy as the most dangerous part of it, the wilful blindness not only to the rise but also to the triumph of Hitler, and so on. They reached a climax of unreality in the eighteen months after his advent to power. The party's (i.e. the Comintern's) line did not change until July 1934. It cannot have been easy for a communist historian to record Italian party leaders trying desperately to retain a faint element of realism in their analysis ('We cannot say that in Italy social-democracy is the main support of the bourgeoisie') and obliged the next day to make a public recantation – and this ten years after the March on Rome.

Nevertheless, even after the Comintern adopted the line of anti-fascist unity (with the enthusiastic support of Togliatti, who joined Dimitrov in the leadership of the International) the Italian party failed to advance. This was all the more surprising since the new line was both eminently sensible and uniquely designed to improve the prospects of the communist parties, virtually all of

[3] Three volumes of Spriano's history have so far been published, covering the period until 1941 (Turin 1967, 1969, 1970). Whether the Comintern archives have been closed for technical reasons – until the death of Stalin they appear not to have been even roughly catalogued, and unexpected discoveries can still, one is told on good authority, be made in them – or for political reasons, their inaccessibility is much to be regretted.

which gained substantial ground in this period. So, of course, did the Italians, in a modest way. Moreover, they remained by far the largest, most active and most serious of the illegal or emigrant anti-fascist organizations. In 1936 there were among the Italian emigration in France some four to five thousand organized Communists, about six hundred members of the Socialist Party and a hundred or so anarchists. Still, it is worth remembering that, according to the CP's own estimates, there were at this time almost half a million Italian workers in that country, of whom the largest and broadest mass organization of the CP did not capture more than fifteen thousand.

The most genuine and publicized achievement of the party also demonstrates its weakness: its intervention in the Spanish Civil War. Italian communists occupied posts of the highest responsibility in this, the last and perhaps greatest of the undertakings of a genuinely international communist movement: Togliatti, Longo, Vidali. The Garibaldi Brigades played a notably heroic and effective part; not only in the defence of Spain but – as the non-communist *Giustizia e Libertà* was, it must be admitted, quicker to see than the CP – in restoring the self-confidence of the Italian left.[4] Yet what we now know is, that the effort of mobilizing the first Italian volunteer force exhausted the resources of the anti-fascist emigration. Of the 3,354 Italians in the International Brigades the dates of arrival of roughly two thousand are known. Approximately a thousand of these arrived in the second half of 1936, four hundred in the first, a little more than three hundred in the second half of 1937, rather less than three hundred in 1938. (Incidentally, of the 2,600 whose immediate provenance can be established, 2,000 came from the French emigration and only 223 directly from Italy.)[5] Since the casualties were heavy, they simply could not be filled, in spite of the party's efforts to step up recruitment: by November 1937 only 20 per cent

[4] The following passage from Lussu (*Giustizia e Libertà*, 28 August 1936) deserves to be quoted: 'Our need to go to Spain is greater than the Spanish Republic's need of us. Italian anti-fascism lacks a revolutionary glory ... We must recognize that we have not known how to do battle against fascism. The small political vanguard of the Italian emigration must generously sacrifice itself in this enterprise. It will acquire experience on the battlefields. It will make its name there. It will become the nucleus that will attract around itself the greater vanguard of tomorrow.'

[5] Spriano, vol. 3, pp. 226–7.

of the Garibaldi Brigade consisted of Italians. In a word, the anti-fascist emigration mobilized itself, and when it had done this it had nobody left to mobilize.

This is the background to another phenomenon that has not been sufficiently well known until Paolo Spriano's work : the apparently persistent campaign of the International against the Italian CP throughout the 1930s. Like so much in the last years of the Comintern, this is a very obscure subject ; for as the International was brought under the direct supervision of the Soviet secret police apparatus – Yezhov himself, the head of the purges, joined the executive at the Seventh Congress and Trilisser-Moskvin, another policeman, the actual secretariat[6] – its activities became increasingly shadowy, in so far as they did not atrophy altogether. (After 1936 it becomes impossible even to identify the leading committees of the International and their membership from published sources.) Togliatti's prominence in the International, Longo's in the International Brigades, have tended to divert attention from the fact that the CI's criticisms became progressively more severe, until the point was reached where the Central Committee of the party was dissolved by Moscow in 1938, the financial aid on which it depended almost wholly was drastically cut in early 1939, and that there was talk of yet further reorganizations of the leadership until well into the war.

No doubt personal animosities and byzantine court intrigues played their part in all this, but the major reason for the CI's dissatisfaction was rational enough: the total failure of the Italian party to make any effective contact with, let alone measurable progress in, Italy itself. It remained what it had long been, a group of a few hundred political emigrants, wholly dependent on the material support of Moscow, plus a large number of prisoners in Mussolini's jails, or in forced residence. In some respects the situation in the first year of Italy's war was even more disastrous than in 1929–35, for then there had been a coherent body of leaders, whereas the Spanish war, the fall of France, and other events had now dispersed even this 'external centre'.

This failure cannot be blamed on 'orders from Moscow' in any literal sense, however plausible this explanation may seem for the period 1927–34. (Even so it underestimates the genuine support

[6] G. Berti, 'Problemi di storia del PCI e dell'Internazionale Communista', *Riv. Stor. Italiana*, LXXXII, March 1970.

which ultra-sectarianism had within the Italian party, especially among the youth whose spokesman was Luigi Longo.) Nor can it be entirely blamed on the errors of the Italian party, whether these were their own or part of a general trend among communists. They themselves failed to see fascism as a general phenomenon, and still tended (when not forced into the official formulae of Moscow) to analyze it as a special problem of one particular rather backward capitalism. And of course, in spite of Gramsci's attempts to think out this problem, they shared the difficulty of all communists in adjusting themselves to a situation so different from the revolutionary world crisis in which they had been formed. Nevertheless, the main reasons for the failure of the PCI were probably objective, and the Comintern underestimated them, because, in spite of its long experience of illegality, fascism had no real precedent.

The powers of the modern state determined to suppress opposition regardless of law and constitution, are enormous, and modern mass labour movements, which cannot function without some sort of legality, are unusually vulnerable to it. The PCI itself had been taken by surprise: how else explain that the fascist raids of late 1926 caught no less than one-third of its effective membership, including its leader Gramsci? Whatever the ideological and propagandist top-dressing, the essence of both the fascist and later the Nazi policy towards the labour movements was not to convert them but to pulverize them. Their organizations were to be dissolved, their leaders and cadres down to local and works level were to be eliminated, and they were to be left, as Trotsky was later to put it 'in an amorphous state'. So long as 'any independent crystallization of the proletariat' (or any other class) was to be prevented, it did not much matter what the workers thought.

But what could an illegal movement do once decapitation and pulverization had been successful? It could maintain – or rather re-establish – contact with existing groups of loyal supporters, and perhaps with luck form some new ones. This became progressively more difficult. The Comintern was quite correct in urging illegal parties to establish an 'internal centre' as the essential base for effective national activity, but the mere attempt to contact surviving members, easily threatened and kept under surveillance, almost automatically led the police to the emissaries of the 'external centre'. And what, in any case, could the illegal organization do? Practically all activities of a labour movement imply some kind of public appearance, which is precisely what they could not permit themselves. On the margins of modern society, or where the state power does not or cannot maintain intensive control, they might maintain themselves better: in the isolated oral and secret universe of villages, in small closed communities where outsiders, including agents of the state, can be more readily isolated. It is probably no accident that as organization in the industrial north collapsed, the centre of the illegal party in the late 1920s and early 1930s shifted to central Italy, which by then had twice as many known members as the north. But in the short run, what difference did this make? When fascism fell, we hear of several touching cases of individuals and groups, out of touch with their party for years, who paid up all their back dues, which they had carefully saved up through the long internal exile of fascism. We know that the militants of the Sicilian village of Piana degli Albanesi took pride in never once omitting to send at least a token demonstration on May Day to the remote mountain glen where the founder of socialism in their region, the noble Nicola Barbato, had addressed them in 1893 and where the bandit Giuliano was to massacre them in 1947. But such examples, however moving, prove the efficacy of the fascist policy. It cut off the party even from its most persistent supporters and prevented effective expression of their loyalty.

What could an illegal movement do under such circumstances? The then familiar refuge of weak illegal oppositions, individual terrorism, was unacceptable to marxists, the experience of tsarist Russia having proved to their satisfaction that it was ineffective.[7] The milder forms of dramatic propaganda by action, such as dropping leaflets from aeroplanes over Milan, favoured by the liberal *Giustizia e Libertà*, did not look very effective either. At this period guerrilla insurrection of the Maoist or Guevarist kind was not yet fashionable. In any case the record of such activity in the nineteenth century, both by Mazzini's followers and by the anarchists, hardly recommended it to communists. To wait passively for a process of internal disintegration to set in, or for some crisis – whether economic or, as it turned out, military – which would once again provide a means to set the masses in action, was equally unacceptable. Communists could hope for such a crisis, and mistakenly thought either the slump or the Abyssinian war

[7] We recall that the Russian terrorists at the peak of their effectiveness consisted of probably not more than five hundred individuals.

might bring it about, but they could not do much to precipitate it. All the International could think of was to urge the PCI to get back into Italy among the masses at all costs, and there was not much else the PCI could think of either. And this task seemed impossible.

We can now see in retrospect that the basis of its subsequent success nevertheless existed or was being established. In the first place, the mass of anti-fascist Italians remained unreconciled. The mass basis of Italian fascism remained narrower than that of Nazism. Secondly, the collapse of anarchism and the passivity of the Socialist Party transferred a substantial body of worker and peasant support at least potentially to communism. To this extent the party's persistent presence, and the fascists' own attitude to communism, established it as the major nucleus of anti-fascist opposition. That there was such a transfer of loyalties in Italy, unlike Germany, was probably due to the very different structure of the left movement in the two countries. There was not in Italy the fatal polarization of the labour movement between mutually hostile parties of very different social structures. The Italian 'red' movement of the early 1920s was still a spectrum of overlapping tendencies and groups. Between the reformist Unitarians at one end and the Communists and anarchists on the other, stood the Maximalists, whose frustrated desire to affiliate to the Comintern together with the PCI's serious plans to reunite with them, demonstrate the common ground between them. Just as it was to prove easier for socialists and communists to establish a working united front in 1934, so it was easier for former socialists to emerge as communists after fascism.

Thirdly, at some time during the 1930s – between 1935 and 1938 – a certain revival of opposition within Italy may be noted. This is most easily documented among the young intellectuals who subsequently made their names both as party leaders (Ingrao, Alicata) and as leaders of the postwar communist hegemony of Italian culture. Spain undoubtedly played an important part in this crystallization of the old and its reinforcement by a new generation of anti-fascists – a new generation which probably, though this is difficult to document, included workers also. At all events the activists in the small and impermanent party cells appear to have been chiefly young people.[8] The immediate impact

[8] Spriano, vol. 3, p. 194.

of the Spanish Civil War is attested both by police sources and by anti-fascist informants, and this, significantly enough, at a time when communist propaganda from abroad had not yet begun to pay major attention to Spain.[9] (While *Giustizia e Libertà* was immediately aware of the full significance of Spain, it is a curious fact that *as late as the end of September 1936* the Central Committee of the PCI – perhaps because of deficient contact with the International, but certainly to its discredit – paid hardly any attention to Spain.)[10] The initial victory of the Republic over the military rising inspired not only the old anti-fascists, but (according to a police informer in Milan) 'even some sectors which had appeared to be firmly converted to fascism'. It demonstrated that fascism was not all-powerful, and hence (as another informer noted in Genoa) raised hopes 'of some sort of political transformations which would more or less rapidly bring about the capitulation of the authoritarian spirit of fascism'.

Yet Spain was not the only factor. How much of the new anti-fascism among young intellectuals, as like as not students from Sicily, Calabria or Sardinia meeting in the capital, was due to the desire to escape from the heavy provincialism of fascist culture to the wider intellectual world, whose luminaries abroad so visibly supported anti-fascism? To the failure of Italian fascism to establish a cultural hegemony as well as a genuine mass basis? (The sense of international *inferiority*, both cultural and otherwise, was much greater in Italy than in Germany, the sense of cultural isolation more oppressive.) Whatever the reasons, by the end of the 1930s anti-fascism in Italy was no longer based only on the generations which had come to political maturity before 1924. It had begun to generate its own youthful dissidents.

Curiously enough – and this was one of its major weaknesses – the PCI seems to have misunderstood the situation, perhaps because of what had by now become an overestimate of the popular strength of fascism. Its policy from 1935 on was that of a broad alliance, but it appears persistently (and in line with international slogans) to have thought in terms of detaching a supposedly large sector of 'sincere' fascists, disappointed with the betrayal of the original fascist ideal, from the regime; and above all not to hurt the susceptibilities of Italian nationalism, which the

[9] *Ibid.*, pp. 81–4.
[10] *Ibid.*, p. 99.

Abyssinian war had shown to be a powerful force.[11] But in fact, as both the non-communist anti-fascist emigrants and some of the new internal anti-fascists observed, this was not the main problem. The major effect of the fascism in Italy, observed the youthful Eugenio Curiel, who finally joined the Communists after maintaining contacts with both Socialists and *Giustizia e Libertà*, was not to convert Italians to fascism. It was:

> infinite scepticism . . . which kills all possible faith in any ideal, which derides the sacrifice of the individual for the sake of the welfare of the community. This is, at bottom, the most conspicuous conquest made by fascism and will remain as its bitterest legacy.[12]

As it happened, this very scepticism which isolated the tiny minorities of active anti-fascists and kept the much larger body of inactive ones passive, was to turn against the fascist regime when Mussolini drove a reluctant and unenthusiastic Italian people into the second world war. Defeat was to give the anti-fascists their chance to revive hope and human self-respect through action. But the masses they were then to mobilize were not to consist to any great extent of the 'sincere' fascists, or even of the inevitable and numerous turncoats. They were to consist of the old and young anti-fascists, and above all of the ordinary Italian workers and peasants, whose conversion to an active and militant resistance was to be dramatic.

It was, there can be no doubt whatever, opposition to the war which gave anti-fascism back its mass basis. It is not significant that in July 1941 yet another attempt to re-establish an 'internal centre' was made. What is significant is that it succeeded. From the autumn of 1941 on the PCI functioned in Italy as it had not been able to since the spring of 1932, when the last head of a functioning 'internal centre' had been arrested in Milan. By the spring of 1943 mass strikes for bread and peace could be organized in the north. The invasion of Italy and the armistice reinforced the new mass movement with the bulk of the cadre of communist leadership – returning from jail, exile

[11] A curious example: In 1939 the PCI detached one of its best military cadres, Ilio Barontini, to establish a guerrilla action in Ethiopia in conjunction with the forces loyal to the emperor. This operation was conducted with the usual efficiency and heroism of good communists, and maintained until May-June 1940. It is entirely to the credit of the party, but until the publication of Spriano's history (pp. 298–9) in 1970, hardly any public reference to this episode was made in the party's publications.

[12] Spriano, vol. 3, p. 273

or anti-fascist resistance in other countries, or emerging into the open. Its three components – the old guard of party leaders, the experienced military cadres of the Spanish war, and the young anti-fascists of the 1930s vintage – together formed a body of leadership which had no equivalent among any other anti-fascist group. It not only took the initiative but provided the great bulk of the armed partisan units in central and northern Italy. Probably well over 80 per cent of them were more or less under communist leadership. They succeeded in mobilizing not merely a large body of inactive anti-fascists, or communists who had dropped out of the struggle,[13] but substantial bodies of new working-class and peasant militants like the famous seven Cervi brothers in Emilia, sons of a prosperous and modern-minded farmer and good Catholic. The results were dramatic. It is improbable that in 1940 there were even three thousand members of the PCI, and most of these were scattered all over the globe or in jail. By the winter of 1944–5 there were four hundred thousand, and the party was growing rapidly. It had established itself in the position which it was never thereafter to lose, as the major party of the left.

Could it have done so but for the war? 'What would have happened if?', is a question which can never be answered with certainty or even a high degree of probability. It is certain that Italian fascism was a more fragile political structure than German National Socialism, that the Italian economy was both more backward and more vulnerable than the German, and that Italians were poorer and more discontented. Very possibly it might have begun to break up slowly from within, as the Franco regime in Spain clearly began to do after fifteen years of fairly stable control from the middle 1950s. It is certain that the feebleness of organized anti-fascism within Italy was out of proportion to the strength of potential anti-fascism, old and new. It is also probable that the Italian Communist Party never lost that organic connection with the organized popular movement – whether among the unionized industrial workers or the 'red' peasants which the KPD so largely lacked. Under the circumstances its heroic and persistent illegal activity would probably have in any case made it into a stronger force after fascism than it had been before. It is also certain that it

[13] However, with some exceptions such as Arrigo Boldrini, an army officer who appears to have had no contact with the party before the summer of 1943, the partisan leaders were men of the left.

possessed a coherent body of leaders of remarkably high quality, which succeeded in avoiding the worst of the internal splits and purges which played such havoc with the leadership of the KPD. But beyond this all is speculation, and pointless speculation. History is what happened, not what might have happened. What happened was that Mussolini created the conditions which allowed the Communist Party to take the lead in a massive movement of national liberation, at least in central and northern Italy, and to emerge from it as the major party of the left.

(1972)

6

CONFRONTING DEFEAT: THE GERMAN COMMUNIST PARTY

Hermann Weber has added about nine hundred pages to the already long bibliography of German communist history, with his massive work *Die Wandlung des deutschen Kommunismus*.[1] The first question prospective readers will ask is : did he have to ? The answer, on the whole, is yes. These two volumes are a monument of erudition and patient, thorough research – seventeen public archives in Western Germany alone have been consulted – though further research remains to be done. The major sources for the history of the KPD in the Weimar Republic are in Moscow, and therefore likely to be inaccessible for quite a while, and in East Berlin, and therefore also inaccessible to researchers without the backing of the Central Committee of the SED, among whom Dr Weber is not going to be numbered. He has had to rely essentially on public records, notably police files (when will students of the British left in the 1920s have as much access to relevant material in our Public Records as historians in other countries ?), on a few private archives, a mass of interviews and memoranda from survivors of the period, printed sources and the literature. Probably he has not missed very much, but a monograph about six years of KPD history designed on this scale must inevitably suffer far more than a less detailed book from the inability to get at crucial documentation.

Still, let us be grateful for what we have until something even better becomes possible. Dr Weber has written at the very least an invaluable work of reference. The statistical data about the KPD's districts in vol. I and the 300-page who's who of its functionaries in vol. II are enough to make the work indispensable. But there is more

[1] Hermann Weber, *Die Wandlung des deutschen Kommunismus* (2 vols.), Frankfurt, 1970.

here than a mere collection of facts and data, or even one of the comparatively rare histories of German Communism which is free from the embittered personal involvement in past party and Comintern infighting, from which older writers find it impossible to escape. Weber has written a rather sensible book, which throws light on problems which go far beyond the interest of students of the KPD.

The problem with which he is essentially concerned is what happens to a revolutionary party in a non-revolutionary situation. The KPD was founded and grew as a revolutionary party, or at least a party of radical and active rejection of, or rather – to use the correct slang – 'confrontation' with, the *status quo*. It was founded when the Empire had collapsed, and the German Councils' Republic might reasonably be expected to follow soon, as the Russian October had followed February; and in so doing inaugurate the world revolution. 1919 was an apocalyptic year. Even Lenin, the most hard-headed of revolutionaries, thought it might bring the great breakthrough. The young German CP brought to its great tasks an able if small marxist leadership, immediately decimated by the assassinations of Luxemburg, Liebknecht and Jogiches, but also a rank and file composed largely of the utopian radicals, quasi-anarchist or socially marginal elements who are likely to flood into small and loosely structured nuclei of radical opposition in times of revolutionary upsurge. Most of these ultra-lefts moved away from the KPD within a year or two, though not without leaving behind a tendency towards 'heroic illusions' about the possibilities of the situation, a certain putschism, and a residuum of ultra-radicalism.

The German 'October' did not take place. On the contrary, the old regime, minus the emperor but plus a passionately and viscerally anti-revolutionary and governmental Social Democracy, re-established itself. What became the mass KPD, after the 1920 merger with the left wing of the Independent Socialists, expressed essentially the profound disappointment of large strata of the German working class with the failure of the social revolution and their embittered economic discontent. It represented all those forces – proletarian and intellectual – which rejected and hated a republic which had few republicans, but plenty of generals, policemen, bureaucrats, tycoons and judges whose reactionary bias was flagrant and incendiary, and which had installed a restoration of economic, social, political and legal injustice.

In social terms, the new KPD attracted the young – in 1926 80 per cent of its leading functionaries were below forty, 30 per cent below thirty and its average age was thirty-four;[2] the unskilled – an unusually high percentage of 13·5 among the top functionaries were drawn from them; the unemployed – in 1927, at the peak of economic stabilization, 27 per cent of the Berlin membership were jobless. Like all working-class organizations, however, its cadre rested largely on the basic rock of skilled proletarians, especially – as so often – the metal-workers. Three-quarters of its leading functionaries had only elementary school education, though at the other extreme 10 per cent were university graduates; among the membership 95 per cent had only been to primary school, 1 per cent to universities. Historically, half its leaders but 70 per cent of its members had entered politics since 1917. The relatively large number of pre-1917 Social Democrats among the functionaries came into it at the time of the merger with the Independent Socialists. Only about 20 per cent of the functionaries in the 1920s had belonged to the Spartacus League or the radical left during the war, so that the direct Rosa Luxemburg traditions were distinctly weak; on the other hand only thirty-six out of the almost four thousand full-time employees of the Social Democratic Party bureaucracy in 1914 were to be found as KPD full timers in the 1920s.

The KPD was new, young, underprivileged, radically hostile to the system and ready for revolution, which seemed to be possible if not probable until its great defeat in the autumn of 1923. This explains the strength within it of the uncompromising, offensive-minded, activist and often sectarian left. There is no doubt that among the various factions and currents of opinions within it, which fought out their differences in the early years with the usual pre-stalinist freedom and vigour (those were the days when it did not need a communiqué to state that discussions had been 'full and frank'), the left enjoyed by far the greatest support – in 1924 perhaps 75 per cent. The right, mostly ex-Spartacists who provided the basic leadership until 1923, was weak, except among the skilled workers – though not the intellectuals. The middle group or 'conciliators' which split away from the right after 1923, as the left took over, represented mainly

[2] At this time the average age of the SPD leadership was fifty-six.

party professionals, though they could count on about a quarter of the membership.

The KPD's problem up to 1923 was how to make the revolution, which seemed within reach, and which was essential not merely for the triumph of world socialism, but for the Soviet Republic itself. The German soviet revolution was the necessary complement to the Russian revolution, and even Lenin was quite prepared in theory to envisage a situation when the home of Marx, Engels, technological progress and economic efficiency would take over as the centre of the socialist world. In 1919 the Comintern regarded Berlin as the logical place for its headquarters, its location in Moscow as temporary. The German CP was treated as an equal – according to Weber even at the end of 1922 – though we may suspect that the wily Radek, whose long experience of the German socialist movement made him the man chiefly responsible for German affairs in Moscow, held distinctly more modest expectations about its chances. The major problem for the KPD in this period was posed by its deep involvement with Moscow; an involvement arising both from the relative age, strength and tradition of the KPD and from the crucial importance of German prospects for Soviet Russia and the whole international revolution. The KPD might not wish to be mixed up in Russian affairs, but it could hardly help being so, especially since Zinoviev was in charge of the Comintern and Radek, a supporter of Trotsky at a crucial stage, was its German expert. Beside this, the internal confusion of the party seemed a minor problem. In the first place the years 1919–23 clarified it somewhat by eliminating both the bulk of the utopian-syndicalist ultra-left and an ex-social-democratic right. In the second place, the prospect of revolution makes differences which might otherwise bulk large, comparatively manageable: in 1917, after all, such fundamental distinctions as those between Marx and Bakunin had not caused much trouble in Russia.

After the defeat of 1923 the problem was essentially what to do in a period of stabilization. 'Bolshevization', which is the main subject of Weber's book, was the answer. This systematic assimilation of other party organizations to the Russian model, and their subordination to Moscow, is generally seen by non-communist historians as a by-product of inner-Soviet developments, which it clearly was to some extent. However, it is Weber's merit to see that this is not the whole, or even the major part, of the truth. He distinguishes several elements in it.

In the first place, as he notes correctly, any effective and lasting organization in modern industrial society tends to be bureaucratized in some degree, including revolutionary parties. Democratic movements and organizations operate somewhere between the two extremes of unlimited internal freedom, bought at the cost of practical effectiveness, and ossified bureaucracy. Weber comments:

> In a labour movement, the democratic tendency always retains some force, since its entire tradition requires an anti-authoritarian, egalitarian and libertarian spirit. Moreover, the leadership is always obliged to support such tendencies from time to time, in order to stimulate the membership to activity and prevent a total paralysis of the party.

The formation of a structured and disciplined KPD out of the merger of men, movements and sects in 1918–20 was itself normal, and unacceptable only to utopians or anarchists. It is the systematic atrophy of internal democracy and over-bureaucratization after 1924 which provide the problem.

In the second place, a revolutionary party needs an unusually strong 'skeleton' of this kind, if only because it is a voluntary organization which must be capable of holding its own against the power structure of state, economy and the mass media, whose resources, influence and strength are far superior. An hierarchical and disciplined 'apparat' of professional revolutionaries (or, in peacetime, professional functionaries) forms easily the most effective cadre of this sort. Its absolute size is secondary: the KPD's corps of full-timers probably remained far smaller than the SPD's in the Weimar Republic. Though this inevitably produced tensions between leaders and rank and file, not to mention a hypertrophy of centralism and atrophy of initiative from below, it was acceptable to German communists for political as well as operational reasons. Just because the KPD emerged in Germany – whose political traditions notably differed from those of Russia – somewhere in an undefined space between social democracy and the libertarian-democratic (not to say utopian-radical) revolutionism which seems to be its natural antithesis in industrial countries, it had above all to define its political location. 'Bolshevization' did so. This was not only because bolshevism had, after all, shown itself to be the *only* successful form of revolution – the others had failed or not even started – but because the 'Party' itself as a disciplined revolutionary army, ready for battle, provided unity and answers to confusing questions. Loyalty bypasses many uncertainties, especially in proletarian movements, which are built on the instinct of unity and solidarity.

These forces would have been operative even without the intervention of Moscow, which Weber only mentions in the third place. It stands to reason that, given the deliberately centralized structure of the Comintern, of which the local parties were merely disciplined 'sections', and the obvious and inevitable dependence of both on the Soviet party, 'bolshevization' would mean stalinization. In other words a process which had no intrinsic connection with the USSR, except inasmuch as it reflected the natural prestige of the organizational and strategic 'model' associated with the party and revolution of Lenin, would be transformed into an extension of Soviet politics. The distinction between the two is evident in the case of the Italian CP, because there it took the form of Togliatti's conscious subordination to the Russian party of a leading cadre formed earlier and independently from it ; a cadre which, though purged and modified by the Russians remained essentially intact and with its own ideas (which it admittedly kept to itself). It is reasonably clear in the British CP, where once again the solidification of the party took place earlier and the nucleus of the party leadership remained unchanged after 1922–3. It is not so clear in Germany, because the turnover of the leading cadre continued to be much greater and was visibly dominated by Moscow.

This was due partly to the heavy Russian involvement of the KPD which we have already noted. What happened in Germany *mattered more* in Moscow than what happened anywhere else in Europe. The triumph of the left within the CP after the failure of 1923 intensified this involvement. It was not imposed by Moscow. Indeed, if anything it marked a (last) assertion of the anti-Russian autonomy of the German party,[3] a suspicion which the leadership of Ruth Fischer and Maslow tried to allay – fatally – by turning itself into the German faction of Zinoviev. It was thus not merely opposed to the general and rather moderate course which Stalin and the bulk of the CPSU were now following, but in addition involved the KPD in the Russian inner-party struggle – on the wrong side. (No faction of any significance in Germany favoured Trotsky.) Moreover, the sectarianism of the left was plainly senseless, though it appealed to the rank

[3] See Weber, vol. I, p. 301.

and file. In a period of stabilization – basically from 1921, unquestionably after 1923 – some form of political realism was necessary: united action with the majority of the organized workers who were in the SPD, work in trade unions, and in Parliament. Direct Comintern intervention in 1925 deposed the left leaders. *Nothing else could have done,* and this established a sinister precedent. For not merely did it transfer the centre of gravity of German inner-party discussion to Moscow, but to a Comintern which was now playing Soviet politics, and which intervened not so much to change policies as to choose loyal followers.

But which followers? The vulgar historiography of the Comintern neglects this question, assuming merely that they were blind executants of Moscow's policy. But two tragic peculiarities of KPD history cannot be so easily written out of the scenario. These were (*a*) the zeal with which it carried out the suicidal line of 1919–33 and (*b*) the remarkable instability of its top leadership. Neither were inevitable. For instance, an automatic reflex of discipline led the British CP in 1939 to reverse its line on the war, to drop the most important leaders associated with it – Pollitt and Campbell – and to carry out the new line with unhesitating loyalty. But everyone who had experience of this episode in its history knows that, but for outside intervention the party would not have altered its line at this time (though a minority might have hankered after such a change), that it reverted with almost audible relief to its old line in 1941, and that Pollitt and Campbell in no sense suffered in the long run for their association with the 'incorrect' policy of 1939.

The truth was that, although increasing numbers of KPD functionaries – especially the young and the unskilled, and those without previous experience in Spartacus or the USPD – were prepared to support *any* party line unconditionally, the basic orientation of the KPD activists was towards the sectarian left. It had begun as a party of revolution, it stabilized itself as one of militant and systematic negative 'confrontation'. Its consistent failure to gain strength in the trade unions reflects this. The Comintern had deposed the ultra-left leadership of 1924–5 only at the cost of taking some account of this mood. Thus, as Weber points out, the ultra-left course was never genuinely disavowed by the KPD and a return to a similar course under Comintern auspices in 1928–9 was welcomed. It meant doing what came naturally. It is perhaps significant – though this is one of the few aspects on which Weber is silent – that the Young Communists seem to have played an altogether subordinate part in the Comintern's German policy. Elsewhere, one of the commonest methods by which Moscow filled the party leaderships with loyal cadres uncommitted to any pre-Comintern ideology, was by the promotion of recruits from the various YCLS. Whether for this or other reasons, youth organizations supplied a significant number of Communist leaders: Rust in Britain, Longo and Secchia in Italy, a very substantial group in France. Togliatti, indeed, is reported to have observed during the great left turn of 1929: 'If we don't give in, Moscow won't hesitate to fix up a left leadership with some kid out of the Lenin School.'[4] So far as one can see, in Weimar Germany the Young Communists produced no leaders of any great significance. They were not required to: there were enough left sectarians to choose from.

The problem arising out of the instability of the leadership is twofold: why was the turnover so large?[5] And why did it lead – as I think most observers must agree – to a progressive lowering of quality? The line from Liebknecht and Luxemburg, through Levi and Meyer, Brandler and Thalheimer, Ruth Fischer and Maslow, to Thaelmann and his group is a distinctly descending one in terms of general political ability, though not in courage and devotion. This is not by any means the case in all other communist parties.

What seems to have happened is that the KPD never succeeded in developing a coherent body of leaders out of Spartacus (whose surviving cadres, after the shedding of quasi-syndicalist elements, tended to be 'right' deviationists), the ex-Independent Socialists (who tended to breed 'left' deviationists), and the post-1920 entrants into the party. The struggle for the formation of a leading group continued until it was merged with 'bolshevization' by

[4] According to an informant of Tasca, quoted in Spriano, *Storia del Partito Comunista Italiano*, vol. 2, p. 228.

[5] In the absence of comparably detailed calculations for other CPS it is impossible to be certain, but it does seem that their turnover was smaller. Thus in 1929 only two members of the KPD's political bureau had survived from 1924 – Thaelmann and Remmele, of whom the latter was subsequently eliminated. In France five political bureau members sat continuously from 1926 to 1932, and another discontinuously, while three – but for Semard's death, quite certainly four – were still members in 1945.

Moscow; and in this struggle the ablest in all groups tended to be eliminated for their prominence, or were unable to establish themselves as leaders of independent standing in the KPD before being reduced to Comintern functionaries.[6] This is perhaps the real tragedy of the murder of Rosa Luxemburg. Spartacus provided what the German left lacked: a potentially coherent and flexible approach to German politics, which did not confuse revolutionism with leftism. If Rosa Luxemburg was not likely to provide an alternative to Lenin internationally, within her own country her prestige might have imposed the Spartacus approach on the new party. It might have provided that party with a nucleus of political leadership and strategy.

For at bottom this was the drama of the KPD: it had no policy for any situation other than one of revolution, because the German left, one might almost say the German labour movement, had never had one. The SPD did not practise politics, but merely waited (in theory) until historic inevitability brought it an electoral majority and hence 'the revolution', while concealing (in practice) a subaltern acceptance of the *status quo* by providing its members with a large collective private world. The German left had spent its time criticizing the *de facto* abandonment of revolutionary or any working-class struggle by the SPD, but had little chance to develop more than a few buds of an alternative policy, which never bore fruit. The German CP settled down to the same attitude as the old SPD, except for its genuinely revolutionary temper: to mobilize, to confront and to wait. It had not time – though quite a few of the early KPD leaders might have had the capacity – to develop a revolutionary politics; in other words, at the least, something political to do when there were no actual barricades to be put up. It lacked that tradition of participation in a going system of radical, or even bourgeois-reformist, politics, which, with all its dangers, provided the proletarian left of other countries with strategic or tactical models for non-insurrectionary periods. When the French CP, 'bolshevized' in every sense, including a fair proportion of its

[6] A case in point may be the late Gerhart Eisler, whose policy as a Weimar leader combined unconditional loyalty to the USSR with opposition to local ultra-leftism. He was actually instrumental at one point in securing a temporary suspension of Thaelmann from the leadership, and subsequently disappeared into Comintern international service, until his return – in various secondary functions – to the German Democratic Republic.

leaders, confronted a problem like fascism, it would automatically think of falling back on a familiar political device, the temporary bloc of the left or the 'people', in defence of the Republic. In fact there are signs that even during the most insanely sectarian phase of 1928–33, these were the reflexes of PCF leaders, though they were still stifled by the Comintern. It was not that someone like Maurice Thorez was less of a good bolshevik than Thaelmann, or even that he was brighter – though he was; but that there was a French tradition of proletarian *political action*, whereas in Germany there was not. There they bred fighters of unparalleled bravery and loyalty and remarkable organizers, but not revolutionary politicians.

Hence the KPD not merely failed in the crucial period of Hitler's rise to power – the prevailing policy in Moscow would have made it almost impossible to succeed even if, what is more than doubtful, the German SPD would have tolerated a common resistance to fascism. It did not even realize that it was failing, until long after it was too late, let alone how catastrophically and irrevocably it had failed. And so it went down to total and final defeat. For the test of its failure lies not in Hitler's victory, nor even in the rapid, brutal and effective destruction of the party which was the most persistent, the bravest, in a sense the *only* active force of opposition under the Nazi dictatorship. *It lies in the failure of the KPD to revive after 1945*, except in the Russian-occupied zone, where political conditions eliminated its potential rivals.[7] When Hitler had been defeated, the old SPD, which had done nothing to prevent his rise and had virtually liquidated itself peacefully after his triumph, revived as the major mass party of the West German working class. The KPD still polled about 6 per cent (1·4 million votes) in 1949, compared to the SPD's 30 per cent, but by 1953 it was down to 2·2 per cent (0·6 million votes) compared to the SPD's 29 per cent, and there is no reason to believe that it would have done all that much better, had it not been formally banned by the federal republic. In a word, after 1945 it lived on rapidly wasting assets. It had failed during the Weimar Republic to establish itself as a permanent factor in the German working-class movement.

[7] The argument that the KPD under Weimar had its greatest bastions in what is now the DDR, is not convincing. In actual fact, the greatest preponderance of KPD over SPD voters in 1932 was to be found in the Rhine-Ruhr area, where the party had about twice as much support as its rival.

Its failure contrasts not only with its striking mass influence in the Weimar days, but also with the record of other – generally smaller – CP's in countries where the anti-Russian reflex might have been expected to weaken them. In Austria, for instance, the Communists continued to poll a steady 5·5 per cent in the first ten postwar years (their support before 1938 had been negligible). In Finland, they never polled less than 20 per cent (perhaps double their interwar score). Both these countries had fought wars against the USSR, or lost territory, or been partly occupied by the Red army. Almost everywhere in Europe the CPs emerged from the period of anti-fascism stronger, and – at least for a time – more deeply rooted in their national working classes than before. In Germany, Hitler had eliminated them as a mass movement.

Yet one cannot conclude the tragic survey of the Weimar KPD entirely on this gloomy note. For it did, after all, achieve what the KPD set out to achieve – a German Socialist Republic, and the fact that this came into existence through the Red army rather than through the efforts of the German movement, would have been perfectly acceptable to the Weimar communists. The German Democratic Republic must be entered on the balance sheet as much as the decisive defeat in the western part of the country. For that republic, which can only be criticized if we also acknowledge its remarkable achievements in very difficult circumstances,[8] is indeed the child of the KPD. To this extent the critique of the party must be qualified. After all, how many other communist parties have succeeded in actually building new societies ? Yet who ever doubted that, if someone ever handed power to them on a plate, the great body of upright, brave, loyal, devoted, able and efficient functionaries and executives who returned from exile and from the concentration camps to do their duty as communists, would do a competent job ?

How left-wing parties behave when they are given power is not an insignificant test: social democratic ones have failed it with great regularity, starting with the German SPD in 1918. But communist parties have always known that they would pass it. The German KPD, however, failed other tests, by which revolutionary movements

[8] Two of these achievements are worth noting: the genuine settling of accounts with the Nazi past of the German people, and the quiet refusal to join, except in the most marginal way, in the show trials, victimizations and executions of communists which disfigured the other east European regimes in the late Stalin period.

must also be judged. Unlike the French and Italian CPs, it failed to become an integral part of its working-class movement, though it had excellent chances of doing so. Its political history proved as impermanent as the Weimar Republic. It failed to develop any policy for operating under conditions of even a temporarily stabilized capitalism, and for this reason it went down before Hitler with the rest of the Weimar Republic. This failure reflected a more general difficulty which faced all the communist parties or indeed all revolutionary socialists in developed industrial countries: how to envisage a transition to socialism in conditions other than the historically exceptional ones of the years after 1917. Yet while the development of other CPs shows some attempt to come to terms with this problem (in so far as they were not prevented by outside influence), that of the KPD does not. While it was a mass force, it did one thing: it held the red flag high. Its worst enemies cannot accuse it of any compromise with reformism, any tendency to allow itself to be absorbed by the system. But confrontation is no policy. In a period of crisis, as in 1929–33, it might attract growing support from those who had nothing to lose – by the spring of 1932, 85 per cent of the party membership was unemployed – but numerical support is not necessarily strength. The 2,500 or so members of the PCI, at the very same time, represented a more serious force than the 300,000 German communists, the 6,000,000 KPD voters.

The history of the KPD is tragic. The great hope of the world in 1919, the only significant mass communist party in the west in 1932, it is little more than an episode in the history of Western Germany. Perhaps it failed for German reasons: because of the inability of the German left to overcome the historic weaknesses of both the bourgeoisie and the proletariat of that great and ambiguous country. But other possibilities for its development can be envisaged, without excessive unrealism. At all events Dr Weber provides us with a wealth of material for assessing a crucial case of failure in the history of the left. Others may perhaps learn from this failure. They should read him with care, and not without compassion.

(1970)

II
ANARCHISTS

7
BOLSHEVISM AND THE ANARCHISTS

The libertarian tradition of communism – anarchism – has been bitterly hostile to the marxist ever since Bakunin, or for that matter Proudhon. Marxism, and even more leninism, have been equally hostile to anarchism as theory and programme and contemptuous of it as a political movement. Yet if we investigate the history of the international communist movement in the period of the Russian revolution and the Communist International, we find a curious asymmetry. While the leading spokesmen of anarchism maintained their hostility to bolshevism with, at best, a momentary wavering during the actual revolution, or at the moment when the news of October reached them, the attitude of the bolsheviks, in and outside Russia, was for a time considerably more benevolent to the anarchists. This is the subject of the present paper.

The theoretical attitude with which bolshevism approached anarchist and anarcho-syndicalist movements after 1917, was quite clear. Marx, Engels and Lenin had all written on the subject, and in general there seemed to be no ambiguity or mutual inconsistency about their views, which may be summarized as follows:

(*a*) There is no difference between the ultimate objects of marxists and anarchists, i.e. a libertarian communism in which exploitation, classes and the state will have ceased to exist.

(*b*) Marxists believe that this ultimate stage will be separated from the overthrow of bourgeois power through proletarian revolution, by a more or less protracted interval characterized by the 'dictatorship of the proletariat' and other transitional arrangements, in which state power would play some part. There was room for some argument about the precise meaning of the classical marxist writings on these problems of transition, but no ambiguity at all about the marxist view that the proletarian revolution would not give rise immediately to communism, and that the state could not be abolished, but would 'wither away'. On this point the conflict with anarchist doctrine was total and clearly defined.

(*c*) In addition to the characteristic readiness of marxists to see the power of a revolutionary state used for revolutionary purposes, marxism was actively committed to a firm belief in the superiority of centralization to decentralization or federalism and (especially in the leninist version), to a belief in the indispensability of leadership, organization and discipline and the inadequacy of any movement based on mere 'spontaneity'.

(*d*) Where participation in the formal processes of politics was possible, marxists took it for granted that socialist and communist movements would engage in it as much as in any other activities which could contribute to advance the overthrow of capitalism.

(*e*) While some marxists developed critiques of the actual or potential authoritarian and/or bureaucratic tendencies of parties based on the classical marxist tradition, none of these critics abandoned their characteristic lack of sympathy for anarchist movements, so long as they considered themselves to be marxists.

The record of the political relations between marxist movements and anarchist or anarcho-syndicalist ones, appeared equally unambiguous in 1917. In fact, these relations had been considerably more acrimonious in the lifetime of Marx, Engels and the Second International than they were to be in that of the Comintern. Marx himself had fought and criticized Proudhon and Bakunin, and the other way round. The major social democratic parties had done their best to exclude anarchists, or been obliged to do so. Unlike the First International, the Second no longer included them, at all events after the London Congress of 1896. Where marxist and anarchist movements coexisted, it was as rivals, if not as enemies. However, though the marxists were intensely exasperated by the anarchists in practice revolutionary marxists, who shared with them an increasing hostility to the reformism of the Second International, tended to regard them as revolutionaries, if misguided ones. This was in line with the theoretical view summarized in (*a*) above. At least anarchism and revolutionary syndicalism might be regarded as a comprehensible reaction against reformism and opportunism. Indeed, it might – and was – argued that reformism and anarcho-syndicalism were part of the same phenomenon : without the one, the other would not have gained so much ground. It could further be argued that the collapse of reformism would also automatically weaken anarcho-syndicalism.

It is not clear how far these views of the ideologists and political leaders were shared by the rank-and-file militants and supporters of the marxist movements. We may suppose that the differences were often much less clearly felt at this level. It is a well-known fact that doctrinal, ideological and programmatic distinctions which are of major importance at one level, are of negligible importance at another – e.g. that as late as 1917 'social democratic' workers in many Russian towns were barely if at all aware of the differences between bolsheviks and mensheviks. The historian of labour movements and their doctrines forgets such facts at his peril.

This general background must be supplemented by a discussion of the differences between the situation in various parts of the world, in so far as these affected the relations between communists and anarchists or anarcho-syndicalists. No comprehensive survey can be made here, but at least three different types of countries must be distinguished :

(*a*) Regions in which anarchism had never been of major significance in the labour movement, e.g. most of north-western Europe (except the Netherlands), and several colonial areas in which labour and socialist movements had hardly developed before 1917.

(*b*) Regions in which anarchist influence had been significant, but diminished dramatically, and perhaps decisively, in the period 1914–36. These must include part of the Latin world, e.g. France, Italy and some Latin American countries, as also China, Japan and – for somewhat different reasons – Russia.

(*c*) Regions in which anarchist influence remained significant, if not dominant, until the latter part of the 1930s. Spain is the most obvious case.

In regions of the first type relations with movements describing themselves as anarchist or anarcho-syndicalist were of no significance to communist movements. The existence of small numbers of anarchists, mainly artists and intellectuals, raised no political problem, and neither did the presence of anarchist political refugees, immigrant communities in which anarchism might be influential, and other phenomena marginal to the native labour movement. This appears to have been the case in, say, Britain and Germany after the 1870s and 1880s, when anarchist trends had played some part, mainly disruptive, in the special circumstances of extremely small socialist movements or socialist movements temporarily pressed into semi-illegality as by Bismarck's anti-socialist law. The struggles between centralized and decentralized types of movement, between bureaucratic and anti-bureaucratic, 'spontaneous' and 'disciplined' movements were fought out without any special reference (except by academic writers or a few very erudite marxists) to the anarchists. This was the case in Britain in the period corresponding to that of revolutionary syndicalism on the continent. The extent to which communist parties showed themselves to be aware of anarchism as a political problem in their countries, remains to be seriously studied by a systematic analysis of their polemical publications (in so far as these did not merely echo the preoccupations of the International), of their translation and/or re-publication of classical marxist writings on anarchism, etc. However, it may be suggested with some confidence that they regarded the problem as negligible, compared to that of reformism, doctrinal schisms within the communist movement, or certain kinds of petty-bourgeois ideological trends such as, in Britain, pacifism. It was certainly entirely possible to be deeply involved in the communist movement in Germany in the early 1930s, in Britain in the later 1930s, without paying more than the most cursory or academic attention to anarchism, or indeed without ever having to discuss the subject.

The regions of the second type are in some respects the most interesting from the point of view of the present discussion. We are here dealing with countries or areas in which anarchism was an important, in some periods or sectors a dominant influence in the trade unions or the political movements of the extreme left.

The crucial historical fact here is the dramatic decline of anarchist (or anarcho-syndicalist) influence in the decade after 1914. In the belligerent countries of Europe this was a neglected aspect of the general collapse of the prewar left. This is usually presented primarily as a crisis of social democracy, and with much justification. At the same time it was also a crisis of the libertarian or anti-bureaucratic revolutionaries in two ways. First, many of them (e.g. among 'revolutionary syndicalists') joined the bulk of marxist social democrats in the rush to the patriotic banners – at least for a time. Second, those who did not, proved, on the whole, quite ineffective in their opposition to the war, and even less effective at the end of the war in their attempts to provide an alternative libertarian revolutionary movement to the bolsheviks. To cite only one decisive example. In France (as Professor Kriegel has shown), the 'Carnet B' drawn up by the Ministry of the Interior to include all those 'considérés comme dangereux pour l'ordre social', i.e. 'les révolutionnaires, les syndicalistes et les anarchistes', in fact contained mainly anarchists, or rather 'la faction des anarchistes qui milite dans le mouvement syndical'. On 1 August 1914 the Minister of the Interior, Malvy, decided to pay no attention to the Carnet B, i.e. to leave at liberty the very men who, in the government's opinion, had convincingly established their intention to oppose war by all means, and who might presumably have become the cadres of a working-class anti-war movement. In fact, few of them had made any concrete preparations for resistance or sabotage, and none any preparation likely to worry the authorities. In a word, Malvy decided that the entire body of men accepted as being the most dangerous revolutionaries, was negligible. He was, of course, quite correct.

The failure of the syndicalist and libertarian revolutionaries, further confirmed in 1918–20, contrasted dramatically with the success of the Russian bolsheviks. In fact, it sealed the fate of anarchism as a major independent force on the left outside a few exceptional countries for the next fifty years. It became hard to recall that in 1905–14 the marxist left had in most countries been on the fringe of the revolutionary movement, the main body of marxists had been identified with a *de facto* non-revolutionary social democracy, while the bulk of the revolutionary left was anarcho-syndicalist, or at least much closer to the ideas and the mood of anarcho-syndicalism than to that of classical marxism. Marxism was henceforth identified with actively revolutionary movements, and with communist parties and groups, or with social democratic parties which, like the Austrian, prided themselves on being markedly left wing. Anarchism and anarcho-syndicalism entered upon a dramatic and uninterrupted decline. In Italy the triumph of fascism accelerated it, but where, in the France of 1924, let alone of

1929 or 1934 was the anarchist movement which had been the characteristic form of the revolutionary left in 1914?

The question is not merely rhetorical. The answer is and must be: largely in the new communist or communist-led movements. In the absence of adequate research this can not yet be adequately documented, but the broad facts seem clear. Even some of the leading figures or well-known activists of the 'bolshevized' communist parties came from the former libertarian movements or from the militant trade union movements with their libertarian *ambiance*: thus in France Monmousseau and probably Duclos. This is all the more striking, since it was rather unlikely that leading members of marxist parties would be drawn from former anarcho-syndicalists, and even less likely that leading figures in the libertarian movement would opt for leninism.[1] It is indeed highly likely that (as the leader of the Dutch CP, De Groot observes, perhaps not without some *parti pris*) that ex-libertarian workers adapted themselves better to life in the new CPs than ex-libertarian intellectuals or petty bourgeois. After all, at the level of the working-class militant, the doctrinal or programmatic differences which divide ideologists and political leaders so sharply, are often quite unreal, and may have little significance, unless *at this level* – i.e. in the worker's specific locality or trade union – different organizations or leaders have long-established patterns of rivalry.

Nothing is more likely, therefore, than that workers previously adhering to the most militant or revolutionary union in their locality or occupation should, after its disappearance shift without much difficulty into the communist union which now represented militancy or revolutionary attitudes. When old movements disappear, such a transfer is common. The old movement may retain its mass influence here and there, and the leaders and militants who have identified themselves with it, may continue to hold it together on a diminishing scale as best they can, in so far as they do not retire *de jure* or *de facto* into an unreconciled inactivity. Some of the rank and file may also drop out. But a large proportion must be expected to transfer to the most suitable alternative, if

[1] Of a small random sample of French communist MPs between the wars, the *Dictionnaire des Parlementaires Français 1889–1940*, gives the following indications about their pre-communist past: Socialist 5; 'Sillon', then socialist 1; trade union activity (tendency unknown) 3; libertarian 1; no pre-communist past 1.

one is available. Such transfers have not been investigated seriously, so that we know no more about what happened to ex-anarcho-syndicalists (and those who had followed their lead) than we know about ex-members or followers of the Independent Labour Party in Britain after the 1930s, or ex-communists in Western Germany after 1945.

If a large part of the rank and file of the new communist parties, and more especially, the new revolutionary trade unions, was composed of former libertarians, it would be natural to expect this to have had some effect on them. On the whole there is little sign of this within the communist parties. To take merely one representative example, the discussions on 'bolshevizing the Communist International' in the Enlarged Executive of that organization, March–April 1925, which dealt specifically with the problem of non-communist influences within the communist movement. There are little more than a half-dozen references to syndicalist and none to anarchist influence in this document.[2] They are confined entirely to the cases of France, Italy and the United States. As for France, the loss 'of the larger part of the former leading officials [of social democratic origins in Germany], and of petty-bourgeois syndicalist origins in France' is noted (p. 38). Treint reported that 'our Party has eliminated all the errors of Trotskyism: all the individualist quasi-anarchist errors, the errors of the belief in legitimacy, of the coexistence of diverse factions in the Party. It has also learned to know the Luxemburgist errors' (p. 99). The ECCI resolution recommended, as one of ten points concerning the French party 'in spite of all former French traditions, establishment of a well-organized Communist Mass Party' (p. 160). As for Italy, 'the numerous and diverse origin of the deviations which have arisen in Italy' are noted, but without reference to any libertarian trends. Bordiga's similarity to 'Italian syndicalism' is mentioned, though it is not claimed that he 'identifies himself completely' with this and other analogous views. The Marxist-Syndicalist faction (Avanguardia group) is mentioned as one of the reactions against the opportunism of the Second International, as is its dissolution 'into trade syndicalism' after leaving the party (pp. 192–3). The recruitment of the CPUSA from two sources – the Socialist Party and syndicalist organizations – is mentioned (p. 45). If we compare these scattered references to the preoccupation of the International

[2] *Bolshevising the Communist International*, London, 1925.

in the same document with a variety of other ideological deviations and other problems, the relatively minor impact of libertarian-syndicalist traditions within communism, or at least within the major communist parties of the middle 1920s, is evident.

This may to some extent be an illusion, for it is clear that behind several of the tendencies which troubled the International more urgently, such traditions may be discerned. The insistence of the dangers of 'Luxemburgism' with its stress on spontaneity, its hostility to nationalism and other similar ideas, may well be aimed at the attitudes of militants formed in the libertarian-syndicalist school, as also the hostility – by this time no longer a matter of very serious concern – to electoral abstentionism. Behind 'Bordighism', we can certainly discern a preoccupation with such tendencies. In various western parties Trotskyism and other marxist deviations probably attracted communists of syndicalist origins, uncomfortable in the 'bolshevized' parties – e.g. Rosmer and Monatte. Yet it is significant that the *Cahiers du Bolchevisme* (28 November 1924), in analyzing the ideological trends within the French CP, make no allusion to syndicalism. The journal divided the party into '20 per cent of Jauresism, 10 per cent of marxism, 20 per cent of leninism, 20 per cent of Trotskyism, and 30 per cent of Confusionism'. Whatever the actual strength of ideas and attitudes derived from the old syndicalist tradition, that tradition itself had ceased to be significant, except as a component of various left-wing, sectarian or schismatic versions of marxism.

However, for obvious reasons, anarchist problems preoccupied the communist movement more in those parts of the world where before the October revolution the political labour movement had been almost entirely anarchist and social democratic movements had been negligible, or where the anarcho-syndicalists maintained their strength and influence during the 1920s; as in large regions of Latin America. It is not surprising that the Red International of Labour Unions in the 1920s was much preoccupied with these problems in Latin America, or that as late as 1935 the Communist International observed that 'the remnants of anarcho-syndicalism have not yet been completely overcome' in the CP of Brazil (whose original membership consisted overwhelmingly of former anarchists). Nevertheless, when we consider the significance of anarcho-syndicalism in this continent, the problems arising from it seem to have caused the Comintern little real preoccupation after the Great

Depression of 1929–30. Its chief criticism of the local communist parties in this respect appears to have been that they were unable to benefit sufficiently from the rapid decline of the anarchist and anarcho-syndicalist organizations and the growing sympathy for communism of their members.[3]

In a word, the libertarian movements were now regarded as rapidly declining forces which no longer posed major political problems.

Was this complacency entirely justified? We may suspect that the old traditions were stronger than official communist literature suggests, at any rate within the trade union movements. Thus it is fairly clear that the transfer of the Cuban tobacco workers' union from anarcho-syndicalist to communist leadership made no substantial difference either to its trade union activities or to the attitude of its members and militants.[4] A good deal of research is needed to discover how far, in former strongholds of anarcho-syndicalism the subsequent communist trade union movement showed signs of the survival of old habits and practices.

Spain was virtually the only country in which anarchism continued to be a major force in the labour movement after the Great Depression, while at the same time communism was – until the Civil War – comparatively negligible. The problem of the communist attitude to Spanish anarchism was of no international significance before the second republic, and in the period of the Popular Front and Civil War became too vast and complex for cursory treatment. I shall therefore omit discussion of it.

[3] 'The growth of discontent among the masses and of their resistance to the attacks of the ruling classes and of imperialism have sharpened the process of disintegration among socialist, anarchist and anarcho-syndicalist organizations. In the most recent period the recognition of the need for a united front with the communists has sunk quite deep roots among rather wide strata of their rank and file. At the same time the tendency for a direct entry into the ranks of the revolutionary unions and communist parties has grown stronger (especially in Cuba, Brazil, Paraguay). After the sixth World Congress there has been a marked drop in the specific weight of anarcho-syndicalism within the labour movements of South and Caribbean America. In some countries the best elements of the anarcho-syndicalist movement have joined the Communist Party, e.g. in Argentina, Brazil, Paraguay and Cuba [. . .]. In other countries the weakening of anarcho-syndicalist influence was accompanied by a strengthening of socialist and reformist organizations (Argentina), the "national-reformist parties" (Mexico, Cuba)' : *Die Kommunistische Internationale vor dem 7. Weltkongress*, p. 472.

[4] I owe this point to Miss Jean Stubbs, who is preparing a doctoral thesis on the Cuban tobacco workers.

The fundamental attitude of the bolsheviks towards anarchists thus was that they were misguided revolutionaries, as distinct from the social democrats who were pillars of the bourgeoisie. As Zinoviev put it in 1920, in discussion with the Italians who were considerably less well disposed towards their own anarchists: 'In times of revolution Malatesta is better than d'Aragona. They do stupid things, but they're revolutionaries. We fought side by side with the syndicalists and the anarchists against Kerensky and the Mensheviks. We mobilized thousands of workers in this way. In times of revolution one needs revolutionaries. We have to approach them and form a bloc with them in revolutionary periods.'[5] This comparatively lenient attitude of the bolsheviks was probably determined by two factors: the relative insignificance of anarchists in Russia, and the visible readiness of anarchists and syndicalists after the October revolution to turn to Moscow, at all events until it was clear that the terms for union were unacceptable. It was no doubt reinforced later by the rapid decline of anarchism and syndicalism, which – outside a small and diminishing number of countries – made it seem increasingly insignificant as a trend in the labour movement. 'I have seen and talked to few anarchists in my life', said Lenin at the Third Congress of the CI (*Protokoll*, Hamburg, 1921, p. 510.) Anarchism had never been more than a minor or local problem for the bolsheviks. An official CI annual for 1922–3 illustrates this attitude. The appearance of anarchist groups in 1905 is mentioned, as is the fact that they lacked all contact with the mass movement and were 'as good as annihilated' by the victory of reaction. In 1917 anarchist groups appeared in all important centres of the country, but in spite of various direct action they lacked contact with the masses in most places and hardly anywhere succeeded in taking over leadership. 'Against the bourgeois government they operated in practice as the "left", and incidentally disorganized, wing of the Bolsheviks.' Their struggle lacked independent significance. 'Individuals who came from the ranks of the anarchists, performed important services for the revolution; many anarchists joined the Russian CP.' The October revolution split them into 'sovietist', some of whom joined the bolsheviks while others remained benevolently neutral, and 'consequent' anarchists who rejected Soviet power,

[5] P. Spriano, *Storia del Partito Comunista Italiano*, vol. 1, p. 77.

split into various and sometimes eccentric factions, and are insignificant. The various illegal anarchist groups active during the Kronstadt rising, have almost totally disappeared.[6] Such was the background against which the leading party of the Comintern judged the nature of the anarchist and syndicalist problem.

It need hardly be said that neither the bolsheviks nor the communist parties outside Russia were inclined to compromise their views in order to draw the libertarians towards them. Angel Pestaña, who represented the Spanish CNT at the Second Congress of the CI found himself isolated and his views rejected. The Third Congress, which discussed relations with syndicalists and anarchists at greater length, established the distance between them and the communists even more clearly, under the impact of some trends within the communist parties and what was believed to be an increase in anarchist and syndicalist influence in Italy after the occupation of the factories.[7] Lenin intervened on this point, observing that agreement with anarchists might be possible on objectives – i.e. the abolition of exploitation and classes – but not on principles – i.e. 'the dictatorship of the proletariat and the use of state power during the transitional period'.[8] Nevertheless, the increasingly sharp critique of anarcho-syndicalist views was combined with a positive attitude towards the movement especially in France. Even in the Fourth Congress the syndicalists were still, in France, contrasted to their advantage not only with the social democrats, but with ex-social democratic communists. 'We have to look for quite a lot of elements for a Communist Party in the ranks of the Syndicalists, in the ranks of the best parts of the Syndicalists. This is strange but true' (Zinoviev).[9] Not until after the Fifth Congress – i.e. during the period of 'bolshevization' does the negative critique of anarcho-syndicalism clearly begin to prevail over the positive appreciation of the movement – but by then it is so far merged with the critique of Trotskyism, Luxemburgism and other intra-communist deviations as to lose its

[6] 'Jahrbuch für Wirschaft, Politik und Arbeiterbewegung' (Hamburg), 1922–3, pp. 247, 250, 481–2.

[7] *Decisions of the Third Congress of the Communist International*, London, 1921, p. 10.

[8] *Protokoll*, p. 510.

[9] *Fourth Congress of the Communist International. Abridged Report.* London, 1923, p. 18.

specific political point.[10] By this time, of course, anarchism and syndicalism were in rapid decline, outside a few special areas.

It is therefore at first sight surprising that anti-anarchist propaganda seems to have developed on a more systematic basis within the international communist movement in the middle 1930s. This period saw the publication of the pamphlet, *Marx et Engels contre l'anarchisme*, in France (1935), in the series 'Elements du communisme', and an obviously polemical *History of Anarchism in Russia*, by E. Yaroslavsky (English edition 1937). It may also be worth noting the distinctly more negative tone of the references to anarchism in Stalin's *Short History of the CPSU* (*b*) (1938),[11] compared to the account of the early 1920s, quoted above.

The most obvious reason for this revival of anti-anarchist sentiment was the situation in Spain, a country which became increasingly important in international communist strategy from 1931, and certainly from 1934. This is evident in the extended polemics of Lozovsky which are specifically aimed at the Spanish CNT.[12] However, until the Civil War the anarchist problem in Spain was considered much less urgent than the social democratic problem, especially between 1928 and the turn in Comintern policy after June–July 1934. The bulk of the references in official CI documents in this period concentrates, as might be expected, on the misdeeds of Spanish socialists. During the Civil War the situation changed, and it is evident that, for instance, Yaros-

[10] Cf. Manuilsky: 'We think, for instance, that so-called Trotskyism has a great deal in common with individualistic Proudhonism [...] It is not by accident that Rosmer and Monatte, in their new organ directed against the Communist Party, resuscitate theoretically the ideas of the old revolutionary syndicalism, mixed with a defence of Russian Trotskyism': *The Communist International*, English edition, no. 10, new series, p. 58.

[11] 'As to the Anarchists, a group whose influence was insignificant to start with, they now definitely disintegrated into minute groups, some of which merged with criminal elements, thieves and provocateurs, the dregs of society; others became expropriators "by conviction", robbing the peasants and small townsfolk, and appropriating the premises and funds of workers' clubs; while others still openly went over to the camp of the counter-revolutionaries, and devoted themselves to feathering their own nests as menials of the bourgeoisie. They were all opposed to authority of any kind, particularly and especially to the revolutionary authority of the workers and peasants, for they knew that a revolutionary government would not allow them to rob the people and steal public property', p. 203.

[12] A. Lozovsky, *Marx and the Trade Unions*, London, 1935 (first edn. 1933), pp. 35–6 and especially pp. 146–54.

lavsky's book is aimed primarily at Spain: 'The workers in those countries where they now have to choose between the doctrine of the anarchists and those of the Communists should know which of the two roads of revolution to choose.'[13]

However, perhaps another – though perhaps relatively minor – element in the revived anti-anarchist polemics should also be noted. It is evident both from the basic text which is constantly quoted and reprinted – Stalin's critique of Bukharin's alleged semi-anarchism, made in 1929 – and from other references, that anarchizing tendencies are condemned primarily because they 'repudiate the state in the period of transition from capitalism to socialism' (Stalin). The classical critique of anarchism by Marx, Engels and Lenin, tends to be identified with the defence of the tendencies of state development in the stalinist period.

To sum up :

The bolshevik hostility to anarchism and anarcho-syndicalism as a theory, strategy or form of organized movement was clear and unwavering, and all 'deviations' within the communist movement in this direction were firmly rejected. For practical purposes such 'deviations' or what could be regarded as such, ceased to be of significance in and outside Russia from the early 1920s.

The bolshevik attitude to the actual anarchist and anarcho-syndicalist movements was surprisingly benevolent. It was determined by three main factors:

(*a*) the belief that the bulk of anarcho-syndicalist workers were revolutionaries, and both objective and, given the right circumstances, subjective allies of communism against social democracy, and potential communist ;

(*b*) the undoubted attraction which the October revolution exercised on many syndicalists and even anarchists in the years immediately following 1917 ;

(*c*) the equally unquestioned and increasingly rapid decline of anarchism and anarcho-syndicalism as a mass movement in all but a very few of its old centres.

For the reasons mentioned above, the bolsheviks devoted little attention to the problem of anarchism outside the few areas in which it retained its strength (and, in so far as the local communist parties

[13] *Op. cit.*, p. 10.

were weak, not much even within those areas) after the early 1920s. However, the rise to international significance of Spain, and perhaps also the attempt to give a theoretical legitimation to the stalinist development of a dictatorial and terrorist state, led to a revival of anti-anarchist polemics in the period between the Great Slump and the end of the Spanish Civil War.

(1969)

8
THE SPANISH BACKGROUND

The Iberian peninsula has problems but no solutions, a state of affairs which is common or even normal in the 'third world', but extremely rare in Europe. For better or worse most states on our continent have a stable and potentially permanent economic and social structure, an established line of development. The problems of almost all of Europe, serious and even fundamental though they may be, arise out of the solution of earlier ones. In western and northern Europe they arose mainly on the basis of successful capitalist development, in eastern Europe (much of which was in a situation analogous to Spain until 1945) on the basis of a soviet-type socialism. In neither case do the basic economic and social patterns look provisional, as, for instance, the patterns of national relations within and between states still so often appear to be. Belgian capitalism or Yugoslav socialism may well change, perhaps fundamentally; but both are obviously far less likely to collapse at slight provocation than the complex *ad hoc* administrative formulae for ensuring the coexistence of Flemings and Walloons, or of various mutually suspicious Balkan nationalities.

Spain is different. Capitalism has persistently failed in that country and so has social revolution, in spite of its constant imminence and occasional eruption. The problems of Spain arise out of the failures, not the successes, of the past. Its political structure is nothing if not provisional. Even Franco's regime, which has lasted longer than any other since 1808 (it has beaten the record of the Canovas era 1875–97), is patently temporary. Its future is so undetermined that even the restoration of hereditary monarchy can be seriously considered as a political prospect. Spain's problems have been obvious to every intelligent observer since the eighteenth century. A variety of solutions have been proposed and occasionally applied. The point is that all of them have failed. Spain has not by any means stood still. By its own standards the economic and social changes of the nineteenth century were substantial, and anyone who has watched the country's evolution in the past fifteen years knows how unrealistic it is to think of it as essentially the same as in 1936. An Aragonese *pueblo* demonstrates this very clearly, if only in the increase of local tractors from two to thirty-two, of motor vehicles from three to sixty-eight, of bank branches from nought to six.) Nevertheless the fundamental economic and social problems of the country remain unresolved, and the gap between it and more developed (or more fundamentally transformed) European states remains.

Raymond Carr, whose remarkable book probably supersedes all other histories of nineteenth- and twentieth-century Spain for the time being,[1] formulates the problem as that of the failure of Spanish liberalism; that is to say of an essentially capitalist economic development, a bourgeois-parliamentary political system, and a culture and intellectual development of the familiar western kind. It might be equally well, and perhaps more profitably, formulated as that of the failure of Spanish social revolution. For if, as Carr admits, liberalism never had serious chances of success, social revolution was, perhaps for this reason, a much more serious prospect. Whatever we may think of the upheavals of the Napoleonic period, the 1830s (which Carr analyzes with particular brilliance), of 1854–6 or 1868–74, there can be no denying that social revolution actually broke out in 1931–6, that it did so without any significant assistance from the international situation, and that the case is practically unique in western Europe since 1848.

Yet it failed; and not only, or even primarily because of the foreign aid given to its enemies. One would not wish to underestimate the importance of Italian and German aid or Anglo-French 'non-intervention' in the Civil War, the greater single-mindedness of Axis than of Soviet support, or the remarkable military achievements of the Republic, which Carr rightly recognizes. It is quite conceivable that, given a different international configuration, the Republic could have won. But it is equally undeniable that the Civil War was a double struggle against armed counter-revolution and the gigantic, and in the last analysis fatal, internal weaknesses of revolution. Successful revolutions, from the

[1] Raymond Carr, *Spain 1808–1939*, Oxford, 1966.

French Jacobins to the Vietnamese, have shown a capacity to win against equally long or even longer odds. The Spanish Republic did not.

There is no great mystery about the failure of Spanish liberalism, though so much of the nineteenth-century history of the country and of its basic social and economic situation is too little known for excessively confident analysis. 'The changes in the classic agricultural structure of Spain between 1750 and 1850 were achieved by a rearrangement of the traditional economy, by its expansion in space, not by any fundamental change' (p. 29). (Carr's explanation that poverty of soil and capital resources made this inevitable, is not entirely convincing.) What it amounted to was that Spain maintained a rapidly growing population, not by industrial and agricultural revolution, but by a vast increase in the extensive cultivation of cereals, which in time exhausted the soil and turned inland Spain into an even more impoverished semi-desert than it already was. Logically, the politics of agricultural inefficiency gave way to those of peasant revolution. 'In the nineties politicians were bullied by the powerfully organized wheat interest; in the twentieth century they were alarmed by the threat of revolution on the great estates.' The alternative, intensive cash crops for export (e.g. oranges) was not generally applicable without prohibitively costly investment, perhaps not even with it; though Carr seems ultra-sceptical of the possibilities of irrigation, though less so of afforestation. Spanish industry was a marginal phenomenon, uncompetitive on the world market, and therefore dependent on the feeble domestic market and (notably in the case of Catalonia) the relics of the empire. It was liberal Barcelona which resisted Cuban independence most ferociously, since 60 per cent of its exports went there. The Catalan and Basque bourgeoisie were not an adequate basis for Spanish capitalism. As Vilar has shown, the Catalan businessmen failed to capture the direction of the national economic policy, and therefore retreated into the defensive posture of autonomism, which the Republic eventually conceded to them and the Basques.

Under these circumstances the economic and social basis of liberalism and its political striking-force, were feeble. As in so many underdeveloped countries, there were two active forces in politics: the urban petty-bourgeoisie, standing in the shadow of the urban plebs, and the army, an institution for furthering the careers of energetic members of the same stratum, and a militant trade union for the most powerfully organized sector of the white-collar unemployed, who had to look to the state because the economy could not employ them. The 'pronunciamento', a curious Iberian invention whose rituals became highly traditional, replaced liberal politics in the first half of the nineteenth century. In the second half it became 'a speculative business enterprise for generals' and in the twentieth century it ceased to have any connection with liberalism.

Revolutions began with a pronunciamento or with what Carr calls the 'primitive provincial revolution' – plebeian risings spreading from town to town by contagion – or both. The fighting poor were essential, but perilous. Local notables, not to mention national ones, retreated from the ever-present danger of social revolution into the 'committee stage', when local power passed to *juntas* of notables with an optional representative or two of the people, while the national government collapsed. 'The final stage was the reimposition, by a ministry that "represented" the revolution, of central government control.' Kiernan's monograph on 1854 describes and explains this process in full detail.[2] Of course in the nineteenth century a proletariat barely existed outside Barcelona, which consequently became the classical revolutionary city of western Europe. The peasantry long remained politically ineffective, or Carlist, i.e. attached to ultra-reactionary politicians and hostile on principle to the towns.

Spanish liberalism was thus squeezed into the narrow space of manoeuvre between the 'primitive revolution', without which nothing would change, and the need to damp it down almost immediately. It was not surprising that a vehicle obliged to brake almost as soon as the foot hit the accelerator, could not get very far. The best hope of the bourgeois moderates was to put some regime in power which would allow the forces of capitalist development to develop; but they never developed enough. Their most usual achievement was to find some formula which neutralized social revolution or the ultra-reactionaries for a while by the combination of at least two of the three forces of 'official' politics: the army, the crown and the 'official' parties. As Carr shows, this was the pattern of Spanish politics: army plus politicians in the 1840s, crown plus politicians after 1875, army

[2] V. G. Kiernan, *The Revolution of 1854 in Spanish History*, Oxford, 1966.

plus crown under Primo de Rivera in the 1920s, and a collapse of the crown when it alienated the other two, as in 1854, 1868 and 1931. When there was no crown there had to be an '*ad hoc* military dictatorship'.

Yet Franco is not simply the successor of Alfonso. For in the twentieth century the forces of social revolution grew stronger than they had been in the nineteenth, because revolution retained its 'primitive' assets while acquiring two new and formidable assets: peasant revolution and the labour movement. It is their failure which poses the major problem of Spanish history and may perhaps throw light on a number of other underdeveloped countries. That failure was due to the anarchists.

This does not mean that the remarkable ineffectiveness of the Spanish revolution is due merely to the historic accident that Spain was colonized by Bakunin more than by Marx. (Even this is not quite an accident. It is characteristic of the cultural isolation of underdeveloped countries in the nineteenth century that so often ideas which were unimportant in the wider world became immensely influential there, like the philosophy of a certain Krause in Spain, or the politics of August Comte in Mexico and Brazil.) The facts of Spanish geography and history are against a nationally coordinated movement, but countries with at least as much regional and more national diversity have achieved one, like Yugoslavia. The self-contained universe of the Spanish *pueblo* long made national changes the result of periodic plebiscites by direct action of its municipalities. But other countries also know the phenomenon of extreme localism, for instance Italy. All the Spanish revolutions, as Carr shows, had an archaic house-style, irrespective of the ideological labels they brandished. It is doubtful whether 'Belmonte de los Caballeros' an Aragonese pueblo, would have behaved differently in 1931–6 had it been organized by the CNT rather than by the socialist UGT. Anarchism succeeded so well, because it was content to provide a mere label for the traditional political habits of revolutionary Spaniards. Yet political movements are not obliged to accept the historic characteristics of their environment, though they will be ineffective if they pay no attention to them. Anarchism was a disaster because it made no attempt to change the style of primitive Spanish revolt, and deliberately reinforced it.

It legitimized the traditional impotence of the poor. It turned politics, which even in its revolutionary form is a *practical* activity, into a form of moral gymnastics, a display of individual or collective devotion, self-sacrifice, heroism or self-improvement which justified its failure to achieve any concrete results by the argument that only revolution was worth fighting for, and its failure in revolution by the argument that anything which involved organization and discipline did not deserve the name. Spanish anarchism is a profoundly moving spectacle for the student of popular religion – it was really a form of secular millennialism – but not, alas, for the student of politics. It threw away political chances with a marvellously blind persistence. The attempts to steer it into a less suicidal course succeeded too late, though they were enough to defeat the generals' rising in 1936. Even then, they succeeded incompletely. The noble gunman Durruti, who symbolized both the ideal of the anarchist militant and conversion to the organization and discipline of real war, was probably killed by one of his own purist comrades.

This is not to deny the remarkable achievement of Spanish anarchism which was to create a working-class movement that remained genuinely revolutionary. Social democratic and in recent years even communist trade unions have rarely been able to escape either schizophrenia or betrayal of their socialist convictions, since for practical purposes – i.e. when acting as trade union militants or leaders – they must usually act on the assumption that the capitalist system is permanent. The CNT did not, though this did not make it a particularly effective body for trade unionist purposes, and on the whole it lost ground to the socialist UGT from the *trienio bolchevique* of 1918–20 till after the outbreak of the Civil War, except where the force of anarchist gunmen and long tradition kept rivals out of the field, as in Catalonia and Aragon. Still, Spanish workers as well as peasants remained revolutionary and acted accordingly when the occasion arose. True, they were not the only ones to retain the reflex of insurrection. In several other countries workers brought up in the communist tradition, or in that of maximalist socialism, reacted in a similiar way when nobody stopped them, and it was not until the middle 1930s that this reflex was actively discouraged in the international communist movement.

Again, neither the Spanish socialists nor the communists can be acquitted of responsibility for the failure of the Spanish revolution. The communists were fettered by the extreme sectarianism of the International's policy in 1928–34, at the very moment when the fall of the monarchy in 1931 opened up possibilities of strategies of alliance which they were not permitted (and probably unwilling) to use until some years later. Whether their weakness would have allowed them to use these effectively at the time is another matter. The socialists veered from opportunism to a strategically blind maximalism after 1934, which served to strengthen the right rather than to unite the left. Since they were visibly much more dangerous to the right than the anarchists (who were never more than a routine police problem), both because they were better organized and because they were in republican governments, the backlash of reaction was much more serious.

Nevertheless, the anarchists cannot escape major responsibility. Theirs was the basic tradition of labour in most parts of the republic which survived the initial military rising, and such deeply rooted traditions are difficult to change. Moreover, theirs was potentially still the majority movement of the left in the republic. They were in no position to 'make' the revolution of which they dreamed. But when the decision of the Popular Front government to resist the military rising by all means, including arming the people, turned a situation of social ferment into a revolution, they were its chief initial beneficiaries. There seems little doubt about the initial preponderance of the anarcho-syndicalists in the armed militia, and none about their domination of the great process of 'sovietization' (in the original sense of the word) in Catalonia, Aragon and the Mediterranean coast which (with Madrid) formed the core of the republic.

The anarchists thus shaped or formulated the revolution which the generals had risen to prevent, but had in fact provoked. But the war against the generals remained to be fought, and they were incapable of fighting it effectively either in the military or political sense. This was evident to the great majority of foreign observers and volunteers, especially in Catalonia and Aragon. There it proved impossible even to get the sixty thousand rifles parading on the city streets, let alone the available machine-guns and tanks, to the under-strength and under-equipped units which actually went to the crucial Aragon front. The inefficacy of the anarchist way of fighting the war has recently been doubted by a new school of libertarian historians (including the formidable intellect of Noam Chomsky), reluctant to admit that the communists had the only practical and effective policy for this purpose, and that their rapidly growing influence reflected this fact. Unfortunately it cannot be denied. And the war had to be won, because without this victory the Spanish revolution, however inspiring and perhaps even workable, would merely turn into yet another episode of heroic defeat, like the Paris Commune. And this is what actually happened. The communists, whose policy was the one which could have won the war, gained strength too late and never satisfactorily overcame the handicap of their original lack of mass support.[3]

For the student of politics in general, Spain may merely be a salutary warning against libertarian gestures (with or without pistols and dynamite), and against the sort of people who, like Ferrer, boasted that 'plutôt qu'un révolutionnaire je suis un révolté'. For the historian, the abnormal strength of anarchism, or the ineffective 'primitive' revolutionism still needs some explanation. Was it due to the proverbial neglect of the peasantry by the marxists of western Europe, which left so much of the countryside to the Bakuninists? Was it the persistence of small-scale industry and the pre-industrial sub-proletariat? These explanations are not entirely satisfactory. Was it the isolation of Spain, which saved Spanish libertarianism from the crisis of 1914–20 which bankrupted it in France and Italy, thus leaving the way open for communist mass movements? Was it the curious absence of intellectuals from the Spanish labour movement, so unusual in twentieth-century underdeveloped countries? Intellectuals were democrats, republicans, cultural populists, perhaps above all anticlericals, and active enough in some phases of opposition: but few of them were socialists and virtually none anarchists. (Their role seems in any case to have been limited – even educated Spain, as Carr says rightly, was not a reading nation – and the café-table or *Ateneo* was not, except in Madrid, a form of nation-wide political action.) At all events the leadership of Spanish revolutionary movements suffered from their absence. At present we cannot answer these questions except by speculation.

We can, however, place the spontaneous revolutionism of Spain

[3] They can be criticized not only for lending themselves to the irrelevant vendettas of Stalin's secret police, but for discouraging not merely the unpopular or counterproductive excesses of the revolution, but the revolution itself, whose existence they preferred not to stress in their propaganda. But the basic point is that they fought to win the war and that without victory the revolution was dead anyway. Had the republic survived, there might be more point to criticisms of their policy which, alas, remain academic.

in a wider context, and recent writers like Malefakis[4] have begun to do so. Social revolutions are not made: they occur and develop. To this extent the metaphors of military organization, strategy and tactics, which are so often applied to them both by marxists and their adversaries, can be actively misleading. However, they cannot succeed without establishing the capacity of a national army or government, i.e. to exercise effective national coordination and direction. Where this is totally absent, what might otherwise have turned into a social revolution may be no more than a nationwide aggregate of waves of local social unrest (as in Peru 1960–3), or it may collapse into an anarchic era of mutual massacre (as in Colombia in the years after 1948). This is the crux of the marxist critique of anarchism as a political strategy, whether such a belief in the virtues of spontaneous militancy at all times and places is held by nominal Bakuninists or by other ideologists. Spontaneity can bring down regimes, or at least make them unworkable, but can provide no alternative suitable to any society more advanced than an archaic self-sufficient peasantry, and even then only on the assumption that the forces of the state and of modern economic life will simply go away and leave the self-governing village community in peace. This is unlikely.

There are various ways in which a revolutionary party or movement can establish itself as a potentially national regime before the actual taking of power or during it. The Chinese, Vietnamese and Yugoslav Communist Parties were able to do so in the course of a prolonged guerrilla war, from which they emerged as the state power, but on the evidence of our century this seems to be exceptional. In Russia a brilliantly led Bolshevik Party succeeded in establishing itself as the leader of the decisive political force – the working class in the capital cities and a section of the armed forces – between February and October 1917, and as the *only* effective contender for state power, which it then exercised as soon as it had taken over the national centre of government, defeating – admittedly with great difficulty and at great cost – the counter-revolutionary armies and local or regional dissidence which lacked this coordination. This was essentially the pattern of the successful

[4] E. Malefakis, *Agrarian Reform and Peasant Revolution in Spain*, New Haven and London, 1970. This book ought to be required reading for all students of the Spanish revolution.

French revolutions between 1789 and 1848 which rested on the capture of the capital city combined with the collapse of the old government and the failure to establish an effective alternative national centre of counter-revolution. When the provinces failed to fall into line and an alternative counter-revolutionary government did establish itself, as in 1870–1, the commune of Paris was doomed.

A revolution may establish itself over a longer period of apparently complex and opaque conflict by the combination of a fairly stable class alliance (under the hegemony of one social force) with certain strong regional bases of power. Thus the Mexican revolution emerged as a stable regime after ten years of murderous civil strife, thanks to the alliance of what was to become the national bourgeoisie with the (subaltern) urban working class, conquering the country from a stable power-base in the north.[5] Within this framework the necessary concessions were made to the revolutionary peasant areas and several virtually independent warlords, a stable national regime being constructed step by step during the twenty years or so after the Sonora base had established itself.

The most difficult situation for revolution is probably that in which it is expected to grow out of reforming politics, rather than the initial shock of insurrectionary crisis combined with mass mobilization. The fall of the Spanish monarchy in 1931 was not the result of social revolution, but rather the public ratification of a very general shift of opinion among the political classes of Spain away from the monarchy. The new Republicans might have been pushed decisively towards the left – more specifically, towards agrarian revolution – by the pressure of the masses. But at the time when they were most susceptible to and afraid of it, in 1931, this did not occur. The moderate socialists may or may not have wanted to organize it, but the communists and anarchists who certainly did, failed in their attempt to do so. One cannot simply blame them for this failure. There were both avoidable and – perhaps predominantly – inevitable reasons why 'CNT and communist recruiters in general were so distant from the prevailing peasant mood that both organizations remained primarily urban based even so late as 1936' (Malefakis). The fact remains that

[5] From the days of Obregon until 1934 the presidents came almost without exception from the state of Sonora.

'peasant rebellion became a significant force after 1933, not in 1931, when it might have been politically more efficacious'. And after 1933 it served to mobilize reaction as effectively as – in the long run more effectively than – the forces of revolution. The Spanish revolution was unable to exploit the historical moment when most successful revolutions establish their hegemony: the spell of time during which its potential or actual enemies are demoralized, disorganized and uncertain what to do.

When it broke out it met a mobilized enemy. Perhaps this was inevitable. But it also faced the battle for survival, which it proved incapable of winning. Probably this was not inevitable. And so we remember it, especially those of us to whose lives it belongs, as a marvellous dream of what might have been, an epic of heroism, the Iliad of those who were young in the 1930s. But unless we think of revolutions merely as a series of dreams and epics, the time for analysis must succeed that of heroic memories.

(1966)

9
REFLECTIONS ON ANARCHISM

The present revival of interest in anarchism is a curious and at first sight unexpected phenomenon. Even ten years ago it would have seemed in the highest degree unlikely. At that time anarchism, both as a movement and as an ideology, looked like a chapter in the development of the modern revolutionary and labour movements that had been definitely closed.

As a movement it seemed to belong to the pre-industrial period, and in any case to the era before the first world war and the October revolution, except in Spain, where it can hardly be said to have survived the Civil War of 1936–9. One might say that it disappeared with the kings and emperors whom its militants had so often tried to assassinate. Nothing seemed to be able to halt, or even to slow down, its rapid and inevitable decline, even in those parts of the world in which it had once constituted a major political force – in France, Italy, Latin America. A careful searcher, who knew where to look, might still discover some anarchists even in the 1950s, and very many more ex-anarchists, easily recognizable by such signs as an interest in the poet Shelley. (It is characteristic that this most romantic school of revolutionaries has been more loyal than anyone else, including the literary critics of his own country, to the most revolutionary among English romantic poets.) When I tried to make contact, about this time, with activists in the Spanish anarchist underground in Paris, I was given a rendezvous at a cafe in Montmartre, by the Place Blanche, and somehow this reminder of a long-lost era of bohemians, rebels and *avant-garde* seemed only too characteristic.

As an ideology, anarchism did not decline so dramatically because it had never had anything like as much success, at least among intellectuals who are the social stratum most interested in ideas. There have probably always been eminent figures in the world of culture who called themselves anarchists (except, curiously enough, in Spain), but most of them seem to have been artists in the wider – or like Pissarro and Signac, the narrower – sense of the word. In any case, anarchism never had an attraction comparable to, say marxism, for intellectuals even before the October revolution. With the exception of Kropotkin, it is not easy to think of an anarchist theorist who could be read with real interest by non-anarchists. There seemed, indeed, no real intellectual room for anarchist theory. The belief in the libertarian communism of self-governing cooperatives as the final aim of revolutionaries, it shared with marxism. The old utopian socialists had thought more deeply and concretely about the nature of such communities than most anarchists. Even the strongest point in the anarchists' intellectual armoury, their awareness of the dangers of dictatorship and bureaucracy implicit in marxism, was not peculiar to them. This type of critique was made with equal effect and greater intellectual sophistication both by 'unofficial' marxists and by opponents of all kinds of socialism.

In brief, the main appeal of anarchism was emotional and not intellectual. That appeal was not negligible. Everyone who has ever studied, or had anything to do with the real anarchist movement, has been deeply moved by the idealism, the heroism, the sacrifice, the saintliness which it so often produced, side by side with the brutality of the Ukrainian Makhnovshchina or the dedicated gunmen and church-burners of Spain. The very extremism of the anarchist rejection of state and organization, the totality of their commitment to the overthrow of the present society, could not but arouse admiration; except perhaps among those who had to be active in politics by the side of the anarchists, and found them almost impossible to work with. It is suitable that Spain, the country of Don Quixote, should have been their last fortress.

The most touching epitaph I have heard on an anarchist terrorist, killed a few years ago by the police in Catalonia, was spoken by one of his comrades, without any sense of irony : 'When we were young, and the Republic was founded, we were knightly but also spiritual. We have grown older, but not he. He was a *guerrillero* by instinct. Yes, He was one of the Quixotes who come out of Spain.'

Admirable, but hopeless, It was almost certainly the monumental ineffectiveness of anarchism which, for most people of my generation – the one which came to maturity in the years of the Spanish Civil War – determined our rejection of it. I still recall in the very earliest days of that war, the small town of Puigcerda in the Pyrenees, a little revolutionary republic, filled with free men and women, guns and an immensity of discussion. A few trucks stood in the *plaza.* They were for the war. When anyone felt like going to fight on the Aragonese front, he went to the trucks. When a truck was full, it went to the front. Presumably, when the volunteers wanted to come back, they came back. The phrase *C'est magnifique, mais ce n'est pas la guerre* should have been invented for such a situation. It *was* marvellous, but the main effect of this experience on me was, that it took me twenty years before I was prepared to see Spanish anarchism as anything but a tragic farce.

It was much more than this. And yet, no amount of sympathy can alter the fact that anarchism as a revolutionary movement has failed, that it has almost been designed for failure.

As Gerald Brenan, the author of the best book on modern Spain, has put it : a single strike of (socialist) miners in the Asturias shook the Spanish government more than seventy years of massive anarchist revolutionary activity, which presented little more than a routine police problem. (Indeed, subsequent research has shown that in the era of maximum bomb-throwing in Barcelona, there were probably not a hundred policemen looking after public order in that city, and their number was not notably reinforced.) The ineffectiveness of anarchist revolutionary activities could be documented at length, and for all countries in which this ideology played an important role in politics. This is not the place for such a documentation. My point is simply to explain why the revival of interest in anarchism today seems so unexpected, surprising and – if I am to speak frankly – unjustified.

Unjustified, but not inexplicable. There are two powerful reasons which explain the vogue for anarchism : the crisis of the world communist movement after Stalin's death and the rise of revolutionary discontent among students and intellectuals, at a time when objective historical factors in the developed countries do not make revolution appear very probable.

For most revolutionaries the crisis of communism is essentially that of the USSR and the regimes founded under its auspices in eastern Europe ; that is to say of socialist systems as understood in the years between the October revolution and the fall of Hitler. Two aspects of these regimes now seemed more vulnerable to the traditional anarchist critique than before 1945, because the October revolution was no longer the only successful revolution made by communists, the USSR was no longer isolated, weak and threatened with destruction, and because the two most powerful arguments for the USSR – its immunity to the economic crisis of 1929 and its resistance to fascism – lost their force after 1945.

Stalinism, that hypertrophy of the bureaucratized dictatorial state, seemed to justify the Bakuninite argument that the dictatorship of the proletariat would inevitably become simple dictatorship, and that socialism could not be constructed on such a basis. At the same time the removal of the worst excesses of stalinism made it clear that even without purges and labour camps the kind of socialism introduced in the USSR was very far from what most socialists had had in mind before 1917, and the major objectives of that country's policy, rapid economic growth, technological and scientific development, national security etc., had no special connections with socialism, democracy or freedom. Backward nations might see in the USSR a model of how to escape from their backwardness, and might conclude from its experience and from their own that the methods of economic development pioneered and advocated by capitalism did not work in their conditions, whereas social revolution followed by central planning did, but the main object was 'development'. Socialism was the means to it and not the end. Developed nations, which already enjoyed the material level of production to which the USSR still aspired, and in many cases far more freedom and cultural variety for their citizens, could hardly take it as their model, and when they did (as in Czechoslovakia and the GDR) the results were distinctly disappointing.

Here again it seemed reasonable to conclude that this was not the way to build socialism. Extremist critics – and they became increasingly numerous – concluded that it was not socialism at all, however distorted or degenerate. The anarchists were among those revolutionaries who had always held this view, and their ideas therefore became more attractive. All the more so as the crucial argument of the 1917–45 period, that Soviet Russia however imperfect, was the only successful revolutionary regime and the essential basis for the success of revolution elsewhere, sounded much less convincing in the 1950s and hardly convincing at all in the 1960s.

The second and more powerful reason for the vogue of anarchism has nothing to do with the USSR, except in so far as it was fairly clear after 1945 that its government did not encourage revolutionary seizures of power in other countries. It arose out of the predicament of revolutionaries in non-revolutionary situations. As in the years before 1914, so in the 1950s and early 1960s western capitalism was stable and looked like remaining stable. The most powerful argument of classic marxist analysis, the historic inevitability of proletarian revolution, therefore lost its force; at least in the developed countries. But if history was not likely to bring revolution nearer, how would it come about?

Both before 1914 and again in our time anarchism provided an apparent answer. The very primitiveness of its theory became an asset. Revolution would come because revolutionaries wanted it with such passion, and undertook acts of revolt constantly, one of which would, sooner or later, turn out to be the spark which would set the world on fire. The appeal of this simple belief lay not in its more sophisticated formulations, though such extreme voluntarism could be given a philosophical basis (the pre-1914 anarchists often tended to admire Nietzsche as well as Stirner) or founded on social psychology as with Sorel. (It is a not altogether accidental irony of history that such theoretical justifications of anarchist irrationalism were soon to be adapted into theoretical justifications of fascism.) The strength of the anarchist belief lay in the fact that there seemed to be no alternative other than to give up the hope of revolution.

Of course neither before 1914 nor today were anarchists the only revolutionary voluntarists. All revolutionaries must always believe in the necessity of taking the initiative, the refusal to wait upon events to make the revolution for them. At some times – as in the Kautsky era of social democracy and the comparable era of postponed hope in the orthodox communist movement of the 1950s and 1960s – a dose of voluntarism is particularly salutary. Lenin was accused of Blanquism, just as Guevara and Regis Debray have been, with somewhat greater justification. At first sight such non-anarchist versions of the revolt against 'historic inevitability' seem much the more attractive since they do not deny the importance of objective factors in the making of revolution, of organization, discipline, strategy and tactics.

Nevertheless, and paradoxically, the anarchists may today have an occasional advantage over these more systematic revolutionaries. It has recently become fairly clear that the analysis on which most intelligent observers based their assessment of political prospects in the world must be badly deficient. There is no other explanation for the fact that several of the most dramatic and far-reaching developments in world politics recently have been not merely unpredicted, but so unexpected as to appear almost incredible at first sight. The events of May 1968 in France are probably the most striking example. When rational analysis and prediction leads so many astray, including even most marxists, the irrational belief that anything is possible at any moment may seem to have some advantages. After all, on 1 May 1968, not even in Peking or Havana did anyone seriously expect that within a matter of days barricades would rise in Paris, soon to be followed by the greatest general strike in living memory. On the night of 9 May it was not only the official communists who opposed the building of barricades, but a good many of the Trotskyist and Maoist students also, for the apparently sound reason that if the police really had orders to fire, the result would be a brief but substantial massacre. Those who went ahead without hesitation were the anarchists, the anarchizers, the *situationnistes*. There are moments when simple revolutionary or Napoleonic phrases like *de l'audace, encore de l'audace* or *on s'engage et puis on voit* work. This was one of them. One might even say that this was an occasion when only the blind chicken was in a position to find the grain of corn.

No doubt, statistically speaking, such moments are bound to be rare. The failure of Latin American guerrilla movements and the death of Guevara are reminders that it is not enough to want a revolution, however passionately, or even to start guerrilla war. No doubt the limits of anarchism became evident within a few days, even in Paris. Yet the fact that once or twice pure voluntarism has produced results cannot be denied. Inevitably it has increased the appeal of anarchism.

Anarchism is therefore today once again a political force. Probably it has no mass basis outside the movement of students and intellectuals and even within the movement it is influential rather as a persistent current of 'spontaneity' and activism rather than through the relatively few people who claim to be anarchists. The question is therefore once again worth asking what is the value of the anarchist tradition today ?

In terms of ideology, theory and programmes, that value remains marginal. Anarchism is a critique of the dangers of authoritarianism and bureaucracy in states, parties and movements, but this is primarily a symptom that these dangers are widely recognized. If all anarchists had disappeared from the face of the earth the discussion about these problems would go on much as it does. Anarchism also suggests a solution in terms of direct democracy and small self-governing groups, but I do not think its own proposals for the future have so far been either very valuable or very fully thought out. To mention only two considerations. First, small self-governing direct democracies are unfortunately not necessarily libertarian. They may indeed function only because they establish a consensus so powerful that those who do not share it voluntarily refrain from expressing their dissent; alternatively, because those who do not share the prevailing view leave the community, or are expelled. There is a good deal of information about the operation of such small communities, which I have not seen realistically discussed in anarchist literature. Second, both the nature of the modern social economy and of modern scientific technology raise problems of considerable complexity for those who see the future as a world of self-governing small groups. These may not be insoluble, but unfortunately they are certainly not solved by the simple call for the abolition of the state and bureaucracy, nor by the suspicion of technology and the natural sciences which so often goes with modern anarchism.[1] It is possible to construct a theoretical model of libertarian anarchism which will be compatible with modern scientific technology, but unfortunately it will not be socialist. It will be much closer to the views of Mr Goldwater and his economic adviser Professor Milton Friedman of Chicago than to the views of Kropotkin. For (as Bernard Shaw pointed out long ago in his pamphlet on the Impossibilities of Anarchism), the extreme versions of individualist liberalism are logically as anarchist as Bakunin.

It will be clear that in my view anarchism has no significant contribution to socialist theory to make, though it is a useful critical element. If socialists want theories about the present and the future,

[1] An illustration of this complexity may be given from the history of anarchism. I take it from J. Martinez Alier's valuable study of landless labourers in Andalusia in 1964–5. From the author's careful questioning it is clear that the landless labourers of Cordova, traditionally the mass basis of Spanish rural anarchism, have not changed their ideas since 1936 – except in one respect. The social and economic activities of even the Franco regime have convinced them that the state cannot simply be rejected, but has some positive functions. This may help to explain why they no longer seem to be anarchists.

they will still have to look elsewhere, to Marx and his followers, and probably also to the earlier utopian socialists, such as Fourier. To be more precise: if anarchists want to make a significant contribution they will have to do much more serious thinking than most of them have recently done.

The contribution of anarchism to revolutionary strategy and tactics cannot be so easily dismissed. It is true that anarchists are as unlikely to make successful revolutions in the future as they have been in the past. To adapt a phrase used by Bakunin of the peasantry: they may be invaluable on the first day of a revolution, but they are almost certain to be an obstacle on the second day. Nevertheless, historically their insistence on spontaneity has much to teach us. For it is the great weakness of revolutionaries brought up in any of the versions derived from classical marxism, that they tend to think of revolutions as occurring under conditions which can be specified in advance, as things which can be, at least in outline, foreseen, planned and organized. But in practice this is not so.

Or rather, most of the great revolutions which have occurred and succeeded, have begun as 'happenings' rather than as planned productions. Sometimes they have grown rapidly and unexpectedly out of what looked like ordinary mass demonstrations, sometimes out of resistance to the acts of their enemies, sometimes in other ways – but rarely if ever did they take the form expected by organized revolutionary movements, even when these had predicted the imminent occurrence of revolution. That is why the test of greatness in revolutionaries has always been their capacity to discover the new and unexpected characteristics of revolutionary situations and to adapt their tactics to them. Like the surfer, the revolutionary does not create the waves on which he rides, but balances on them. Unlike the surfer – and here serious revolutionary theory diverges from anarchist practice – sooner or later he stops riding on the wave and must control its direction and movement.

Anarchism has valuable lessons to teach, because it has – in practice rather than in theory – been unusually sensitive to the spontaneous elements in mass movements. Any large and disciplined movement can order a strike or demonstration to take place, and if it is sufficiently large and disciplined, it can make a reasonably impressive showing. Yet there is all the difference between the CGT's token general strike of 13 May 1968 and the ten millions who occupied their places of work a few days later without a national directive. The very organizational feebleness of anarchist and anarchizing movements has forced them to explore the means of discovering or securing that spontaneous consensus among militants and masses which produces action. (Admittedly it has also led them to experiment with ineffective tactics such as individual or small-group terrorism which can be practised without mobilizing any masses and for which, incidentally, the organizational defects of anarchism do not suit anarchists.)

The student movements of the past few years have been like anarchist movements, at least in their early stages, in so far as they have consisted not of mass organizations but of small groups of militants mobilizing the masses of their fellow students from time to time. They have been obliged to make themselves sensitive to the mood of these masses, to the times and issues which will permit mass mobilization.

In the United States, for instance they belong to a primitive kind of movement, and its weaknesses are evident – a lack of theory, of agreed strategic perspectives, of quick tactical reaction on a national scale. At the same time it is doubtful whether any other form of mobilization could have created, maintained and developed so powerful a national student movement in the United States in the 1960s. Quite certainly this could not have been done by the disciplined small groups of revolutionaries in the old tradition – communist, Trotskyist or Maoist – who constantly seek to impose their specific ideas and perspectives on the masses and in doing so isolate themselves more often than they mobilize them.

These are lessons to be learned not so much from the actual anarchists of today whose practice is rarely impressive, as from a study of the historic experience of anarchist movements. They are particularly valuable in the present situation, in which new revolutionary movements have often had to be built on and out of the ruins of the older ones. For let us not be under any illusions. The impressive 'new left' of recent years is admirable, but in many respects it is not only new, but also a regression to an earlier weaker, less developed form of the socialist movement, unwilling or unable to benefit from the major achievements of the international working-class and revolutionary movements in the century between the Communist Manifesto and the Cold War.

Tactics derived from anarchist experience are a reflection of this relative primitiveness and weakness, but in such circumstances they may be the best ones to pursue for a time. The important thing is to know when the limits of such tactics have been reached. What happened in France in May 1968 was less like 1917 than like 1830 or 1848. It is inspiring to discover that, in the developed countries of western Europe, any kind of revolutionary situation, however momentary, is possible once again. But it would be equally unwise to forget that 1848 is at the same time the great example of a successful spontaneous European revolution, and of its rapid and unmitigated failure.

(1969)

III
MARXISM

10

KARL MARX AND THE BRITISH LABOUR MOVEMENT

The Marx Memorial Lecture, which I have the honour to give this year, commemorates the death of Karl Marx. This is why it is held on 15 March. However, we are this year celebrating not only the 85th anniversary of Marx's death, but the 150th of his birth, and we are still within a few months of the centenary of the publication of the first volume of *Capital*, his most important theoretical work, and of the 50th anniversary of the great October revolution, the most far-reaching practical result of his labours. There is thus no shortage of anniversaries in tidy round figures, all connected with Karl Marx, which we can celebrate simultaneously on this occasion. And yet there is perhaps an even more suitable reason why tonight is a good night to remind ourselves of the life and work of the great man – the man whose name is now so familiar to all that he no longer has to be described, even on the commemorative plaque which the Greater London Council has at last put up on the house in Soho where he lived in poverty and where now the customers of a well-known restaurant dine in affluence.

It is a reason which Marx, with his sense of the irony of history, would have appreciated. As we gather here tonight, banks and stock exchanges are closed, financiers are gathering in Washington to register the breakdown of the system of international trade and payments in the capitalist world ; to stave off, if they can, the fall of the almighty dollar. It is not impossible that this date will go down in the history books like the date 24 October 1929, which marks the end of the period of capitalist stabilization in the 1920s. It is certain that the events of the past week prove more vividly than any argument the essential instability of capitalism ; its failure so far to overcome the internal contradictions of this system on a world scale. The man who devoted his life to demonstrating the internal contradictions of capitalism, would appreciate the irony of the accident that the crisis of the dollar should come to a head precisely on the anniversary of his death.

My subject for tonight, which was fixed long before this, is Marx and British labour; that is to say what Marx thought about the British labour movement and what that movement owes to Marx. He did not, at least in his later years, think much of British labour, and his influence on the movement, though significant, has been less than he or later marxists would have wished. Hence the subject does not lend itself to the usual rhetoric, not that a historian is specially qualified to practise it. It is an occasion for realistic analysis, and I shall try to be realistic.

What was Marx's opinion of the British working class and its labour movement?

Between the time that he became a communist and his death, British labour passed through two phases: the revolutionary phase of the Chartist period and the phase of modest reformism which succeeded it in the 1850s, 1860s and 1870s. In the first phase the British labour movement led the world in mass organization, in political class-consciousness, in the development of anti-capitalist ideologies such as the early forms of socialism, and in militancy. In the second phase it still led the world in a special form of organization, namely trade unionism and probably also in the narrower form of class consciousness which simply consists in recognizing the working class as a separate class, whose members have different (but not necessarily opposed) interests to other classes. However, it had abandoned the effort and perhaps even the hope of overthrowing capitalism, and accepted not only the existence of this system, seeking merely to improve the condition of its members within it, but also, and increasingly, it accepted – with certain specific exceptions – the bourgeois-liberal theories about how much improvement could be achieved. It was no longer revolutionary, and socialism virtually disappeared from it.

No doubt this retreat took longer than we sometimes think: Chartism did not die in 1848 but remained active and important for several years thereafter. No doubt, looking at the mid-Victorian decades with the wisdom of hindsight, we can observe that the retreat concealed elements of a new advance. Thanks to the experience of those decades the revived labour movement of the

1890s and of our own century would be much more firmly and permanently organized and would consist of a real 'movement' rather than a succession of waves of militancy. Nevertheless, there can be no doubt that it was a retreat; and in any case Marx did not survive long enough to see the subsequent revival.

Marx and Engels had high hopes of the British labour movement in the 1840s. More than this, their hopes of European revolution depended to a great extent on changes in the most advanced capitalist country, and the only one with a conscious movement of the proletariat on a mass scale. This did not occur. Britain remained relatively unaffected by the revolution of 1848. However, for some time after this Marx and Engels continued to hope for a revival of both the British and the continental movements. By the early 1850s it became clear that a new era of capitalist expansion had opened, which made this much less likely, and when even the next of the great world slumps – that of 1857 – did not in fact lead to a revival of Chartism, it became clear that they could no longer expect very much from the British labour movement. Nor in fact did they expect very much from it, for the remainder of Marx's lifetime, and their references to it express a growing disappointment. Marx and Engels were not, of course, the only ones to express this disappointment. If they deplored the 'lack of mettle of the old Chartists' in the movement of the 1860s, so did non-marxist survivors of the heroic period, like Thomas Cooper.

Two observations are perhaps worth making in passing at this point. The first is that this 'apparent bourgeois infection of the British workers',[1] this 'embourgeoisement of the English proletariat'[2] will remind many of us of what has been happening to the British labour movement in an even more headlong period of capitalist expansion and prosperity through which we have been living. Marx and Engels were, of course, careful to avoid the superficiality of the academic sociologists of the present, who think that 'embourgeoisement' means that workers are turning into modest copies of the middle class, a sort of mini-bourgeoisie. They were not, and he knew they were not. Nor did Marx believe for a moment that the expansion and prosperity from which many workers undoubtedly benefited, had created an 'affluent society' from which poverty had been banished, or was likely to be.

[1] Marx to Engels, 16 April 1863.

[2] Engels to Marx, 7 October 1858.

Indeed, some of the most eloquent passages in *Capital I* (cap. 23 section 5) deal precisely with the poverty of those years of capitalist triumph in Britain, as illustrated by the parliamentary inquiries of that time. Nevertheless, he recognized the adaptation of the labour movement to the bourgeois system ; but he regarded it as a historical phase, and indeed, as we know, it was a temporary phase. A socialist labour movement in Britain had disappeared; but it was to reappear.

The second observation, which also has its relevance for the present, is that the mid-Victorian decades did not lead Marx to turn himself into a Fabian or a Bernsteinian revisionist (which is the same thing as a Fabian in marxist costume). They led him to alter his strategic and tactical perspectives. They may have led him to become pessimistic about the short-term prospects of the working-class movement in western Europe, especially after 1871. But they neither led him to abandon the belief that the emancipation of the human race was possible nor that it would be based on the movement of the proletariat. He was and continued to be a revolutionary socialist. Not because he overlooked the contrary tendencies or underestimated their force. He had no illusions whatever about the British labour movement of the 1860s and 1870s – but because he did not regard them as historically decisive.

How did Marx explain this change in the character of the British labour movement ? In general, by the new lease of life which the economic expansion after 1851 gave to capitalism – that is to say by the full development of the capitalist world market in those decades – but more specifically by the world domination or world monopoly of British capitalism. This thesis first appears in the correspondence of Marx and Engels around 1858 – after the failure of the hopes they had placed in the 1857 slump – and is repeated at intervals thereafter ; mostly, it should be noted, in letters by Engels. Consequently, Engels also expected the end of this world monopoly to bring about a radicalization of the British labour movement, and in the 1880s Engels did indeed repeatedly observe that both these things were happening or could be expected to happen.

The best-known passage is probably that in the introduction to the first English translation of *Capital I* (written in 1886), but his correspondence in those years returns to this argument time and again, sometimes in order to explain why the revived socialist movement in Britain was not yet making enough progress, more often in a spirit of optimism; for Engels was perhaps more sanguine in his political expectations than Marx, and perhaps also a shade more inclined to see economic changes as inevitably bringing about political results than his comrade. He was, of course, right in principle. The so-called Great Depression of 1873–96, did mark the end of the British world monopoly and also the rebirth of a socialist labour movement. On the other hand he evidently underestimated both the capacity of capitalism as a whole to continue its expansion, and the capacity of British capitalism to safeguard itself against the social and political consequences of its relative decline by imperialism abroad and a new type of domestic policy.

Marx himself spent less time – at least after the 1850s – in discussing these broad economic perspectives and more time in considering the political implications of the increasing feebleness of British labour. His basic view was that:

> England, as the metropolis of world capital, as the country which has hitherto ruled the world market, is for the time being the most important country for working-class revolution; moreover, it is the only country in which the material conditions for this revolution have developed to a certain degree of maturity. Hence the most important task of the International is to accelerate the social revolution in England.[3]

But if the British working class had the material requisites for revolution,[4] it lacked the willingness to make a revolution, that is to say to use its political power to take over power, as it might have done at any time after the parliamentary reform of 1867. Perhaps we should add in passing that this peaceful road to socialism, on the possibility of which for Britain Marx and Engels insisted at various times after 1870,[5] was not an alternative to revolution, but simply a means of 'removing legally such laws and institutions as stand in the way of working-class development' in bourgeois-democratic countries; a possibility which evidently did not exist in non-democratic constitutions. It would not remove the obstacles which stood in the

[3] Marx to Meyer and Vogt, 9 October 1870.

[4] Marx, *Confidential Circular*, 1870 (*Werke*, vol. 16, p. 415).

[5] Marx, *Speech after The Hague Congress 1872* (*Werke*, vol. 18, p. 160); Marx, *Konspekt der Debatten über das Sozialistengesetz* (K. Marx–F. Engels, *Brief an A. Bebel., W. Liebknecht, K. Kautsky und Andre* 1, p. 516); F. Engels, Preface to English translation of *Capital I*.

way of the working class but which did not happen to take the for of laws and institutions, e.g. the economic power of the bourgeoisi and it might easily turn into violent revolution in consequence of t insurrection of those with a vested interest in the old *status quo* ; t point was that if this happened the bourgeoisie would be rebe against a legal government, as (to quote Marx's own examples) t south was against the north in the American Civil War, t counter-revolutionaries were in the French revolution and – w might add – in the Spanish Civil War of 1936–9. Marx's argume was not concerned with any ideal choice between violence an non-violence, or gradualism and revolution, but with the realistic u of such possibilities as were open to the labour movement in an given situation. Of these, in a bourgeois democracy, Parliament w clearly a central one.

Yet the British working class was plainly not ready to make use any of these possibilities, even the formation of an independe labour party or independent political behaviour by such individu workers who happened to get elected to Parliament. Witho waiting for the long-term tendencies of historical development change the situation, there were several things to do : and one the great merits of Marx's writings is to show that communists ca and must avoid both the error of waiting for history to happen, an the error of opting for unhistorical methods such as Bakunini anarchism and pointless acts of terrorism.

In the first place, it was essential to educate the working class political consciousness 'by a continuous agitation against the hosti attitude shown towards the workers in politics by the ruling classes', i.e. by producing situations which demonstrated this hostility. Th might, of course, imply organizing confrontations with the rulin class, which would lead it to drop its appearance of sympathy. Th Marx welcomed the police brutality during the Reform demo strations of 1866 : ruling-class violence could provide 'a revolutio ary education'. So long, of course, as it isolated the police, and n those who fought them. Marx and Engels were scathing about th Fenian terrorist actions in Clerkenwell, which had the opposit effect.

In the second place, it was essential to ally with all sections non-reformist workers. That is why, as he wrote to Bolte (2 November 1871) he worked with the followers of Bronterre O'Brier

[6] Marx to Bolte, 23 November 1871.

relics of the old socialism of Chartist days, on the Council of the International:

> In spite of the crack-brained ideas, they constitute a counterweight to the trade unionists. They are more revolutionary . . . less nationalist and quite immune to any form of bourgeois corruption. But for that, we should have thrown them out a long time ago.

However, Marx's main recipe for revolutionizing the British situation was through Ireland; i.e. by the indirect means of supporting colonial revolution and in doing so destroying the major bond which linked the British workers to the British bourgeoisie. Originally, as Marx admitted, he had expected Ireland to be liberated through the victory of the British proletariat.[7] From the late 1860s he took the opposite view – namely that the revolutions in the backward and colonial countries would be primary and would themselves revolutionize the metropolitan ones. (It is interesting that at much the same time he began to have these hopes for a revolution in Russia, which sustained him in his later years.)[8] Ireland acted as a fetter in two ways: by splitting the English working class along racial lines, and thus by giving the British worker an apparent joint interest with his rulers in exploiting someone else. This was the sense of Marx's famous statement that 'a nation which oppresses another cannot itself be free'. Ireland was thus at one moment the key to England – more than this to the advance of progress in the world in general:

> If we are to accelerate the social development of Europe, we must accelerate the catastrophe of official (i.e. ruling class) England. This requires a blow in Ireland, which is the weakest point of Britain. If Ireland is lost, the British 'empire' goes and the class struggle in England, which has up to now been sleepy and slow, will take more acute forms. But England is the metropolis of capitalism and landlordism in the entire world.

I have spent some time on the details of Karl Marx's attitude to the British labour movement – mainly in the 1860s and early 1870s when he was closely involved with it through the International. He wrote about it in those days not so much as a general historical analyst, but rather as a political strategist and tactician, considering concrete political situations. The situation of the 1860s has passed away for good, and nobody would claim, least of all Marx himself,

[7] Marx to Engels, 10 December 1869.

[8] Marx to Laura and Paul Lafargue, 5 March 1870.

that what he had to say about it in detail applies to any other period. On the other hand it is always instructive to see a marxist master-strategist and tactician at work – and we must remember that, as Engels liked to recall, Marx was a master-tactician in the rare periods when he had the chance to be.

As it happened, he failed to 're-electrify the British labour movement', and this failure, as he realized, condemned the international movement to wait for very much longer, and when the movement revived, Britain and the British working class no longer played the potentially central role in it that they might have done, while Britain was 'the metropolis of capitalism and landlordism everywhere'. As soon as he realized that the strategy of the 1860s had failed, Marx ceased to concern himself very much with the British labour movement. However, at this point we may logically turn to the other half of the question about Marx and British labour, namely the effect which Marx and his teaching had upon the labour movement in this country.

Let us first be clear on the limits – on what were probably the historically inevitable limits of this influence. It was not likely to produce a revolutionary labour movement in a country which lacked the experience and tradition of revolution, and any situations – then or later – which could be even faintly described as revolutionary or pre-revolutionary. It was not likely to produce a mass labour movement inspired and organized by marxism, because when marxism appeared on the scene, a powerful, well-organized, politically influential labour movement already existed on a national scale in the form of trade unionism, consumers' cooperation and Liberal-Labour leaders. Marxism did not precede the British labour movement. It was not even coeval with it. It appeared a third of the way through its lifetime to date. It is no use looking abroad and observing that marxism played or plays a much larger part in the labour movements of some countries than in ours, because, since history does not develop uniformly, we cannot expect the same developments everywhere. The peculiarity of Britain is that it was the oldest, for a long time the most successful and dominant, and almost certainly the stablest capitalist society, and that its bourgeoisie had to come to terms with a proletarian majority of the population long before any other. The influence of marxism has been inevitably circumscribed by this situation.

On the other hand we could expect marxism to play an important part in the formation of that new – or renewed – stage of the British worker's class-consciousness, which led them to abandon confidence in the permanence and viability of capitalism, and to place their hopes in a new society – socialism. We could expect it to play an important part in forming the new ideology, the strategy and tactics of a socialist labour movement. We could expect it to create nuclei of leadership, political vanguards if you like – I am using the term in a general sense here and not only in the specific leninist sense. How large or important these were, how significant the part they played within the larger movement, might be uncertain and unpredictable. In other words, we could have expected marxism to have a significant, but almost certainly not a decisive influence in shaping the British labour movement of the twentieth century. This is a pity, but that is another question. We may perhaps be reconciled to this relatively modest role of marxism if we look at some continental movements in which the influence of marxism was initially far greater, so much so that the entire labour movement took the form of marxist social-democratic mass parties, but nevertheless these movements were basically as moderate and reformist as the British, if not more so; for instance in Scandinavia.

Now in the two respects which I have singled out, the influence of Marx was unquestionably great – much greater than is commonly realized. Ideologists of right-wing labour have searched desperately for alternative founding fathers of British socialism, from John Wesley to the Fabians, but their search has been vain. Methodism in particular, non-conformist protestantism in general, have undoubtedly coloured a lot of the British labour movement, and in a few special cases such as the farm labourers and some of the miners, provided both a framework of organization and a cadre of leaders, but their contribution to what the movement thought and tried to achieve – to its socialism – has been minimal. The contribution of Marx has been capital, if only because Marx's analysis is the only socialist analysis which has stood the test of time. The archaic British forms of socialism – Owenism, O'Brienism, etc. did not revive, though an essentially 'agrarian' analysis of capitalism long remained influential. Fabianism, in so far as it had a specific analysis of capitalism (e.g. the specific economic theory of the *Fabian Essays*) never got off the ground. It survived and became influential merely as a more 'modern' formulation of what moderate labour leaders had always done, namely pursuing piecemeal reforms within the framework of capitalism.

In so far as the British labour movement developed a theory about how capitalism worked – about the nature of capitalist exploitation, the internal contradictions of capitalism, the fluctuations of the capitalist economy such as slumps, the causes of unemployment, the long-term tendencies of capitalist development such as mechanization, economic concentration and imperialism, these were based on the teachings of Marx, or were accepted in so far as they coincided with them or converged with them.

In so far as the British labour movement developed a programme for socialism – based on the socialization of the means of production, distribution and exchange, and rather later, on planning, it was once again the basis of a simplified marxism. I am not claiming that the entire ideology of the movement was so based. It is clear, for instance, that some very important parts of it, e.g. the attitude to international questions and peace or war, were based substantially on an older and powerful liberal-radical tradition. Nor am I claiming that the ideology of all parts of the movement was so based. Its right-wing leaders, especially when they got anywhere near government office, always looked for some alternative source of economic inspiration drawn from bourgeois liberalism – whether in the form of the free-trade orthodoxy of the Lib-Labs and Philip Snowden, the LSE-type marginalism of the Early Fabians, or the Keynesian analysis of the Labour Party ideologists since 1945. But if we go down to the grass roots – to the men and women who canvassed for elections, who collected dues and led industrial movements at shop and factory level, and so on: their theory, and very often their practice, were much the same as that of the members of officially marxist organizations; and the other way round. I do not say that they got this theory from reading *Capital* or even *Value, Price and Profit*, any more than the sort of sub-Freudianism which is the basis of American conversations about personal problems is necessarily based on a reading of Freud. Their theory derived from Marx insofar as they were socialists, because the basic theory of socialism, at least in the respects I singled out above, was the one formulated in a marxist manner; generally it must be admitted, a very simplified manner.

In one way or another this had become part of their political lives.

This was natural, because marxism – or at all events some sort of simplified version of marxism – was the first kind of socialism to reach Britain during the revival of the 1880s, the one most persistently propagated by devoted pioneers at a thousand street corners, and the one most persistently and ubiquitously taught at a thousand classes run by socialist organizations, labour colleges or freelance lecturers; and because it had no real rival as an analysis of what was wrong with capitalism. It was also natural, because the marxist organizations formed and still form by far the most important school for the militants and activists of the labour movement, and this is in spite of the sectarianism which has often plagued them. This is perhaps most obvious at the real grass roots of the British movement, in the unions. From the days of the young John Burns and Tom Mann, to those of the militants of today, marxist organizations of one kind or another have provided the education of the union activists. It has been one of the greatest historic weaknesses of the old ILP, and of its successor, the parliamentary Labour left, that it has had and has such feeble roots in the industrial movements. Conversely, taking account of their relatively modest size, the marxist organizations – whether SDF, Socialist Labour Party, the Communist Party, etc. have had a disproportionately large influence among the union activists. It is true that many of these changed their political opinions as their careers advanced, but if we are talking about Marx's influence, we cannot leave even them out of account.

It would be easy to illustrate the disproportionate influence of Marx, and of the relatively tiny organizations of marxists, on the wider labour movement. The marxist organizations themselves have often underrated it, because they have measured it not against reality, but against their ideal of a marxist mass labour movement; whereas in fact their historical importance has been as groups of cadres or potential cadres, of leaders and brains rather than of followers. Their importance has so far lain not so much in converting vast masses of workers into members of a mass marxist movement or the acquisition of voters, but in their role within a great, politically and ideologically heterogeneous but powerful class movement bound together by class-consciousness and solidarity, and increasingly also by the anti-capitalism which the marxists were the first to find words for when socialism revived in the 1880s. Because this movement has so often fallen short of their expectations, they have often been disappointed in it. But that disappointment was also often due to unrealistic expectations. The General Strike was a magnificent demonstration of the movement's strength; but it was not, and was not even faintly within sight of being, a revolutionary or even a pre-revolutionary situation.

However, just because the expectations of marxists have so often been unrealistic, they have sometimes obscured the realistic ones. Because the lack of success of marxists has so often been due to factors beyond their or anyone else's control, they have sometimes overlooked the failures which might have been avoidable. Marx's own failure in the 1860s was inevitable. Historians may well conclude that no conceivable wisdom, tactical brilliance or organizational effort was likely to bring about the realization of Marx's strategic hopes at that point; though this does not mean that they were not worth pursuing. On the other hand many of the errors of the British Social Democrats were avoidable, though perhaps historically likely. That peculiar combination of sectarianism and opportunism which Lenin recognized in the SDF and which is the occupational risk of so many marxist organizations operating under conditions of capitalist stability, is not inevitable.

The SDF ought to have played a much larger part in the trade union revival of the 1880s, if it had not dismissed trade unions as 'mere palliatives'; its own militants were wiser. The British marxists – with the exception of the SLP – failed to grasp, let alone to lead, the great labour unrest of 1911–14, though this was the first occasion since the Chartists when masses of rank-and-file British workers not only organized on a large scale, but also demonstrated strong anti-capitalist sentiments, and even some evidence of that revolutionary spirit which Marx had called for. They left the leadership mainly to syndicalists and other members of what we would today call the 'new left', though of course many of these – Tom Mann is the best example – had gone through the school of marxism and were to return to marxist organizations. The reason for this failure was the opposite to 'impossibilist' sectarianism. It was due to the failure to discern a new phase in the political consciousness of the workers behind the emotional phrases, the unorthodox and often rather unimpressive theorizing, the irrationalism and what a later generation was to call the 'mindless militancy' of the new movement. As it happens the war and the Russian revolution once again saved the British Socialist Party from some of the results of its errors.

Indeed, in a curious way history has time and again compensated, at least in part, for the errors of British marxists, both by proving Marx right and by demonstrating the inadequacy of the alternatives – whether reformist or revolutionary – which were suggested. It did so by demonstrating, time and again, the fragility of that capitalist system whose stability and strength provided the main argument for both reformists and ultra-revolutionaries. For the reformist argued, with Bernstein and the Fabians, that there was no point in talking about revolution when capitalism looked like lasting for as long as anyone could predict; the only sensible course was to get used to its stability and concentrate on improvements within it. On the other hand the ultra-revolutionaries argued, like so many pre-1914 syndicalists, that there was no point in hoping that history would raise the consciousness of the workers to a new level, because historical development seemed to produce capitalist permanence. It made more sense to raise it by the propaganda of action, by inspiring 'myths', by the sheer effort of the revolutionary will.

Both were wrong in their prescriptions, though not entirely wrong in their critique of the 'sit-back-and-wait-for-history-to-do-the-job-for-us' determinism of orthodox social democracy. Both were wrong because in one way or another the instability and the growing contradictions of capitalism have reasserted themselves periodically: e.g. in war, in some form or other of economic disruption, in the growing contradiction between the advanced and the under-developed countries. The very fact that the ultra-left existed and became a significant force was a symptom of the acuteness of these contradictions before 1914, and it is so today. And whenever history once again proved that Marx's analysis of capitalism was a better guide to reality than Rostow's or Galbraith's, or whoever was in fashion at the time, men tended to turn again to the marxists in so far as they were neither too sectarian nor too opportunist; that is to say in so far as they avoided the double temptation of revolutionaries who operate for long periods under conditions of stable capitalism.

So we may conclude that Marx's influence on British labour could not be expected to be as great as his enthusiastic followers would like it to be. Nevertheless it was, is, and is likely to be, rather greater than both they and the anti-marxists have often supposed. At the same time it was and is smaller (within the limits of historical realism) than it might have been but for the errors of British marxists at crucial stages of the development of the modern labour and socialist movement; errors both of the 'right' and of the 'left': errors which are not confined to any marxist organization, great or small. However, we cannot make Marx himself responsible for them. What both he and Engels had expected of the British labour movement after the Chartist era was modest enough. They had simply expected that it would once again establish itself as an independent political as well as trade unionist class movement, that it should found its own political party, and rediscover both the confidence in British workers as a class and the decisive weight of the working class in the politics of Britain. They were too realistic to expect more in their lifetime, and indeed the labour movement did not quite achieve even these modest objectives before Engels's death.

The British marxists would have done well to listen to Engels's advice, while he was alive, for it was very sound. Nevertheless, even if they had, within a few years of his death the British labour movement had come to a point where Engels's opinions about it, and even less those of Marx who had said so little on the subject after the early 1870s, were no longer of much specific relevance to the situation. If Marx's theory was to be a guide to action for British marxists, they would henceforth have to do the work themselves. They would have to learn the method of Marx, and not only his text, or that of any of his successors. They would have to make their own analysis of what was happening in British capitalism and of the concrete political situations in which the movement found itself. They would have to work out the best ways to organize, their perspectives and programmes, and their role in the wider labour movement. These are still the tasks of those who wish to follow Marx in Britain, or in any other country.

(1968)

11

THE DIALOGUE ON MARXISM

The purpose of my talk is to start discussion on the basis of two questions: why is marxism flourishing today? and how is it flourishing today? You may say that both these beg another question, namely: is it flourishing today? Well, is it? The answer must be yes and no. Marxist socialist movements are on the whole not particularly successful at the moment, and the international communist movement is split, and thus greatly weakened.

It may be that this is to some extent offset by the tendency of other movements, such as those of national and social liberation in many of the emerging countries, to draw closer to marxism, to learn from it, perhaps even to accept it as the basis of their theoretical analysis. It may be that the present phase is temporary. Nevertheless, the general picture of the international labour movement today by no means encourages a state of euphoria.

On the other hand, there can be no doubt whatever that the intellectual appeal of marxism, and I should add the intellectual vitality of marxism, has increased quite remarkably in the past ten years or so. This applies inside and outside communist parties, inside and outside countries of strong marxist labour movements. It applies, for instance, to some extent among students and other intellectuals in countries like West Germany and the United States, in which marxist political organizations are either illegal, or negligible, or both. If you want a rough measure of it, you can find it in the number and circulation of various openly marxist books, which is much greater today, I fancy, than it was say in the 1930s, even at the height of the *Left Book Club*.

You can also find it in the general respect for Marx and marxism which exists in certain fields of academic work, such as history and sociology, though this does not mean that Marx, while respected, is also accepted. I think there can be no doubt that we are at present living through a period when marxism is flourishing, though marxist labour movements may not always be.

What is strange about this situation is that in the developed capitalist countries it occurs during a period of unexampled prosperity, and what is more, after the major marxist organizations – the communist parties – were fairly heavily discredited intellectually by the revelations of the Twentieth Congress of the Soviet Communist Party. The situation during the last major advance of marxism in the 1930s and 1940s was quite different; marxism advanced because capitalism was obviously in crisis, quite possibly, as many thought, its final crisis, because it was in a political crisis, as shown by the advance of fascism and war, because communists were the best anti-fascists, and lastly, because of the direct appeal of the Soviet Union. And marxism consequently advanced overwhelmingly in the form of a strengthening of communist parties.

The most popular marxist case against capitalism was that it would not work; against liberal bourgeois democracy, that it was ceasing to exist, being replaced by fascism. I do not say that this was all of the marxist analysis, but it was certainly the part which struck home most immediately. None of these three powerful arguments operate very strongly today in the developed capitalist countries.

Why then did marxism not merely survive, but in many ways revive in the past ten years? Clearly the first conclusion is, that its strength does not depend on such elementary failures of capitalism as mass unemployment and economic collapse. Of course in countries where the case against capitalism (in the form of imperialism or neo-imperialism) remains obvious, where starvation and misery are widespread, the arguments for marxism are much simpler. But just because they are not so simple in Britain and France as in Peru and India, I am in this talk concentrating on the situation in the advanced capitalist countries.

Yet having established that marxism flourishes today, we must nevertheless look at the peculiar situation in which its revival is taking place. Not to beat about the bush, just because it is so entirely different from that of the 1930s and 1940s, a general trend towards marxism is combined with a disintegration of the traditional marxist analysis. In the years immediately after the war attempts were still being made to maintain the old arguments. Capitalist stability, it was said, was not going to last. Well, perhaps in the long view this is true, but it has certainly lasted for the best part of twenty years, which few marxists expected. The liberation of the colonial and semi-colonial peoples, some argued, was a sham. Well, this is certainly true in the same sense that mere political independence is not enough, and can lead to an informal type of economic domination which we now call 'neo-colonialism'. Nevertheless, it has made a fundamental difference to the political configuration of most parts of the world, which few marxists predicted or were immediately prepared for.

The advance of socialism, most of us thought, would not necessarily be the unaided work of the communists, but it would certainly depend on the efforts of a single united worldwide communist movement organized round the Soviet Union. But for various reasons this single world communist movement has tended to develop tensions within it, and even to split, and our regrets do not alter the facts. Other ways of national and social liberation, perhaps even of achieving socialism, emerged in some colonial and semi-colonial countries independently of the communists, or where the communists were so weak as not to play a major role. Lastly, within marxism itself the end of stalinism brought a major crisis, and much rethinking. This is the setting for the 'dialogue on marxism' which is my subject.

This dialogue therefore takes two major forms : a discussion between marxist and non-marxists, and a discussion between different kinds of marxists, or rather between marxists holding different views on various theoretical and practical topics, both within communist parties, between supporters of rival communist parties (in some rather unfortunate countries) and between communist and non-communist marxists. None of these forms is new. For instance, until the first great split within the marxist movements during and after the first world war and the October revolution, it was accepted that a constant process of debate was normal within the social democratic parties.

Even the Russian Social Democratic Labour Party did not actually split organizationally until just before the first world war, though we have mistakenly learned to think of bolsheviks and mensheviks as separate much earlier. And, as we are now remembering, even after the revolution discussion between widely different viewpoints on ideological and practical matters was accepted as normal in the Soviet Communist Party and the international communist movement until, certainly, around 1930. Still, for a generation – say from 1930 to 1956 – the dialogue of marxism atrophied.

This applies both to the dialogue between marxists and non-marxists and between different views within marxism. As for the non-marxists, we were very keen to confront them, to tell them what marxism was, to expound and propagate it, to polemize against its adversaries. But we did not believe that there was anything we could learn from them ourselves. A conversation in which one partner is expected to listen and the other not, is not a dialogue. The terms in which we spoke of such confrontations reflected this. We spoke of the 'battle of ideas', of 'partisanship' in intellectual discussion, even – at the peak of sectarianism in the early 1950s – of 'bourgeois' versus 'proletarian' science.[1]

Increasingly we eliminated all elements other than those of Marx, Engels, Lenin and Stalin or what had been accepted as orthodox in the Soviet Union: any theories of art other than 'socialist realism', any psychology other than Pavlov's, even at times any biology other than Lysenko's. Hegel was pushed out of marxism, as in the *Short History of the CPSU*, even Einstein roused suspicions, not to mention 'bourgeois' social science as a whole. The more unconvincing our own official beliefs were, the less we could afford a dialogue, and it is interesting that we spoke more often of the 'defence' of marxism than of its power to penetrate. And of course this was natural. How could we discuss, say, the history of the Soviet Union, if we left Trotsky out of it, or thought of him as a foreign agent? At most we could write books and reviews proving to ourselves that we need not listen to those who took a different view.

After Stalin it became increasingly clear that this would not do, and for two reasons: first, because it deprived socialism itself of important tools of research and planning, as notably in economics and the social sciences. (One of the ironies of the situation was, that some of the economic ideas which we deprived ourselves of had actually been developed by marxists in Russia during the 1920s, for

[1] A French communist philosopher and critic has written as follows of this period: 'In our philosophic memory we recall this as the time of the intellectuals in arms, pursuing error into all its hiding places, as the time when we philosophers wrote no books, but turned every book into politics, and cut the world – arts, literature, philosophy, science – with a single blade into the pitiless blocs of class division' (L. Althusser, *Pour Marx*, Paris, 1965, p. 12).

instance, much of the modern theory of economic development and the techniques of planning and national accounting.) Second, because we largely deprived ourselves of marxism as a means of propaganda. People might well, as during the war in resistance movements, join communist parties for class reasons or because there were the best fighters against Hitler. They might then become marxists, and our very effective methods of education helped them to do so. But very few people after the 1930s became communists because of the scientific power of Marx's ideas.

As for the discussion between different kinds of marxists, for a generation this hardly seemed to arise. Most marxists were communists: in or very close to the communist parties. Those who were not, were – or seemed – negligible, and indeed were often unknown, because they represented no important movements. And we vaguely assumed that those who were no longer communists, or who had at one time or another parted company with Lenin, had either ceased to be marxists then, or had somehow never been 'real' marxists. We begged a lot of questions in this way, but they did not seem to be important questions. Plekhanov, for instance, was the father of marxism in Russia and we read some of him with admiration, as Lenin had done. We did not read those writings of his which did not agree with Lenin, because they were not available, and even had they been (like Kautsky's later writings), we would – I think understandably – have judged that they must be wrong, because he himself had been so obviously proven wrong by history. Conversely, we assumed that all those who wrote under the auspices of the Communist Party were marxists, which is by no means inevitable. We were wrong on both counts.

In Britain the impossibility of maintaining this attitude became obvious after 1956, when a high proportion of marxist intellectuals left the Communist Party. It was obviously impossible to argue seriously that, say, Christopher Hill stopped being a marxist historian at the moment when he stopped holding a party card, implausible to argue that he had never been a marxist, and meaningless to argue that he had left the party because at some stage in the past he had stopped being a marxist without telling anyone about it including himself. We had to learn to live with the fact that the marxist intellectuals who were in the Communist Party were only a part – and not as in the past the overwhelming majority – of the intellectuals who called themselves marxists.

The development of different trends within the communist movement made the old assumption even less tenable. It is quite true that a number of ex-communists also became ex-marxists and indeed anti-marxists in due course, as had always happened, and this seemed to justify the old attitude. But equally, and especially in the past ten years, we have found plenty of non-marxists becoming marxists (or calling themselves marxists) without ever joining, or wanting to join, the Communist Party. In fact today it is impossible to make the simple statement on which many of us were brought up : there is one and only one 'correct' marxism and it is to be found in Communist Parties.

This does not mean that there is no 'correct' marxism. Only, it cannot be any longer institutionally defined, and it is by no means as easy to know what in any instance it is, as we once thought. In saying that the discussion is open among marxists I am not saying that on any point it can never conclude, though I think I would say that discussion on some points (not always the same) must go on indefinitely, because marxism is a scientific method, and in the sciences discussion – and discussion between people holding different views on the basis of science – is the only and permanent method of progress. Each problem solved simply produces more problems for further discussion.

But what I am also saying is that, at present, opening questions is much more important than closing them, even if it were easier to close them than seems likely just now. I may suspect – and I do suspect – that a lot of the people now calling themselves marxist aren't, and a lot of theories being put forward under marxist auspices are very far from Marx. But this applies to marxists in communist parties or in socialist countries just as much as to marxists outside both. And anyway, we must also ask ourselves which is at present more important, to define what marxism isn't – which will sooner or later sort itself out anyway – or to discover, or rediscover what it is. I think it is the latter, certainly that is the more difficult task.

For much of marxism must be rethought and rediscovered, and not only by communists. The post-Stalin period has not answered questions, it has asked them. If I may quote a French communist intellectual :

> Those who impute to Stalin not only his crimes and faults, but also all our disappointments of all kinds, may well find themselves disconcerted by the discovery that the end of philosophic dogmatism has not given us back

marxist philosophy . . . It has produced a genuine freedom for research, but also a sort of fever. Some people have rushed to call philosophy what is only the ideological commentary on their feeling of liberation and on their taste for freedom. But temperatures go down as surely as stones thrown into the air. What the end of dogmatism has done is to give us back the right to make an exact inventory of our intellectual possessions, to name both our wealth and our poverty, to think out and to formulate in public our problems, and to set about the rigorous task of real research.[2]

Communists increasingly realize that what they learned to believe and to repeat was not just 'marxism', but marxism as developed by Lenin, as frozen, simplified and sometimes distorted under Stalin in the Soviet Union. That 'marxism' is not a body of finished theories and discoveries, but a process of development; that Marx's own thought, for instance, went on developing throughout his life. That marxism doubtless has potential answers, but often no actual answers to the specific problems we face, partly because the situation has changed since Marx and Lenin, partly because neither of them may actually have said anything about certain problems which existed in their time, and are important to us.

Non-communist marxists must learn that the errors, oversimplifications and distortions of the Stalin period, or even of the entire period of the Communist International, do not mean that no valuable and important contributions were made to marxism, in this period and in the international communist movement. There are no shortcuts to marxism: neither the appeal to Lenin against Stalin, nor to Marx, nor to the young Marx against the older Marx. There is only hard, and long, and in the present circumstances perhaps inconclusive work.

Fortunately all this is widely recognized today and the work is going on. To mention only the very striking revitalization of theory within communist parties. This has been most impressive in recent years, both inside and outside socialist countries, though it has been held up by the reluctance of older cadres, whose career was identified with stalinism, to admit the mistakes they were associated with. (This is particularly marked in the field of the history of the communist movements themselves. With the exception of the Italian Communist Party, which has encouraged the frank and self-critical analysis of its own history and that of the Soviet Union, I can think of no communist party which has written a scientifically acceptable

[2] *Ibid.*, p. 21.

history of itself – certainly neither the French nor the Soviet party – and several, such as ours, which has shied away from the task of writing its history at all.)[3]

There is still in many communist parties a great deal of what might be called darning holes in socks. For instance, Roger Garaudy's phrase 'realism without limits' does not face the question whether the aesthetic theories we used to accept as marxist are valid or not; it merely allows us to admire Kafka, or Joyce, or other people who used to be taboo in the heyday of 'socialist realism' by pretending that they are 'realists' too in some indefinable sense. There is even in communist parties, particularly in eastern Europe, a tendency to go in for simple empiricism and to cover the results by saying 'of course we are marxists'.

I think, and I have the authority of the late Oscar Lange for thinking so, that some of the recent innovations in Soviet economic theory are not – or not yet – marxist, but simply the insertions of bits of liberal economic theory such as marginal utility analysis into the great holes left open for so many years by the failure of Soviet economists to do their job. This is the sort of thing which is rightly criticized by the Chinese, though I confess that their own solution, which seems to me to be that of going back to the simple primary-school marxism of the old days, is in its way just as much an evasion of the real problems of analysis.

Nevertheless, there is real and lively theoretical activity. For instance, one of the most promising signs is the revival of discussion of Marx's so-called Asiatic mode of production which has been going on since about 1960 in France, Hungary and the GDR, Britain, Czechoslovakia, Japan, Egypt and several other countries, and since 1964 also in the Soviet Union and even – though critically – in China. For we must remember that this concept of Marx was abandoned by the international communist movement between 1928 (when the Chinese criticized it) and the early 1930s (when it was banned in the Soviet Union) and has since been beyond the theoretical pale.[4]

What is the nature of this discussion today? It is, obviously, about

[3] I am not underestimating the genuine efforts at self-critical analysis of works like Palme Dutt's *Three Internationals*. But they certainly do not go as far as it is possible and necessary to go today.

[4] For a survey of these discussions, see G. Sofri, *Il modo di produzione asiatico*, Turin, 1969.

the applicability of the marxist analysis to the world today; or rather, since it plainly cannot be applied literally in the old form, about the modifications in the analysis which must be made to fit the world today.[5] And the 'world today' must include the socialist as well as the non-socialist world. There has been very little marxist analysis of that. In political terms this means it is about the perspectives for the victory of socialism in non-socialist countries and of its further development in socialist ones. This implies, but does not exhaust, the discussion of a number of more theoretical problems. It is evident that some of these have no very direct or discernible relevance to immediate or any other politics, though this was not always recognized. For instance, whether we finally decide that the history of China at some time in the past can be analyzed in terms of Marx's 'asiatic mode' or not will make no difference to the politics of the Chinese Communist Party now or in the future. But though a distinction between the theoretical and practical aspects of these debates can be made, in reality they cannot be sharply separated.

Politically, it seems to me that the major problem in non-socialist countries is that of how many and what different roads there are to socialism. Since the October revolution there has been a tendency to assume that there was basically at any time only one, though with local variations. The centralized organization of the world communist movement as well as its later domination by the CPSU only emphasized this rigidity. It still haunts the Soviet-Chinese discussions. Now two observations must be made, of which one poses fewer problems for the marxists than the other. The first is that, quite obviously, the road to socialism cannot be the same in, say, Britain and Brazil, or its perspectives equally bright or gloomy in Switzerland as in Colombia. The task of marxists is to divide the countries of the world into realistic groupings and to analyze properly the very different conditions of progress in each group, without trying to impose any uniformity (such as 'peaceful transition' or 'insurrection') on all of them. This is not so difficult in principle, but as it involves jettisoning a lot of past analyses and policies, it is not so easy in practice.

Much more difficult is to recognize that ways of progress to liberation and even socialism may have developed, in which the

[5] Anyone who has any doubts on this score should read again so typical a marxist statement of the 1930s as John Strachey's *Why you should be a Socialist*, or of the early 1950s as Palme Dutt's *Crisis of Britain*, or for that matter Kuusinen's *Fundamentals o, Marxism-Leninism*.

traditional communist parties or labour movements play only a subordinate part. I am thinking here of cases such as Cuba, Algeria, Ghana and perhaps others. Or in more general terms to ask ourselves whether our ideas of the role of communist parties in the advance to socialism may not have to be rethought in certain cases. For instance, as a current discussion in the Italian CP suggests, whether the split between social democratic and communist parties which arose after 1914 is any longer justifiable in certain countries today. In posing such questions, or rather in stating that they are being posed, I am not giving or even suggesting any answers. I am merely saying that such problems are no longer avoidable by closing our eyes to their existence.

Within the socialist world (and in so far as we think about future socialism in non-socialist countries), several problems are also posed, whether we like it or not, by reality. They are economic problems such as the best agrarian policy in such countries (given the rather striking failures of most of them in this field), or the best ways of economic planning, allocation of resources and goods, etc. They are political problems such as the best forms of organizing the institutions of such countries (given the very striking drawbacks of such institutions in many of them). They are problems of bureaucracy, or freedom of expression, etc. They are also, alas, international problems, as the difficult relations between different socialist states show only too clearly; including above all (as Togliatti pointed out in his Memorandum) the role of nationalism in socialist countries. Here again in stating that the problems exist, I am not implying any answers must not be begged by phrases such as that such things are due to hangovers from the pre-socialist past, that they are due to revisionism or dogmatism, or that they would all disappear if things were 'liberalized'.

All these problems imply theoretical discussion, and in some cases the willingness to break with long-established attitudes (as Lenin for one always was), or to enter entirely new territory. We are not used to this, so much so that we forget that marxists have done so in the past. For instance after the October revolution in Russia they had to enter a territory virtually unsurveyed by Marx, except in a few very general sentences, namely the problem of economic development in backward countries. And because they did so, marxism is today a genuine world movement, for after all, what gives it its most obvious appeal in the world today is, the analysis of the imperialist phase of capitalism, which is very much post-Marx, and the discovery of ways of turning backward countries into modern ones, which is the major theoretical discovery of the Soviet marxists in the 1920s. Moreover, some of these things also bring us back to the dialogue between marxists and non-marxists, for they involve learning from the achievements of non-marxist scientists. It is irrelevant that, if marxism had not ossified, it would itself have kept abreast and no doubt ahead of the best achievements of science. In many ways it did not, and we must now learn as well as teach.

This brings me to my conclusion. We are in a situation in which marxism is splintered, both politically and theoretically. We must, for the foreseeable future, learn to live with it. It is no good regretting the days when it wasn't. We are in a situation where marxism has to catch up in two ways. It has to liquidate the heritage of the sort of intellectual ice-age through which it passed (which does not mean that it should automatically reject everything that was said and done during that age), and we have to absorb all that is best in the sciences since we stopped serious thinking on the subject. I am deliberately using brutal terms, for they need to be used. We must ask as well as explain; above all we must ask ourselves. We must be prepared to be wrong. We must stop pretending to have all the answers, because we obviously haven't. And more than anything else, we must learn again to use marxism as a scientific method.

This we have not done. We have persistently done two things which are incompatible with any scientific method; and we have done them not just since the later days of Stalin, but earlier. First we have known the answers and just confirmed them by research; second we have confused theory and political debate. Both are deadly. We said for instance: 'We know the transition from feudalism to capitalism proceeds by revolution everywhere', because Marx says so, and because if it didn't, then history might not after all proceed by revolutions but by gradualism and the social democrats might be right. Therefore our research will show (a) that the revolution of the 1640s in Britain was bourgeois; (b) that before it Britain was a feudal country; and (c) that thereafter it was a capitalist country. I do not say that the conclusions were wrong, though (b) seems to me to be most doubtful; but this was no way of arriving at them. For if it turned out that the facts did not check with the conclusions, then we simply said, to hell with the facts.

There are historical reasons why we said so, going back to before

1914, but they do not concern us at this moment. And whether or not the facts will suit communists or social democrats has nothing to do with marxism. The fact that the conditions of the British working class are not absolutely deteriorating throughout history suits liberals and social democrats but not revolutionaries. We would be fools and not marxists if for this reason we denied it. Marxism is a tool for changing the world by knowledge, which we as politicians then use. It is not a means of scoring debating points in politics. Many of our most talented older communists have wasted much of their time as writers of marxist theory by failing to observe this distinction.

We must go back to marxism as a scientific method. Perhaps the most promising sign of the present world – and British – situation, which is otherwise not very promising, is that more and more marxists are going back to it in this way. And the proof of what can be achieved is the fact that socialism, based on marxism, has made most progress in the world even at the period when marxism did its best to make itself ineffective.

(1966)

12

LENIN AND THE 'ARISTOCRACY OF LABOUR'

The following brief essay is a contribution to the discussion of Lenin's thought, on the occasion of the hundredth anniversary of his birth. The subject is one which can be conveniently treated by a British marxist, since the concept of an 'aristocracy of labour' is one which Lenin clearly derived from the history of British nineteenth-century capitalism. His concrete references to the 'aristocracy of labour' as a stratum of the working class appear to be exclusively drawn from Britain (though in his study notes on imperialism he also notes similar phenomena in the 'white' parts of the British Empire). The term itself is almost certainly derived from a passage by Engels written in 1885 and reprinted in the introduction to the 1892 edition of the *Conditions of the Working Class in 1844* which speaks of the great English trade unions as forming 'an aristocracy among the working class'.

The actual phrase may be Engels's, but the concept was familiar in English politico-social debate, particularly in the 1880s. It was generally accepted that the working class in Britain at this period contained a favoured stratum – a minority but a numerically large one – which was most usually identified with the 'artisans' (i.e. the skilled employed craftsmen and workers) and more especially with those organized in trade unions or other working-class organizations. This is the sense in which foreign observers also used the term, e.g. Schulze-Gaevernitz, whom Lenin quotes with approval on this point in the celebrated eighth chapter of *Imperialism*. This conventional identification was not entirely valid, but, like the general use of the concept of an upper working-class stratum, reflected an evident social reality. Neither Marx nor Engels nor Lenin 'invented' a labour aristocracy. It existed only too visibly in the second half of nineteenth-century Britain. Moreover, if it existed anywhere else, it was clearly much less visible or significant. Lenin assumed that, until the period of imperialism, it existed nowhere else.

The novelty of Engels's argument lay elsewhere. He held that this aristocracy of labour was made possible by the industrial world monopoly of Britain, and would therefore disappear or be pushed closer to the rest of the proletariat with the ending of this monopoly. Lenin followed Engels on this point, and indeed in the years immediately preceding 1914, when the British labour movement was becoming radicalized, tended to stress the second half of Engels's argument, e.g. in his articles *English Debates on a Liberal Workers' Policy* (1912), *The British Labour Movement in 1912*, and *In England, the Pitiful Results of Opportunism* (1913). While not doubting for a moment that the labour aristocracy was the basis of the opportunism and 'Liberal-Labourism' of the British movement, he did not appear as yet to emphasize the international implications of the argument. For instance, he did not apparently use it in his analysis of the social roots of revisionism (see *Marxism and Revisionism*, 1908, and *Differences in the European Labour Movement*, 1910). Here he argued rather that revisionism, like anarcho-syndicalism, was due to the constant creation on the margins of developing capitalism, of certain middle strata – small workshops, domestic workers etc. – which are in turn constantly cast into the ranks of the proletariat, so that petty-bourgeois tendencies inevitably infiltrate into proletarian parties.

The line of thought which he derived from his knowledge of the labour aristocracy was at this stage somewhat different, and it is to be noted that he maintained it, in part at least, to the end of his political life. Here it is perhaps relevant to observe that Lenin drew his knowledge of the phenomenon not only from the writings of Marx and Engels, who commented frequently on the British labour movement, and from his personal acquaintance with marxists in England (which he visited six times between 1902 and 1911), but also from the fullest and best-informed work on the 'aristocratic' trade unions of the nineteenth century, Sidney and Beatrice Webb's *Industrial Democracy*. This important book he knew intimately, having translated it in his Siberian exile. It provided him, incidentally, with an immediate understanding of the links between the British Fabians and Bernstein: 'The original source of a number of Bernstein's contentions and ideas', he wrote on 13 September 1899, to a correspondent, 'is in the latest books written by the Webbs'. Lenin continued to quote information drawn from the Webbs many years later, and specifically refers to *Industrial Democracy* in the course of his argument in *What Is To Be Done?*

Two propositions may be derived in part, or mainly from the experience of the British labour aristocracy. The first was 'that all subservience to spontaneity of the labour movement, all belittling of the role of "the conscious element", of the role of Social Democracy means, whether one likes it or not, the growth of influence of bourgeois ideology among the workers'. The second was that a purely trade unionist struggle 'is necessarily a struggle according to trade, because conditions of labour differ very much in different trades, and consequently, the fight to improve these conditions can only be conducted in respect of each trade'. (*What Is To Be Done?* The second argument is supported by direct reference to the Webbs.)

The first of these propositions appears to be based on the view that, under capitalism, bourgeois ideology is hegemonic, unless deliberately counteracted by 'the conscious element'. This important observation leads us far beyond the mere questions of the labour aristocracy, and we need not pursue it further here. The second proposition is more closely linked to the aristocracy of labour. It argues that given the 'law of uneven development' within capitalism – i.e. the diversity of conditions in different industries, regions, etc. of the same economy – a purely 'economist' labour movement must tend to fragment the working class into 'selfish' ('petty bourgeois') segments each pursuing its own interest, if necessary in alliance with its own employers, at the expense of the rest. (Lenin several times quoted the case of the 'Birmingham Alliances' of the 1890s, attempts at a joint union-management bloc to maintain prices in various metal trades; he derived this information almost certainly also from the Webbs.) Consequently such a purely 'economist' movement must tend to disrupt the unity and political consciousness of the proletariat and to weaken or counteract its revolutionary role.

This argument is also very general. We can regard the aristocracy of labour as a special case of this general mode. It arises when the economic circumstances of capitalism make it possible to grant significant concessions to its proletariat, within which certain strata of workers manage, by means of their special scarcity, skill, strategic position, organizational strength, etc. to establish notably better conditions for themselves than the rest. Hence there may be historic situations, as in late-nineteenth-century England, when the aristocracy of labour can almost be identified with the effective trade union movement as Lenin sometimes came close to suggesting.

But if the argument is in principle more general, there can be no doubt that what was in Lenin's mind when he used it, was the aristocracy of labour. Time and again we find him using phrases such as the following : 'the petty-bourgeois craft spirit which prevails among this aristocracy of labour' (*The Session of the International Socialist Bureau*,' 1908), the English trade unions, insular, aristocratic, philistinely selfish', 'the English pride themselves on their "practicalness" and their dislike of general principles ; this is an expression of the craft spirit in the labour movement' (*English Debates on a Liberal Workers' Policy*, 1912), and 'this aristocracy of labour . . . isolated itself from the mass of the proletariat in close, selfish, craft unions' (*Harry Quelch*, 1913). Moreover, much later, and in a carefully considered programmatic statement – in fact in his *Draft Theses on the Agrarian Question for the Second Congress of the Communist International* (1920), the connection is made with the greatest clarity :

> The industrial workers cannot fulfil their world-historical mission of emancipating mankind from the yoke of capital and from wars if these workers concern themselves exclusively with their narrow craft, narrow trade interests, and smugly confine themselves to care and concern for improving their own, sometimes tolerable, petty-bourgeois conditions. This is exactly what happens in many advanced countries to the 'labour aristocracy' which serves as the base of the alleged Socialist parties of the Second International.

This quotation, combining the earlier and the later ideas of Lenin about the aristocracy of labour, leads us naturally from the one to the other. These later writings are familiar to all marxists. They date in the main from the period 1914–17, and form part of Lenin's attempt to provide a coherent marxist explanation for the outbreak of the war and especially the simultaneous and traumatic collapse of the Second International and most of its constituent parties. They are stated most fully in the famous Chapter 8 of *Imperialism*, and the article *Imperialism and the Split in Socialism*, written a little later (autumn 1916) and complementing it.

The argument of *Imperialism* is well known though the glosses of *Imperialism and the Split* are not so widely known. Broadly speaking it runs as follows. Thanks to the peculiar position of British capitalism –

'vast colonial possessions and monopolist position in the world markets' – the British working class tended already in the mid-nineteenth century to be divided into a favoured minority of labour aristocrats and a much larger lower stratum. The upper stratum 'becomes bourgeois', while at the same time 'a section of the proletariat allows itself to be led by people who are bought by the bourgeoisie, or at least are in their pay'. In the epoch of imperialism what was once a purely British phenomenon is now found in all the imperialist powers. Hence opportunism, degenerating into social-chauvinism, characterized all the leading parties of the Second International. However, 'opportunism cannot now triumph in the working class movement of any country for decades as it did in England' because world monopoly has now to be shared between a number of competing countries. This imperialism, while generalizing the phenomenon of the aristocracy of labour, also provides the conditions for its disappearance.

The relatively cursory passages of *Imperialism* are expanded into a rather fuller argument in *Imperialism and the Split*. The existence of a labour aristocracy is explained by the super-profits of monopoly, which allows the capitalists 'to devote a part (and not a small one at that!) to bribe their own workers, to create something like an alliance between the workers of a given nation and their capitalists against the other countries'. This 'bribery' operates through trusts, the financial oligarchy, high prices, etc. (i.e. something like joint monopolies between a given capitalism and its workers). The amount of the potential bribe is substantial – Lenin estimated it as perhaps one hundred million francs out of a billion – and so, under certain circumstances, is the stratum which benefits from it. However, 'the question as to how this little sop is distributed among labour ministers, "labour representatives" ... labour members of war industrial committees, labour officials, workers organized in narrow craft unions, office employees, etc. etc. is a secondary question'. The remainder of the argument, with exceptions to be noted below, amplifies but does not substantially alter, the argument of *Imperialism*.

It is essential to recall that Lenin's analysis was attempting to explain a specific historic situation – the collapse of the Second International – and to buttress specific political conclusions which he drew from it. He argued first, that since opportunism and social chauvinism represented only a minority of the proletariat, revolutionaries must 'go down lower and deeper, to the real masses', and second, that the 'bourgeois labour parties' were now irrevocably sold to the bourgeoisie, and would neither disappear before the revolution nor in some way 'return' to the revolutionary proletariat, though they might 'swear by the name of Marx' wherever marxism was popular among the workers. Hence revolutionaries must reject a factitious unity between the revolutionary proletarian and the opportunist philistine trend within the labour movement. In brief, the international movement had to be split, so that a communist labour movement could replace a social democratic one.

These conclusions applied to a specific historical situation, but the analysis supporting them was more general. Since it was part of a specific political polemic as well as a broader analysis, some of the ambiguities of Lenin's argument about imperialism and the labour aristocracy are not to be scrutinized too closely. As we have seen, he himself pushed certain aspects of it aside as 'secondary'. Nevertheless, the argument is in certain respects unclear or ambiguous. Most of its difficulties arise out of Lenin's insistence that the corrupted sector of the working class is and can only be a minority, or even, as he sometimes suggests polemically, a tiny minority, as against the masses who are not 'infected with "bourgeois respectability"' and to whom the marxists must appeal, for 'this is the essence of marxian tactics'.

In the first place, it is evident that the corrupted minority could be, even on Lenin's assumptions, a numerically large sector of the working class and an even larger one of the organized labour movement. Even if it only amounted to 20 per cent of the proletariat, like the labour organizations in late-nineteenth-century England or in 1914 Germany (the illustration is Lenin's), it could not simply be written off politically, and Lenin was too realistic to do so. Hence a certain hesitation in his formulations. It was not the labour aristocracy as such, but only 'a stratum' of it which had deserted economically to the bourgeoisie (*Imperialism and the Split*). It is not clear which stratum. The only types of workers specifically mentioned are the functionaries, politicians, etc. of the reformist labour movements. These are indeed minorities – tiny minorities – corrupted and sometimes frankly sold to the bourgeoisie, but the question why they command the support of their followers is not discussed.

In the second place, the position of the mass of the workers is left in some ambiguity. It is clear that the mechanism of exploiting a monopoly of markets, which Lenin regards as the basis of 'opportunism', functions in ways which cannot confine its benefits to one stratum only of the working class. There is good reason to suppose that the 'something like an alliance' between the workers of the given nation and their capitalists against the other countries (and which Lenin illustrates by the Webbs' 'Birmingham Alliances') implies some benefits for all workers, though obviously much larger ones for the well-organized and strategically strong labour aristocrats among them. It is indeed true that the world monopoly of nineteenth-century British capitalism may have provided the lower proletarian strata with no significant benefits, while it provided the labour aristocracy with substantial ones. But this was because there was, under the conditions of competitive, liberal '*laissez-faire*' capitalism and inflation no mechanism other than the market (including the collective bargaining of the few proletarian groups capable of applying it), for distributing the benefits of world monopoly to the British workers.

But under the conditions of imperialism and monopoly capitalism this was no longer so. Trusts, price maintenance, 'alliances', etc. did provide a means of distributing concessions more generally to the workers affected. Moreover, the role of the state was changing, as Lenin was aware. 'Lloyd Georgism' (which he discussed most perceptively in *Imperialism and the Split*) aimed at 'securing fairly substantial sops for the obedient workers, in the shape of social reforms (insurance, etc.)'. It is evident that such reforms were likely to benefit the 'non-aristocratic' workers relatively more than the already comfortably situated 'aristocrats'.

Finally, Lenin's theory of imperialism argues that the 'handful of the richest, privileged nations' turned into 'parasites on the body of the rest of mankind', i.e. into collective exploiters, and suggests a division of the world into 'exploiting' and 'proletarian' nations. Could the benefits of such a collective exploitation be confined entirely to a privileged layer of the metropolitan proletariat ? Lenin was already keenly aware that the original Roman proletariat was a collectively parasitic class. Writing about the Stuttgart Congress of the International in November 1907 he observed :

> The class of those who own nothing but do not labour either is incapable of overthrowing the exploiters. Only the proletarian class, which maintains the whole of society, has the power to bring about a successful social revolution. And now we see that, as the result of a far-reaching colonial

policy the European proletariat has partly reached a situation where it is not its work that maintains the whole of society but that of the people of the colonies who are practically enslaved . . . In certain countries these circumstances create the material and economic basis for infecting the proletariat of one country or another with colonial chauvinism; of course this may perhaps be only a temporary phenomenon, but one must nevertheless clearly recognize the evil and understand its causes . . .

'Marx frequently referred to a very significant saying of Sismondi's to the effect that the proletarians of the ancient world lived at the expense of society whereas modern society lives at the expense of the proletarians' (1907). Nine years later, in the context of a later discussion, *Imperialism and the Split* still recalls that the 'Roman proletariat lived at the expense of society'.

Lenin's analysis of the social roots of reformism is often presented as if it dealt only with the formation of a labour aristocracy. It is of course undeniable that Lenin stressed this aspect of his analysis far more than any other, and for purposes of political argument, almost to the exclusion of any other. It is also clear that he hesitated to follow up other parts of his analysis, which seemed to have no bearing on the political point he was at this time overwhelmingly concerned to make. However, a close reading of his writings shows that he did consider other aspects of the problem, and that he was aware of some of the difficulties of an excessively one-sided 'labour aristocratic' approach. Today, when it is possible to separate what is of permanent relevance in Lenin's argument from what reflects the limits of his information or the requirements of a special political situation, we are in a position to see his writings in historical perspective.

If we try to judge his work on the 'aristocracy of labour' in such a perspective, we may well conclude that his writings of 1914–16 are somewhat less satisfactory than the profound line of thought which he pursued consistently from *What Is To Be Done?* to the *Draft Theses on the Agrarian Question* of 1920. In fact, though much of the analysis of a 'labour aristocracy' is applicable to the period of imperialism, the classic nineteenth-century (British) model of it, which formed the basis of Lenin's thinking on the subject, was ceasing to provide an adequate guide to the reformism of, at least, the British labour movement by 1914, though as a stratum of the working class it was probably at its peak in the late-nineteenth and early-twentieth century.

On the other hand, the more general argument about the dangers of 'spontaneity' and 'selfish' economism in the trade union movement, though illustrated by the historic example of the late-nineteenth-century British labour aristocracy, retains all its force. It is indeed one of the most fundamental and permanently illuminating contributions of Lenin to marxism.

(1970)

13
REVISIONISM

The history of ideas is a tempting subject for the intellectual, for after all it deals with his own trade. It is also an extremely misleading and confusing one, and never more so than when vested interest, practical politics or other untheoretical matters are involved. Nobody will understand the split between the eastern and western churches in terms of theological discussion alone, or expect a purely intellectual history of the debate on cigarettes and lung cancer to reveal anything except the power of bias and self-delusion. Marx's famous reminder that it is not men's consciousness that determines their material existence but the other way round is never more to the point than where the printed word seems to be the primary reality, even though in fact, but for certain practical phenomena, it would not exist or be significant. It was not the intellectual merits of Keynes's *General Theory* which defeated Treasury orthodoxy, but the great depression and its practical consequences.

'Revisionism' in the history of socialist and communist movements illustrates the dangers of an isolated history of ideas particularly well, because it has always been almost exclusively an affair of intellectuals. But the number of articles, books and authors which a political tendency produces is notoriously a poor measure of its practical importance, except of course among intellectuals. Guild socialism, an articulate and much described creed, deserves at best a footnote in the actual history of the British labour movement. Trotskyism in the Soviet Russia of the 1920s had more numerous and abler spokesmen than the 'right-wing deviation', but its actual support among the party cadres outside the universities was almost certainly very much less. Conversely, of course, neither the number nor the nature of the arguments used by theoreticians tells us much about the actual movements with which they may be associated.

The German Social Democratic Party condemned Bernstein

almost unanimously, but in fact the policy of its reformist leaders was if anything more moderate than the one he recommended. The Hungarian revisionists of 1956 claimed to return to a purer and more democratic leninism, but, as Mr W. Griffith rightly points out in one of the few useful contributions to the subject in the Congress for Cultural Freedom's symposium *Revisionism*,[1] the actual direction of events in Hungary during those hectic days was away from any kind of leninism. In brief, a study of 'revisionism' which is chiefly, as the present book claims, a set of 'essays in the history of marxist ideas' is likely to confuse rather than to illuminate.

This is not to deny the interest of the study of ideas as such, though even in this specialized and rarefied atmosphere we must beware of the occupational hazard of both the theorists and the heresy-hunters, that of overestimating the unambiguity and the compelling force of intellectual concepts. The capacities of the human mind, given enough incentive, to put almost any practical construction on almost any theory, are easily under-rated. It might seem difficult to turn orthodox marxism, the specific annunciation of revolution by the proletariat, into an ideology of gradualism, or of bourgeois liberalism. But plenty of western social democratic marxists did the first, by arguing that the time for revolution had not yet arrived because capitalism had not yet worked itself into its final polarization, and the Russian 'legal marxists' (who are barely referred to in this book) did the second, by using Marx's argument that there was a phase of historical development (namely, now) when liberal capitalism was progressive and should be encouraged. There were historical reasons for both these apparently perverse procedures: the strength of the marxist framework in continental labour movements which local gradualists (unlike the British Fabians) were loath to abandon or the absence of any powerful intellectual tradition in Russia which allowed businessmen to feel self-confident and socially useful, even for a limited historical space of time. Nevertheless, the phenomenon of a theory being, without much apparent modification, turned into its practical opposite, should warn the enthusiastic historian of pure doctrine, as also the believers in *post hoc ergo propter hoc*.

It is evidently dangerous to confuse the context of an idea with its consequences. Thus we know that the 'Hegelian' strain in early

[1] Leopold Labedz (ed.), *Revisionism, Essays on the History of Marxist Ideas*, London 1962.

marxist analysis ('alienation') has strongly attracted the revisionists of the 1950s. It enables them to devise a case against capitalism, the 'alienating society' which survives the comforts of the age of affluence, while at the same time stressing the humanist aspects of Marx, his moral passion and concern for freedom. Yet, as Mr Daniel Bell points out, this argument is relatively new. In the 1930s 'alienation' played a negligible part in, or was absent from, both orthodox and dissident marxist argument, and the retreat from Hegel, enshrined in the *Short History of the CPSU* passed with little comment. Moreover, the few Hegelian marxists or near-marxists were either, like Ernst Bloch and the Frankfurt group, outside politics and party struggle or, like Lukács and Lefebvre, loyal stalinist communists. Conversely, if unorthodox or 'liberal' and 'gradualist' marxism had any philosophical affiliations it was (as with Bernstein, the 'legal marxists', and lately with Kolakowski) Kantian, rather than Hegelian; a tendency scarcely mentioned in this book.

Is it therefore likely that what attracted 'revisionists' to the Hegelian Marx was not so much what they were to find in him in the 1950s – Lukács's own deductions from him were far from liberal – but the fact that he was defined as heterodox, and that his champions, exposed to the nagging and thundering of the party hacks, therefore attracted the critical young. To read 'revisionism' back into the Marx of 1844 or the Lukács of 1923 is, to a much greater extent than either the orthodox or the authors of this symposium appear to realize, hindsight. It is also to oversimplify the process by which ideas, some more and some less suitable for the purpose, are adapted to certain political attitudes, because the attitude requires the idea rather than the other way round.

Such procedures are not the only ones likely to confuse the reader of this book who seeks chiefly to discover what 'revisionism' as an historical phenomenon is about. Though one would not suppose so from a symposium which ranges impartially over Bernstein and Trotsky, Bukharin and Otto Bauer, Luxemburg, Plekhanov, Deborin, Lukács and Tito, historically 'revisionism' consists of two relatively brief periods in the doctrinal history of marxism, one round the turn of the last century, the other since the 1950s. Both have certain things in common. Both occurred at times when the course of events – in particular the strength and prosperity of capitalism in the western world – appeared to throw grave doubts on the predictions of its imminent demise which marxists believed, and hence on the general analysis on which these were thought to be based. Both were therefore associated with a 'crisis in marxism' (the term was coined by T.G.Masaryk in 1897), i.e. with attempts to revise or supplement it, or to look for satisfactory or realistic bases for socialist action. Both these periods of hesitation proved temporary, but while they lasted they were chiefly confined to the countries in which the old-fashioned revolutionary perspectives of marxism had grown dim or pointless. Those in which they were not remained largely immune.

As in 1896–1905 the Russians, the Poles, the Bulgarians and the Serbs were the strongest defenders of the old verities of class struggle and revolutionary forward sweeps, so in the 1950s Asia, Africa and Latin America remained largely untroubled by the events which convulsed the communist parties of Europe. It is in these countries that the Chinese, now the defenders of old truth against new dilution, have sought or found most of their support within communist movements.

In both cases, moreover, the trademark 'revisionism' was or ought to be applied not, as the editor of this volume suggests, to all unofficial deviations from accepted marxist orthodoxy, but only to one type: that situated in the political topography of socialism on the right. This was quite clear in 1900, when 'revisionism' meant the marxist Fabianism of Bernstein and was coined to describe it. It was not so clear in the 1950s, when orthodox communists leaders hastened to apply the name, which clearly suggested the abandonment of class struggle, revolution and socialism to all who were familiar with it, to all dissidents to whom it could be plausibly attached. Paradoxically in this respect they had much in common with the present symposium. Nevertheless it is clear in this period also that on the global issues which divided 'revisionists' from their opponents – the stability and prospects of capitalism, gradualism versus old-style revolution, the virtues of bourgeois democracy or bourgeois thought, and the like – the 'revisionists' were those who stood on the right of the communist spectrum.

Of course they included various degrees of moderation, and it might well be desirable to confine the name to those who, in theory or fact, moved from their original leninism to something hard to distinguish from western social democracy or liberalism, for instance to Mr Djilas. In practice such a distinction is impossible to maintain clearly, partly because many east European revisionists of this kind prefer, for obvious reasons, the camouflage of leninist argument, partly because static distinctions falsify the nature of ideas which are still in evolution, partly because everyone likes to have some revisionist on his right wing from whom he can demonstratively distinguish himself. Nevertheless it has some meaning. Mr Gomulka, though clearly a right-winger by the standards of classical communist discussion, was plainly a communist and likely to remain one. This was not the case with several of the young Polish revisionists of the *Po Prostu* circle.

In one respect, of course, the two episodes are unlike. The revisionism of the 1950s was largely preoccupied with the internal problems of socialism – especially with stalinism – which did not exist in 1900. It therefore became inextricably tangled up with several traditional debates within the socialist movement such as that between libertarian and state socialism and with the Soviet controversies of the 1920s. These had no original connection with right-wing revisionism. On the contrary, they were often raised by the utopian or non-utopian left or at all events by those who, like Rosa Luxemburg and Trotsky, had impeccable credentials as radical revolutionists, and vociferous opponents of the original revisionism. Moreover, in the reaction against stalinism it was natural for communists to search for precedent and inspiration among non-stalinist or pre-stalinist marxists, and almost any neglected or divergent marxist might do. Hence interminable confusion. Thus stalinist suppression and the soundness of his criticisms of many Soviet tendencies made Trotsky popular among some revisionists. At the same time the wing of the communist movement which then most clearly represented the Trotskyite approach to world revolution was without doubt the Chinese.

None of these confusions is effectively dissipated by the symposium of twenty-seven studies, on rather haphazardly chosen subjects, several already published in one form or another, which Mr Leopold Labedz has edited. It will give the reader a convenient conspectus of the work of some relatively undocumented thinkers, some interesting arguments (e.g. about Lukács) and some information about writers, journals or groups of mainly secondary importance in the West. Except for two lesser chapters on India and Japan, it neglects the extra-European world entirely. Except for Mr Galli's Italian chapter, it pays little attention to the crises within the western communist parties, which are an obvious part of the phenomenon of 'revisionism'. Professor Coser in an essay on the United States actually succeeds in not mentioning the American CP at all, and Mr Duvignaud, in what is admittedly the most parochial of all the chapters, leaves us entirely in the dark about the French political situation – e.g. about the role of the Algerian war in crystallizing discontent within the CP – and omits even such leading dissident marxists as Lucien Goldmann and Serge Mallet.

Some of these omissions are no doubt due to the inevitable difficulties of editing a symposium, the quickest but also one of the least satisfactory ways of making a book. Others, however, are due to the general limitations of the historical approach which this work appears to represent. We still await the book which will put the 'revisionism' of the 1950s in its perspective as an historic phenomenon. The present collection of essays may feed a temporary curiosity among amateur 'students of communism' and 'sovietologists', but it is doubtful whether its permanent mark on the literature of modern communism will be great.

(1962)

14
THE PRINCIPLE OF HOPE

In our age men distrust the western universe and do not expect much of the future except perhaps Crusoe's luck, a personal island off the beaten track. To resist the assaults of the large machines made by and of men, to survive the consequences of collective human lunacy, are the highest ambitions of Atlantic intellectuals. Even the dream of the hungry, a continent filled with T-bone steaks and television quizzes, turns into a reality of ulcers and fatty degeneration. A modest wariness seems the best posture for man: lack of passion his least harmful social goal.

Can we, after all, it is argued, hope for anything better than that the human race will just avoid blowing up its planet, that political institutions will maintain a gentle order among foolish or sinful men, with perhaps a little improvement here and there; that a tacit truce be established between ideals and realities, individuals and collectivities? It is probably no accident that the four major states of the west were at the end of the 1950s presided over by paternal or avuncular images drawn (in Europe at least) from memories of the last age of stability which our continent recalls, that before 1914.

An entire generation was educated into such emotional middle age in the affluent but insecure societies of the postwar west, and its ideologists have been those of despair or scepticism. Fortunately the education has been ineffective. Already the late products of the 1950s, works like Mr Daniel Bell's *End of Ideology* or Professor Talmon's *High Tide of Political Messianism*, are oddly out of tune with the passionate, turbulent, confused but hopeful atmosphere of that international phenomenon, the intellectual 'new left'. Perhaps it is time for Ernst Bloch's *Das Prinzip Hoffnung*.[1] The historian of the future may well see this noble and massive work – all 1,657

[1] Ernst Bloch, *Das Prinzip Hoffnung*, 2 vols., Frankfurt, 1959.

pages of it testifying to its subject – standing outside the 1960s as the arch used to stand outside Euston station: symbolically, though not functionally, anticipating new departures.

Hope is Professor Bloch's subject and indeed has been so since his unduly neglected career as a philosopher of men's dreams began with *Geist der Utopie* (1918) and *Thomas Münzer als Theologe der Revolution* (1921). Hope bore him through the years of American exile when the present work was written (1938–47). It appears before us now in both an East and a West German edition, as revised in 1953 and 1959.

It is a strange, overcrowded, sometimes absurd, but nevertheless superb work. The British reader may find it well-nigh incredible, for in our country the old-fashioned philosopher as our grandparents knew him is dying out like the bison of the prairies, hunted down by the mathematical logicians and the definers of askable questions. The German reader will recognize in him a splendid specimen of traditional German romantic philosophy, a sort of marxist Schelling, as one reviewer has with some justice called him. But even in his native country philosophers such as he are now rare. No doubt, like several other aspects of traditional German culture, they found it easier to survive in East Germany under a crust of doctrinaire marxism than in the Americanized West. At all events it has struck at least one West German critic as 'irritating' that so magnificently and archetypically German a phenomenon as Professor Bloch's philosophy should come from 'beyond the Elbe'. However, he has remained a somewhat isolated figure since his transfer to the Federal Republic.

The starting point of Professor Bloch's argument is the empirical observation that man, in spite of the gloomier *littérateurs*, is a hoping animal. To be unsatisfied, to wish to envisage a more general state when things could be other (i.e. better) than they are, is the most elementary form of this fundamental human urge. Its highest form is Utopia – the construction of perfection which men seek or try to realize or which at least hangs above them like an intellectual sun. Such Utopia is not confined to the building of ideal commonwealths. There are images of desire everywhere: in our dreams of perfect bodily health and beauty, pushing back sickness, old age and even death: in those of a society without want. There are the images of a world transformed by the technical control of nature, the dream buildings or cities imperfectly reflected in all but the most modestly functional architecture of real life. The Utopia of a lost or undiscovered Eden or Eldorado haunted the explorers; the dream landscape of perfection – 'a world more adequately fitted to man' – haunts poetry, opera and painting. There are the perspectives of absolute wisdom.

But for Professor Bloch Utopia is more even than this wide range of 'anticipations, images of desire, the contents of hope'. It lies in all men who strive to 'realize themselves', i.e. to realize here and now the ideal of full humanity which we know to be latent in ourselves. It lies in the dream of eternity in this life, as in Faust's longing for the moment of life which shall be everlasting: 'Verweile doch, du bist so schön'. This dream of the present intensified into eternity finds its expression for Bloch in the art of music. It lies finally in the revolt against the limits of man's life and fate, in the images of hope against death, which find a mythical expression in our religions.

But hope, desire of change, Utopia, are not merely fundamental aspects of human behaviour. They represent reality because for Professor Bloch they echo the fundamental fact of change in nature, which is itself thereby oriented towards the future. Life itself, being in evolution, 'unfinished' and, therefore, changeable and perfectible, gives man scope for Utopia and is its objective counterpart. There is for Professor Bloch a materialist-utopian tradition in philosophy from which he would claim descent: that of the 'Aristotelian left', which took the master's doctrine of entelechy as its starting point and developed a concept of self-moving and self-creating matter. Some late Greeks, the medieval Islamic Aristotelians, an entire body of heretical Christian thought culminating in Giordano Bruno, belong to this tradition; so in spite of his deliberate philosophic idealism, does Hegel, at least in part. And so, using this tradition to help turn Hegelianism right side up, does Marx, in whom the utopian tradition and utopian hope reach their first really adequate practical and philosophical expression. For in Marx the gap between the wish and its fulfilment, the present and the future, is at last closed.

Hope is a fact, but for Professor Bloch also a desirable one. The object of his work is not merely its study but its propagation: the philosopher must be not only analyst but enthusiast. To teach men to hope in the right way and for the right things, to recognize what hoping implies, is his primary purpose. Consequently it is essential to criticize what denies, or rather what obscures and diverts hope, for *desiderium* ('dreaming forwards') is so deeply rooted in man that even the most pessimistic (indeed, especially the most pessimistic) attitudes can be shown to be merely diversions rather than denials of the utopian urge; even Angst or the concept of 'nothingness'. Those who really deny Utopia are those who create a closed and middling world from which the great avenues opening upon perfection are hedged off: the bourgeoisie.

For the bourgeois world replaces Utopia by 'adjustment' or escape – the society without want or unhappiness, by window-shoppinga nd the *New Yorker* ad. life; the anti-philistine life by gangster-romance; the undiscovered Eden by holidays in Positano and Chianti bottles as lampstands. Instead of hope there are lies, instead of truth, a mask. (For the middle-class ideal of the period before industrialism, as exemplified in Dutch seventeenth-century painting and Biedermeier interiors, Professor Bloch has respect and a certain tenderness. It can hardly be fitted even into his extended concept of Utopia, though he tries; de Hooch paints 'those tiny sharp pictures that carry homesickness within them'. But it had clarity and honesty, and in it 'the corner grocery of happiness was made to look like a genuine treasure chamber'.) And yet the nature of hope is such that there is truth even in the lies of capitalism. The desire for a 'happy end', however commercially exploited, is man's desire for the good life; our ever-deceived optimism, superior to unconditional pessimism, the belief that something can be done about it.

Professor Bloch's attacks against the theories which stand in the way of the recognition of hope, and especially his contemptuous dissection of Freudian and even more contemptuous dismissal of Adlerian and Jungian psychoanalysis, are therefore essential to his argument. However, though they sometimes coincide with what used to be marxist orthodoxy, they must not be confused with it. His critique of the fashions of the west is not indiscriminate: if he rejects philosophical pragmatism or functionalism in architecture, and brushes aside D.H.Lawrence (not without some silent sympathy from some of us) as a 'sentimental penis-poet', he cherishes Schönberg and respects abstract painting. Moreover, his arguments are strictly his own, for whatever his conclusions, Professor Bloch's philosophical provenance is un-marxist, or rather only one-third marxist.

He is in fact a surviving German 'natural philosopher' of the Coleridgean era who has turned revolutionary; a natural rebel against mechanical rationalism, a natural denizen of that world of semi-mystical cosmic harmonies, vital principles, living organisms, evolution, the interplay of polar opposites, and so on, in which Herder, Schelling or for that matter Goethe, not to mention Paracelsus and Jacob Boehme, moved. (It is highly characteristic of Professor Bloch's book that Paracelsus should be referred to more often in it than Descartes, Hobbes, Locke and Darwin put together.) Admittedly marxism has, via Hegel, deeper roots in this tradition than is commonly allowed. As late as *Anti-Duehring* Engels still writes a characteristic passage exalting Kepler above Newton and, indeed, a specific defence of the positive aspects of 'nature philosophy'. Still, the other two acknowledged components of marxism, the British and the French, have quite a different pedigree, and indeed its strength lies in the combination of both the 'classical' and the 'romantic' traditions of thought, if the term may be used in this context. But Professor Bloch is almost wholly a 'romantic'.

Hence both the strength and the weakness of his work. His views about the natural sciences will strike Anglo-Saxon readers as wilfully absurd, perhaps because we live in an age when the major advances in science are made by mathematics and a sophisticated neo-mechanism. But if his critiques may strike scientists as incomprehensible for the same reason as Goethe's rejection of Newton's optics, neither are the aberrations of fools. On the other hand Professor Bloch's approach gives him great penetration into the logic of what appears to be irrational (such as the world of visionary and symbolic statement), a navigational mastery of the oceans of the human heart, and a deep understanding of men's aspirations. These are the gifts of the artist, and indeed Professor Bloch is an artist, with a major writer's psychological insight and a remarkable style, where concise and gnomic foothills flank sinewy mountain ranges of prose, broken by cascades of noble rhetoric, and on which the glaciers of wit sparkle and glow.

But he is not an artist who has strayed into philosophy. He is a philosopher who also requires the techniques of the artist, for whom it is equally essential not only, say, to make an acute analysis of the middle-class preconceptions of Freud but also to express Spinoza's aspirations metaphorically but not vaguely as 'to see the world as a crystal, with the sun at its zenith, so that nothing throws a shadow'. Romanticism has taught Professor Bloch that there are things not readily expressible, at present in quantities or verifiable propositions, which nevertheless 'are there' and ought to be expressed. What is left of love when Kinsey has counted its orgasms, sample inquiries have measured its attitudes, physiologists described its mechanism and analysts the propositions which can be made about it, is still meaningful, and not only subjectively to lovers.

Das Prinzip Hoffnung is a long, discursive and sometimes repetitive book. To attempt any summary of its content beyond the briefest and driest oversimplification is quite impracticable, for it is a work of gigantic size and encyclopaedic range. (How many philosophical books, marxist or otherwise, contain analyses of the relation between music and medieval scholastic logic, discussions of feminism as a variant of Utopia, of Don Juan, Don Quixote and Faust as myths, of Natural Law in the eighteenth century, the evolution of Rosicrucianism, the history of town planning, yoga, the baroque, Joachim of Fiore, fun-fairs, Zoroaster, the nature of dancing, tourism and the symbolism of the alchemists?) Probably most readers will enjoy the book mainly for its variety and as the sum of often profoundly brilliant, sometimes rather peculiar, always stimulating, parts. Probably few readers will follow the author all the way, though none will fail to discover in him flashes of dazzling insight or – embedded in page-long paragraphs like flakes of mica in granite – the most polished of aphorisms.

However, even the most critically inclined should make the attempt to follow him to the end of his journey, where man, 'ein unterdrücktes und verschollenes Wesen', finds that 'the true Genesis is not at the beginning but at the end', where Blake fuses with Marx, and alienation ends in man's discovery of his true situation. For it is not every day that we are reminded, with so much wisdom, erudition, wit and mastery of language, that hope and the building of the earthly paradise are man's fate.

(1961)

15
THE STRUCTURE OF CAPITAL

A few years ago an able and acute observer of marxism could suggest that the history of its evolution as a theory was virtually at an end; or at all events at a standstill. It is plainly not possible to take such a view today. The cracking of the apparently smooth and firmly frozen surface of stalinism in the Soviet Union and of the unified and apparently integrated international communist movement has not merely produced, or revealed, equivalent cracks in the systematic compendium of dogma elaborated in the 1930s, and brilliantly simplified for pedagogic purposes in the *Short History of the CPSU*. The thaw of the ice-cap also watered the numerous plants of heterodoxy, schism or mere unofficial growth which had survived on the margin of, or under, the giant glacier. The hundred flowers bloomed, the schools began once again to contend, in a manner unfamiliar to all except the elderly who could throw their minds back to the 1920s or the old who recalled the days before 1914. Marxism, which had apparently aspired to turn itself – and by *force majeure* had largely turned itself – into a closed system, communicating with the outside world chiefly by a series of operations designed to show that it had no need to do so, was opened up again.

If we leave aside, as lacking much theoretical interest, the attempts to retain something like the old orthodoxy unchanged (as in China or among some groups of sectarians in other countries), and the moves to accept useful theories and techniques from the 'bourgeois' world without integrating them into the nominally unmodified marxist system (as happened to some extent in the Soviet Union), the marxist re-thinking of the past ten years has, broadly speaking, followed four paths. First, it has attempted something like an archaeological operation, by identifying the strata of theoretical thinking which had gradually accumulated on top of Marx's original thought, and for that matter pursuing the evolution of the great man's ideas themselves through its various stages. Second, it has sought to identify and to pursue the various original theoretical developments made from time to time on the basis of marxism, but for various reasons officially expelled from, or never absorbed into, the main corpus of its ideas. Third, it has attempted to come to terms, where this seemed apposite, with the various intellectual developments which had taken place outside marxism, and once again were deliberately extruded from it in the stalinist period. Last, it has tried to return to an analysis of the world (i.e. primarily of its social, economic and political developments) after a long period when the official interpretation had become increasingly remote from reality.

Among the pre-stalinist currents of marxism, one has long proved to be particularly fruitful and attractive to the re-thinkers, the 'central European' strain, to use George Lichtheim's convenient term. Most of the rare communist writers who retained any reputation as independent minds in the 1940s and early 1950s belonged to this tradition, e.g. George Lukács, Henri Lefebvre or, nourished in the Italian rather than German version of Hegelianism, Gramsci. The central Europeans formed part of that passionate reaction against the evolutionist positivism and mechanical determinism to which the theoretical leaders of the Second International had tended to reduce marxism, and which, in one form or another, provided the intellectual base for a return to revolutionary ideology in the year preceding and following the October revolution. For a brief period after the collapse of syndicalism (which had absorbed part of this left-wing revulsion against the Kautskys of the pre-1914 era) virtually all the rebel currents flowed together into the single cataract of bolshevism. After Lenin's death they began to diverge again, or rather the gradual and systematic construction of a single channel of official theory called 'leninism' forced the rest out of the main stream. Yet though Lenin's own thought was one of the forms of this re-assertion of revolutionary theory against 'revisionism' and 'reformism', and by far the most important in practice, it had been by no means the only one. Luxemburg and Mehring in Germany, the central-European Hegelians, and others, converged with Lenin in practice as revolutionaries, but were in no sense leninist in origin or intellectual procedures.

Politically the central European strain was revolutionary, not to say ultra-left. Socially, it was not so much a collection of intellectuals – all ideological schools are that – as one of men and women whose taste ran to agitation, writing and discussion rather than organization and the (bolshevik) executive life. In theory it was above all hostile to the Darwinian and positivist versions of marxism *à la* Kautsky, and suspicious even of those aspects of the mature Marx and Engels which might have encouraged determinism rather than voluntarism. Even the young Gramsci in Turin reacted to the October Revolution by calling for a 'revolt against Marx's *Capital*'. Philosophically it tended to stress – against the more official theorists of social democracy and the revisionists – the Hegelian origins of Marx and such of his youthful writings as were then available. The publication of the *Fruehschriften* by Landshut and Mayer in 1932 was to provide the central Europeans with what has turned out to be their basic text, the 1844 Manuscripts, and their basic operational tool, 'alienation'. By this time, however, the political situation had changed. The central Europeans no longer stood on the extreme left of the movement, a place now occupied by the Trotskyists (though in the west most of these, as J. P. Nettl has pointed out, were in fact Luxemburgians). Their passionate voluntarism, their own contempt for bourgeois science and their idealization of proletarian consciousness had been selectively absorbed into, even exaggerated by, the official Soviet doctrine. The main advantage the central Europeans retained was the capacity to combine the passion for social revolution, even the readiness to accept the Jesuit discipline of the communist parties, with the interests of mid-twentieth-century western intellectuals – such as *avant-garde* culture and psychoanalysis – and a version of marxist theory which, against the apparent trend of events in the Soviet Union itself, reaffirmed the humanist Utopia of Marx. War and resistance brought them political reinforcements, especially in France, from revolutionary intellectuals to whom the discovery of German philosophy (in this instance not mediated by marxism) gave a justification for the assertion of human liberty, the act of this assertion and struggle, and therefore the function of the 'engaged' intellectual. Via the phenomenologists Sartre moved into something like a position as honorary central European, and eventually into what he at any rate considered marxism. The collapse of stalinism relieved what had become an increasingly intolerable pressure on the central Europeans within the communist movement – stalinist theory had shown a diminishing toleration for the Hegelian or pre-1848 elements in Marx – and left them as the most obvious ideological nucleus for critical communist thought. Paradoxically a strain of ideas which began on the ultra-left ended on the right wing of the revolutionary movement.

Sooner or later a reaction was to be expected. It has now emerged under the leadership of Louis Althusser, a philosopher who has left the shadows of the great École Normale Supérieure of the Rue d'Ulm for the limelight of Parisian intellectual celebrity; or at any rate celebrity in the fifth and sixth *arrondissements*, which is even harder to achieve. His rise has been curiously sudden. Before 1965 he was virtually unknown even to the left-wing public, except as the author of an essay on *Montesquieu* and a selection from *Feuerbach*. In that year no fewer that three volumes came out as the first offerings of a series called '*Théorie*' under M. Althusser's direction: a collection of papers under the title *Pour Marx*[1] and two volumes essentially recording the papers presented at an intensive seminar by M. Althusser and his followers called *Lire Le Capital*.[2] (The laconic titles are part of the Althusserian trademark.) Their success has been startling. It is no reflection on the very considerable gifts of the author – not least his gallic combination of evident intelligence, lucidity and style – to observe that he has been lucky in the moment of his emergence. The atmosphere of the Althusserian Quartier Latin is the one in which every self-respecting left-wing secondary schoolboy or student is a Maoist or at least a Castroite, in which Sartre and Henri Lefebvre are ancient monuments and the self-lacerations of the intellectual ex-communists of 1956 as incomprehensible as the 'opportunism' of Waldeck-Rochet and Roger Garaudy. A new generation of rebels requires a new version of revolutionary ideology, and M. Althusser is essentially an ideological hard-liner, challenging the political and intellectual softening around him. It is typical that, though a member of the communist party, he should choose as his publisher François Maspero, the mouthpiece of the ultra-left.

[1] Louis Althusser, *Pour Marx*, Paris, 1960.

[2] Louis Althusser, Jacques Rancière and Pierre Macherey, *Lire Le Capital* (vol. 1); Louis Althusser, Étienne Balibar and Roger Establet, *Lire Le Capital* (vol. 2), Paris, 1960.

This does not make him into a 'neo-stalinist' as his detractors have suggested. The eloquent and rather moving pages of intellectual autobiography with which *Pour Marx* opens show no indulgence to stalinism, but their target is not so much 'le contagieux et implacable système de gouvernement et de pensée [qui] provoquait ces délires' – the Althusserian prose is in the classic tradition – but the 'conditions of theoretical void' in which French communism grew up and which stalinism helped to conceal behind that 'primacy of politics' which was in any case congenial to the French. It led those philosophers who were not content to 'confine themselves to commentaries and meagre variations on the theme of Great Quotations' in sheer intellectual self-defence either to deny the possibility of any philosophy, or to maintain some sort of dialogue with their professional colleagues by 'disguising themselves – dressing up Marx as Husserl, as Hegel, as the humanist and ethical Young Marx – at the risk of sooner or later confusing the mask with the face'. The end of stalinist dogmatism did not 'give us back marxist philosphy in its integrity'. It merely revealed its absence. Yet – and here M. Althusser leaves a moderately well-beaten track and at the same time allows himself scope for a good deal of private innovation – its absence was not due merely to the defects of the French intellectual left. It was not there because marxist philosophy, 'founded by Marx in the very act of founding his theory of history, has still largely to be constructed'; M. Althusser's ambitious purpose is to construct it.

In one sense this position has similarities with some tendencies of thought in the Stalin era, for one of the characteristics of that period was the systematic assertion of the absolute originality of Marx: the sharp cut which sundered him from Hegel and his own Hegelian youth, and from the utopian socialists (Roger Garaudy was obliged to revise his *Sources françaises du socialisme scientifique* on these grounds in the late 1940s). M. Althusser also talks of the *coupure* in Marx's evolution, and, while placing it, with most students, around 1845, seems reluctant to accept anything as fully 'marxist' before the *Poverty of Philosophy* and the *Communist Manifesto*.[3] But of course the stalinist theories had no doubt about what marxist philosophy was. M. Althusser is just prepared to

[3] Althusser has since pushed the frontiers of the 'pre-marxist' Marx steadily further forward, until little before 1875 is acceptable as properly non-Hegelian. Unfortunately this eliminates the bulk of Marx's writings.

admit that certain thinkers in the past began to ask the crucial question how, e.g., the purpose of *Capital* differs from that of political economy – Lenin, Labriola, Plekhanov, Gramsci and various Italian scholars following the underestimated Galvano Della Volpe, the Austro-marxists (who fell into neo-kantianism), and some Soviet commentators (who were incompletely aware of the implications of their analyses). But he denies that there is as yet a satisfactory answer.

For there is none in Marx himself. Just as classical political economy did not quite see the point of what it observed, and what Marx formulated for it, so that Adam Smith gives, as it were, the right answer to questions he had not consciously asked, so Marx himself surpassed his own insight, leaving us to recognize where it was he was going :

> What political economy does not see is not something pre-existing which it might have seen but did not, but something it has itself produced in its operation of knowing [*connaissance*], and which did not exist before this operation. It is precisely the production [of knowledge] which is identical with that object. What political economy does not see is what it makes: its production of a new answer without question, and at the same time its production of a new latent question carried within that new answer (*Lire Le Capital* I, pp. 25–6).

Marx himself suffers from the same weakness, which is the inevitable concomitant of the process of understanding. He was a far greater man than Adam Smith, because, while unable to emerge fully into his own novelty, he reaches out for 'his' question, formulating it somewhere or other, perhaps in a different context, searching for the answer 'by multiplying the images suitable for its presentation'. We, however, can know what he lacked: 'le concept de l'Efficace d'une structure sur ses effets' (*ibid.*, pp. 33–4). In discovering this lack we can not only begin to grasp marxist philosophy – the philosophy which Marx founded but did not construct – but also advance beyond it. For

> a science progresses, that is to say lives, only by paying extreme attention to its points of theoretical fragility. In this respect it holds its life less by what it knows than by what it does not know; on the absolute condition of circumscribing that non-known, and of formulating it rigorously as a problem.

It will be evident that the core of M. Althusser's analysis is epistemological. The nature of his exercise is the exploration of Marx's process of understanding and his main method an intensely detailed critical reading of the works, using all the resources of linguistic, literary and philosophical discipline. The first reaction of his own critical readers may well be that the methods and concepts he applies are not necessarily those emerging by his own favourite process of epistemological advance, from Marx himself. To say that 'along other roads contemporary theory in psychoanalysis, in linguistics, in other disciplines like biology and perhaps in physics has confronted the problem without realizing that Marx had "produced" it much earlier', may be true; but it is not impossible that the problem has been discovered in Marx because of the new and considerable vogue for linguistic 'structuralism' and Freud in France. (Indeed, while structural-functionalist elements are easily recognized in Marx, it is by no means so clear what Freud has to contribute to the understanding of *Capital*.) But if in fact these are to some extent insights from the outside ('nous devons ces connaissances bouleversantes . . . à quelques hommes : Marx, Nietzsche et Freud') it may be wondered whether the critical effort is merely confined to 'making manifest what is latent' in Marx.

A second reflection is that the Althusserian type of analysis finds it difficult, if not impossible, to get outside the formal structure of Marx's thought. M. Althusser is aware of this characteristic ('at no point do we set foot on the absolutely uncrossable frontier which separates the "development" of specification of the concept from the development and particularity of things') and appears to justify it by abstract argument ('we have demonstrated that the validation of a scientific proposition as knowledge in a given scientific practice was assured by the interplay of particular forms, which guarantee the presence of scientificity [*scientificité*] in the production of knowledge, in other words by specific forms which confer the character of – true – knowledge upon an act of knowledge'). Yet even if this is true and this method of validation can be applied as easily to *Capital* as to mathematical propositions (which is not obvious) all mathematicians know that a considerable gap still remains between their demonstrations and such real life phenomena – for instance, the evolution and operation of the capitalist system – as may be found to correspond to their discoveries. One can agree with M. Althusser's profound and persistent dislike of empiricism, and still feel uneasy about his apparent dismissal of any exterior criterion of practice such as actual historical development, past or future ('nous considérons le résultat sans son devenir'). For in fact Marx did get down to the difficult problem of the concrete. If he had not, he would not have written *Capital* but would have remained within the sphere of generality which dominates that marvellous and neglected *Introduction to the Critique of Political Economy*, which is in many respects the key work of the Althusserian Marx, as the 1844 Manuscripts are the key work of the Hegelian-humanist Marx whom he rejects.

And indeed, as soon as M. Althusser descends from the level where marxism establishes what history or economics can or cannot do ('the mathematical formalization of econometrics must be subordinate to conceptual formalization') and turns to its actual subject matter, he says little that is new or interesting. He produces a brilliant critique of the vulgar-marxist views on 'base' and 'superstructure' and a satisfying formulation of their interaction. But such practical applications of the general principle as are used to illustrate it are taken from marxists who have used a more direct and less intellectually self-contained route.

While students like M. Godelier[4] face the concrete problems of historic periodization raised by Marx, and have, for instance, taken a leading part in the rediscovery and re-analysis of the 'Asiatic mode of production' which is one of the more interesting intellectual results of the revival of original thought among communist intellectuals since Stalin, E.Balibar's long discussion of historical materialism (*Lire Le Capital*, vol. 2) remains resolutely on the heights of what one might call meta-history.

Moreover, M. Althusser's type of approach, valuable though it is, simplifies away some of Marx's problems – for instance, that of historic change. It is right to show that the marxian theory of historical development is not 'evolutionist' or 'historicist' in the nineteenth-century sense, but rests on a firm 'structuralist' foundation : development is the totality of all combinations, actual or possible, of the limited number of the different elements of 'production' which analysis defines ; those actually realized in the past make up the succession of socio-economic formations. Yet one might object to this, as to the not dissimilar Lévi-Straussian view, that by itself it does not explain how and why one socio-economic

[4] Maurice Godelier, *Rationalité et irrationalité en economie*, Paris, 1966.

formation changes into another but merely establishes the limits outside which it is senseless to speak of historic development. And also that Marx spent an extraordinary amount of his time and energy trying to answer these questions. M. Althusser's work demonstrates, if demonstration be still needed, the remarkable theoretical power of Marx as a thinker, his status and originality as a 'philosopher' in the technical sense of the word, and argues persuasively that he is far from a mere Hegel transposed from idealism to materialism. Yet even if his reading of Marx is correct, it is only a partial reading.

This does not diminish the force of his analysis as a tool of negative criticism. Whatever we may think of the polemical formulation of his contentions ('from the point of view of theory marxism is no more an historicism than it is a humanism'), the strength of his objections to the Hegelian and 1844 Manuscripts interpretation of Marx is substantial, the acuteness of his analysis of certain weaknesses of the thought of Gramsci (and their reasons) or of Sartre is impressive, the critique of 'model-building' including that of Weberian ideal types, is to the point. This is due to some extent to the personal abilities of the man whom *Le Monde* (reporting the special session of the French Communist Party's Central Committee devoted to the discussion of his and M. Garaudy's views) calls a 'philosophe de grande qualité', a quality revealed among other things in the intellectual respect he thinks he owes to some of those he criticizes. Nevertheless, it is also due to the thinker and the cause who so evidently inspire his passionate study.

One reads him with attention, even with excitement. There is no mystery about his capacity to inspire the intelligent young, and though it may be feared that the Althusserian school whom he will certainly gather round him will be more scholastic than sparkling, the net effect of his irruption into marxist theoretical debate may be positive. For his procedure is, almost by definition, that of asking rather than answering questions: of denying that the right answers have merely to be re-established even by the closest textual scrutiny of authority, because they have as yet to be worked out. For M. Althusser the relation between Marx and his readers is one of activity on both sides, a dialectical confrontation which, like reality, has no end. It is curious and characteristic that the philosopher (who has also, as in one essay of *Pour Marx*, doubled as a dramatic critic) chooses the metaphor of theatre – needless to say that of Brechtian theatre – to describe both Marx's process of exposing what lies beyond him (the *Darstellung* of 'ce mode de présence de la structure dans ses effets, donc la causalité structurale elle-même') and the readers' relation to him :

> C'est alors que nous pouvons nous souvenir de ce terme hautement symptomatique de la '*Darstellung*', le rapprocher de cette 'machinerie', et le prendre au mot, comme l'existence même de cette machinerie en ses effets : la mode d'existence de cette mise-en-scène, de ce théâtre qui est à la fois sa propre scène, son propre texte, ses propres acteurs, ce théâtre dont les spectateurs ne peuvent en être, d'occasion, spectateurs, que parce qu'ils en sont d'abord les acteurs forcés, pris dans les contraintes d'un texte et de rôles dont ils ne peuvent en être les auteurs, puisque c'est, par essence, un théâtre sans auteur (*Lire le Capital*, vol. 2, p. 177).

But the pleasure of reading an intelligent and original thinker ought not to blind us to his weaknesses. M. Althusser's approach to Marx is certainly not the most fruitful. As the above discussion has suggested tactfully, it may even be doubted whether it is very marxist, since it plainly takes no interest in much that Marx regarded as fundamental, and – as his subsequent writings, few though they are, make increasingly clear – is at loggerheads with some of Marx's most cherished arguments. It demonstrates the new-found post-stalinist freedom, even within communist parties, to read and interpret Marx independently. But if this process is to be taken seriously, it requires genuine textual erudition such as M. Althusser does not appear to possess. He certainly seems unaware both in *Pour Marx* and *Lire Le Capital* of the famous *Grundrisse*, though they have been available in an excellent German edition since 1953, and one may even suspect that his interpretation has preceded his reading of some of the texts with which he is acquainted. To this extent he still suffers from the after-effects of the stalinist period, which created a gap between the older generation of enormously learned Marx-scholars and both the political activists and the younger neo-marxists.

Moreover the revival of marxism requires a genuine willingness to see what Marx was trying to do, though this does not imply agreement with all his propositions. Marxism, which is at once a method, a body of theoretical thinking, and collection of texts regarded by its followers as authoritative, has always suffered from the tendency of marxists to begin by deciding what they think

Marx ought to have said, and then to look for textual authority for the chosen views. Such eclecticism has normally been controlled by a serious study of the evolution of Marx's own thought. M. Althusser's discovery that the merit of Marx lies not so much in his own writings, but in allowing Althusser to say what he ought to have said, removes this control. It is to be feared that he will not be the only theorist to replace the real Marx by one of his own construction. Whether the Althusserian Marx or other analogous constructs will turn out to be as interesting as the original is, however, quite another question.

(1966)

16
KARL KORSCH

The search for a viable post-stalinist marxism has tended to be at the same time a search for viable pre-stalinist marxian thinkers. There is no logical reason why this should be so, but the psychological motives which lead men (especially young men) to seek not only truth but also its teachers, are very strong. In any case we owe to it the rediscovery – one might almost say the discovery – of several interesting writers. Karl Korsch (1886–1961) is the most recent of these. A number of circumstances conspired to maintain him in obscurity during his lifetime. Though a communist for the first half of the 1920s, his writings were not attached to any 'deviation' of substance, or were in their time lumped with the heterodoxies of the Lukács of *Geschichte und Klassenbewusstsein* unjustly, though not without some plausibility. He thus had no chance of surviving the Stalin era as the guru of any organized body of marxists, however small. The Spanish anarcho-syndicalists, to whom he was drawn, were not a body likely to transmit, or even to understand, a theorist who was nothing if not sophisticated, and who belonged to a highly developed academic tradition. Hitler's victory buried his writings of the 1920s, Hitler's bombs the surviving stock of his *Karl Marx* published in London in 1938 in the Chapman and Hall series on *Modern Sociologists*, and which had in any case barely been noticed in the atmosphere of Anglo-Saxon marxism of those days.

The unexpected revival of interest in marxism among West German intellectuals in the 1960s has restored him to life. *Marxismus und Philosophie* (1923–31) was published in 1966 with a long introduction by Erich Gerlach and some minor texts of the 1920s;[1] *Karl Marx*, in a full scholarly edition by Goetz Langkau, in 1967.[2]

[1] Karl Korsch (ed. Erich Gerlach), *Marxismus und Philosophie*, Frankfurt, 1966. (English edition 1970).

[2] Karl Korsch, *Karl Marx*, Frankfurt, 1967.

6—R * *

At first sight the interest of Korsch seems to lie in the fact that he brought to marxism the comparatively rare combination of a German academic – he achieved the uncomfortable distinction of a professional chair at the ultra-right-wing university of Jena – of an active politician, Thuringian minister and Reichstag deputy, and of a passionate revolutionary. However, what is more important is his membership of that 'central European left' which was formed, in the years before and during the first world war, as a theoretical resistance movement to the Kautskyan orthodoxies of the Second International, and for a more or less short time, merged with 'bolshevism' after the October revolution. Korsch shared with most of this remarkably able generation of thinkers the conviction that German Social Democracy had justified its political passivity with a version of marxism which, in effect, turned it into a form of nineteenth-century positivist evolutionism. The left must turn from the politically misleading determinism of the natural sciences to philosophy (i.e. to the philosophic Marx of the 1840s), if only because marxist orthodoxy had lightly pushed this aside. The object was not to close marxism as a metaphysical 'system', but to open it. It was to oppose the constant – and hitherto uncompleted – philosophical critique of reality and ideology (including that of marxism itself) to the sterile certainties of positivism.

It is a matter of debate how far this return to a marxist philosophy was achieved at the cost of a systematic 're-Hegelianization' of Marx, such as was common elsewhere on the central European left. At all events the convergence between Korsch and Lukács proved to be only temporary. For from the start Korsch seems to have differed from his contemporaries in some important respects. His original pre-marxist critique of orthodoxy, developed in London before 1914, had asked not so much for revolution as for a positive content in socialism, such as he discovered both in syndicalism and, curiously enough, in the Fabian Society which he had then joined. Syndicalism he saw as an authentic proletarian conception of socialism, perhaps the inevitable form of such a conception. The Fabians, he thought, introduced a voluntarist element into socialism by their insistence on the socialist education of the people and a 'positive formula for socialist construction' by their discussions about the control of industry.

Though this line of thought differed from those of other anti-Kautskyans, it converged with them. All the left-wing rebels called for activism and planning and rejected historical determinism, all of them denied that Marx's 'man sets himself only such historical tasks as he can solve' meant that the solution of these tasks would be as automatic as their solubility. On the other hand Korsch differed from what we may call the east European wing of this new left in as much as he concentrated entirely on the problems of capitalism in the advanced industrial countries. Indeed, it is arguable that his rediscovery is due to this fact. For there has never been much difficulty in knowing, or at least in proposing, what marxists should do in underdeveloped countries. The problem ever since the later nineteenth century has been to suggest what they should do in countries of stable industrialism and no visible revolutionary perspectives. Korsch concentrated on this problem though unfortunately he had no solution for it.

Korsch's 'western' orientation accounts for the consistent theoretical critique of bolshevism which made him, even in his communist period, far less committed to the Russian (as distinct from the desired western) revolution than, say, Rosa Luxemburg, and led him rapidly to abandon any positive judgement of the Soviet Union. At this point he diverged from his friend and admirer Bertolt Brecht, and for that matter from many others on the central European left. For him leninism was as wrong as Kautskyanism, and for the same reasons. Indeed, he acutely pointed out that crucial concepts of leninism, such as the view that socialism enters the proletarian movement through intellectuals, could be derived from Kautsky. Philosophically Korsch's points against *Materialism and Empiriocriticism* were well taken. In concentrating on the defence of 'materialism' (which was not a serious issue), Lenin directed his fire against the unreal enemy of 'idealism' and left undisturbed the real danger, a 'materialist conception coloured by natural science'. This had been the fundamental current of bourgeois thought in philosophy, the natural and social sciences, and formed the major model for the vulgarization of marxism itself. Hence Lenin's perfectly sincere desire to remain a Hegelian was idle; he was forced back on to a simplified, indeed a pre-Hegelian, view of the opposition between materialism and idealism, which in turn led to an oversimplified view of what Marx's 'standing the Hegelian dialectic on its feet' meant, a vulgarization of the concept of the unity of theory and practice. Ultimately he was led to a position which was to inhibit the ability of marxism to contribute to the further development of the empirical sciences of nature and society.

He admitted that Lenin had not so much claimed to practise philosophy, as to criticize philosophical tendencies which appeared to him to be noxious for various reasons of party policy. But could marxists deal with philosophy or any other field of thought exclusively in terms of its usefulness or harmfulness in politics ? They could not.

The criticism of Lenin is in many respects just, but Korsch dismissed the factors which made leninism not merely another version of Kautskyan theory, but an entirely different historical phenomenon, a revolutionary theory for the underdeveloped world. He admitted that it was such a theory, though reluctantly. He denied that it formed 'an adequate theoretical expression for the practical needs of the present phase of the class struggle'. Indeed after his expulsion from the German Communist Party he increasingly assimilated the Soviet Union to fascism. Both were aspects of the *étatiste* and totalitarian counter-revolution which followed the short-lived upsurge of the revolutionary movement in 1917–23 and sought to prevent its recurrence. Historically absurd, such a view is plausible only on the assumption that bolshevism was a 'flight from the theoretical and practical demands of the industrial proletariat', reflecting the situation of the 'backward east' which still faced the problem of making its bourgeois revolution. Korsch made this assumption. He observed the revolutionary movement of the underdeveloped world and dismissed it as an irrelevance to the industrial proletariat of the industrial countries.

The difficulty of this position was that it left him without a revolutionary alternative for the west, once the tide of postwar rebellion had receded. Indeed, it left him with no concrete political perspective at all, after the failure of the Spanish anarcho-syndicalists. There are signs that, like other long-frustrated and disappointed revolutionaries, Korsch began to feel that the future was slightly less black after 1956, but since he wrote nothing of substance in his final years, we need not speculate how he might have modified his views.

Inevitably, as disillusion increased, the process of 'developing' marxism turned into one of criticizing it ; or rather of shedding so much of it that it was doubtful, in spite of Korsch's disclaimers, that the remainder could still be properly called marxism. Dialectics, for instance, was not a 'superlogic' to be handled like ordinary logic – a reasonable point – but the way in which during a revolutionary era, classes, groups and individuals produced new ideas, dissolved existing systems of knowledge and 'replaced them with more flexible systems, or better still, with no system at all, but with the wholly unconfined and free use of thought applied to the constantly changing process of development'. If we combine this with the rejection of most of Marx's actual propositions about the real world as what Mr Gerlach calls the 'dogmatization of the result of marxist research which have historically limited validity, the speculative instead of empirical derivation of development', not much of the actual corpus of Marx's writings was left. What remained was a method for an empirical social science, which derived from Marx chiefly a welcome refusal to identify itself with the natural sciences, and a proletariat, organized as a party, which could use this method for its purposes. There was no clear reason why marxism should be, or tend to become, the form of consciousness of the proletariat, and in future it would at best be one of the elements in proletarian theory, if indeed the revolutionary movement in its revival could be confined to the proletariat. Marx himself would be seen 'merely as one among many precursors, founders and developers of the socialist movement of the working class'.

It would thus seem that in the period of 'counter-revolution' Korsch found himself in the very difficulty that he noted in Marx and Engels after 1848: in the absence of realistic revolutionary perspectives the 'unity of theory and practice' was impossible to maintain, and there was an inevitable shift from 'practice' to theoretico-empirical research. However, it is extremely doubtful whether the Korschian adaptation to this situation, unlike the marxian one, can be properly described as 'still a comprehensive theory of social revolution'. Its practical side is reduced to platitude and hope. Its theoretical side provides a systematic bridge from what most Anglo-Saxons would (perhaps wrongly) call metaphysics to modern scientific method, as in the argument that Hegel, whose method was not all that different from the axiomatic procedures of modern natural sciences, could not be regarded as in conflict with empirical research, and in Korsch's exploration of mathematical models in the social sciences, such as the 'field theory' of his friend Kurt Lewin in psychology, and perhaps the theory of games. Unquestionably the reminder that the most committed social science must be subject to the usual tests of truth is valuable. Whether it has much specific connection with marxism, except as it were a biographical one, is another question.

It is relevant to stress this evolution to Korsch's political and theoretical analysis, because it forms a necessary background to his writings, and, though fairly explicit in *Marxismus und Philosophie* (or rather in the polemical introduction to the second edition of this work), is far from explicit in *Karl Marx*, a work which is in any case not easy of access to the non-specialist. It does not follow that the extreme position which he expressed in the period around 1950 – a phase of acute discouragement for more than one thinker brought up in the marxian tradition – is also that of works written in the 1920s or 1930s. However, these also mark points along a single line of development. This does not diminish the interest of these works both for the student of Marx, and for the student of the ulterior transformations and modifications of marxist thought. Korsch had an erudite and critical knowledge of the master's works, an admirable marxist awareness of the historic changes which underlay his and his followers' theoretical developments, and a point of view which makes his exposition refreshingly different from the fashions which have prevailed over the last generation.

Thus it is useful to remind young men brought up on catch phrases about 'alienation' or 'sociology' that Marx is above all an economist, in as much as the 'critique of political economy' increasingly formed an analytical backbone of his theory, while the other aspects of the analysis were increasingly reduced to incidental, if penetrating and brilliant *aperçus*. This is not epoch-making, but needs saying at a time when *Capital* may be seen by some as a treatise of epistemology or sociology : 'Marx's materialist science of society is not sociology but economics.' It is equally useful to subject the historical process of the 'reception' of marxism in late-nineteenth-century Germany and Europe to a cool, balanced and convincing analysis. Korsch shows that 'revisionism' was not a rejection of a formerly predominant theory and practice of revolutionary marxism, but as it were the twin of a formalized marxist orthodoxy which emerged at the same time, each a response of revolutionary theory to non-revolutionary actuality. And so on.

Such observations are helpful, but not world-shaking. And though Korsch evidently thought otherwise, it is hard to get excited about the propositions to which he himself attached crucial importance. No doubt in the 1920s the application of historical materialism to the study of marxism itself was unusual, but it is so no longer :

> So long as the material basis of existing bourgeois society can only be attacked and shaken, but not overthrown, by the practical revolutionary struggle of the proletariat, the revolutionary theory of the proletariat can only criticize the socially anchored forms of thought of the bourgeois era, but cannot finally go beyond them.

The recognition that marxism is 'incomplete' is in itself not enough. Korsch's statement remains on the level of platitude, though the kind of platitude which can stimulate those not habituated to it. It is fair enough : but where do we go next ? In the last analysis it is his failure to advance beyond this level which prevents Korsch from making a major contribution to the development of marxism. He is well worth reading, because he was both intelligent and learned. He wrote with some force and lucidity, compared with the habitual prose-style of central European marxist theorists, though this is unlikely to emerge from English translations. What he says is often worth listening to though some of his best insights, such as those about the essentially proletarian character of syndicalism, antedate his marxian period and have no necessary connection with it. But in the end, there is no major reason today why we should have to read him.

Applying his own criteria, and those of marxism to this failure, we may perhaps say that it reflects the essential predicament of the 'western' communist current to which Korsch belonged. It was a political non-starter. To be a social revolutionary between the wars usually meant in one way or another to choose bolshevism, even in a heretical form. Until the early 1920s, and in Spain until the late 1930s, it might still look as though it could also mean choosing something like syndicalism, but this was a horse which was already visibly collapsing under the rider who wished to urge it towards the goal of successful revolution. There was no other choice for a revolutionary, though marxism would have permitted various forms of theoretical adaptation and development which fitted it for non-revolutionary operation. For emotionally understandable reasons, Korsch rejected such 'revisionist' adaptations. Since he also rejected bolshevism, he was left isolated, theoretically and practically sterile and not a little tragic, an ideological St Simeon on his pillar.

(1968)

IV
SOLDIERS AND GUERRILLAS

17
VIETNAM AND THE DYNAMICS OF GUERRILLA WAR

Three things have won conventional wars in this century; greater reserves of manpower, greater industrial potential and a reasonably functioning system of civilian administration. The strategy of the United States in the past two decades has been based on the hope that the second of these (in which it is supreme) would offset the first, in which the USSR was believed to have the edge. This theory was based on faulty arithmetic in the days when the only war envisaged was one against Russia, for the Warsaw Pact powers have no greater population than NATO. The West was merely more reluctant to mobilize its manpower in conventional ways. However, at present the argument is probably more valid, for some of the Western states (like France) will almost certainly stay neutral in any world war that is likely, and China alone has more men than all the Western powers likely to fight in concert. At all events, whether the arguments were right or wrong, the United States has since 1945 put its money entirely on the superiority of its industrial power, on its capacity to throw into a war more machinery and more explosives than anyone else.

Consequently, it has been badly shaken to discover that a new method of winning wars has been developed in our time, and that it more than offsets the organization and industrial power of conventional military operations. That is guerrilla war, and the number of Goliaths who have been felled by Davids with slingshots is now very impressive: the Japanese in China, the Germans in wartime Yugoslavia, the British in Israel, the French in Indo-China and Algeria. At present the United States itself is undergoing the same treatment in South Vietnam. Hence the anguished attempts to pit bombs against small men behind trees, or to discover the gimmick (for surely there must be one?) which allows a few thousand ill-armed peasants to hold at bay the greatest military power on earth. Hence also the simple refusal to believe that it can be so. If the United States is baffled it must be due to some other – measurable and bombable – reason: to the aggressive North Vietnamese, who actually sympathize with their southern brothers and smuggle trickles of supplies to them; to the terrible Chinese who have the nerve to possess a common border with North Vietnam; and no doubt eventually to the Russians. Before common sense flies completely out of the window, it is therefore worth taking a look at the nature of modern guerrilla war.

There is nothing new about operations of a guerrilla type. Every peasant society is familiar with the 'noble' bandit or Robin Hood who 'takes from the rich to give to the poor' and escapes the clumsy traps of soldiers and policemen until he is betrayed. For as long as no peasant will give him away and as long as plenty will tell him about the movements of his enemies, he really is as immune to hostile weapons and as invisible to hostile eyes as the legends and songs about such bandits invariably claim.

Both the reality and the legend are to be found in our age, literally from China to Peru. Like the military resources of the bandit, those of the guerrilla are the obvious ones; elementary armaments reinforced by a detailed knowledge of difficult and inaccessible terrain, mobility, physical endurance superior to that of the pursuers, but above all a refusal to fight on the enemy's terms, in concentrated force, and face to face. But the guerrilla's major asset is non-military and without it he is helpless: he must have the sympathy and support, active and passive, of the local population. Any Robin Hood who loses it is dead, and so is any guerrilla. Every textbook of guerrilla warfare begins by pointing this out, and it is the one thing that military instruction in 'counterinsurgency' cannot teach.

The main difference between the ancient, and in most peasant societies endemic, form of bandit operation and the modern guerrilla is that the Robin Hood type of social bandit has extremely modest and limited military objectives (and usually only a very small and localized force). The test of a guerrilla group comes when it sets itself such ambitious tasks as the overthrow of a political regime or the expulsion of a regular force of occupiers, and especially when it sets out to do this not in some remote corner of a country (the 'liberated area') but over an entire national territory. Until the early twentieth century hardly any guerrilla movements faced this test; they operated in extremely inaccessible and marginal regions – mountain country is the commonest example – or opposed relatively primitive and inefficient governments native or foreign. Guerrilla actions have sometimes played an important part in major modern wars, either alone in exceptionally favourable conditions, as with the Tyrolese against the French in 1809, or more usually, as ancillaries to regular forces – during the Napoleonic wars, for example, or in our century in Spain and Russia. However, by themselves and for any length of time, they almost certainly had little more than nuisance value, as in southern Italy where Napoleon's French were never seriously inconvenienced by them. That may be one reason why they did not much preoccupy military thinkers until the twentieth century. Another reason, which may explain why even revolutionary soldiers did not think much about them, was that practically all effective guerrillas were ideologically conservative, even if socially rebellious. Few peasants had been converted to left-wing political views or followed left-wing political leaders.

The novelty of modern guerrilla war, therefore, is not so much military. The guerrillas of today may have at their disposal much better equipment than did their predecessors, but they are still invariably much worse armed than their opponents (they derive a large part of their armament – in the early stages, probably most of it – from what they can capture, buy or steal from the other side, and not, as Pentagon folklore holds, from foreign supplies). Until the ultimate phase of guerrilla war, when the guerrilla force becomes an army, and may actually face and defeat its adversaries in open battle, as Dienbienphu, there is nothing in the purely military pages of Mao, Vo Nguyen Giap, Che Guevara or other manuals of guerrilla warfare, which a traditional *guerrillero* or band leader would regard as other than simple common sense.

The novelty is political, and it is of two kinds. First, situations are now more common when the guerrilla force can rely on mass support in widely different areas of its country. It does so in part by appealing to the common interest of the poor against the rich, the oppressed against the government; and in part by exploiting nationalism or the hatred of foreign occupiers (often of another colour). It is, once again, only the folklore of military experts that 'peasants want only to be left alone'. They don't. When they have no food, they want food; when they have no land, they want land; when they are cheated by the officials of a remote capital, they want to get rid of them. But above all they want rights as men and when ruled by foreigners, to get rid of the foreigners. One ought to add that an effective guerrilla war is possible only in countries in which such appeals can be successfully made to a high percentage of the rural population in a high proportion of the country's territory. One of the major reasons for the defeat of guerrilla war in Malaya and Kenya was that these conditions did not obtain: the guerrillas were drawn almost entirely from among the Chinese or Kikuyu, whereas the Malays (the rural majority) and the rest of Kenya remained largely outside the movement.

The second political novelty is the nationalization not only of support for the guerrillas but of the guerrilla force itself, by means of parties and movements of national and sometimes international scope. The partisan unit is no longer a purely local growth; it is a body of permanent and mobile cadres around whom the local force is formed. They link it with other units into a 'guerrilla army' capable of nationwide strategy and of being transformed into a 'real' army. They also link it with the non-combatant national movement in general, and the politically decisive cities in particular. This implies a fundamental change in the character of such forces: it does *not* mean that guerrilla armies are now composed of hard-core revolutionaries infiltrated from outside. However numerous and enthusiastic the volunteers, the outside recruitment of guerrillas is limited partly by technical considerations, partly because many potential recruits, especially from among city intellectuals and workers, are simply not qualified; they lack the sort of experience which only guerrilla action or peasant life can give. Guerrillas may be started by a nucleus of cadres, but even a totally infiltrated force such as the Communist units which maintained themselves for some years after 1945 in Aragon (Spain) soon had to begin systematically recruiting among the local population. The bulk of any successful guerrilla force is always likely to consist of local men, or of professional fighters who were once recruited as local men, and the military advantages of this are immense, as Che Guevara has pointed out, for the local man 'has his friends, to whom he can make a personal appeal for help: he knows the terrain and all the things that are likely to happen in the region; and he will also have the extra enthusiasm of the man who is defending his own home'.

But if the guerrilla force is an amalgam of outside cadres and local recruits, it will nevertheless have been entirely transformed. It will not only have unprecedented cohesion, discipline and morale, developed by systematic education (in literacy as well as military techniques) and political training but unprecedented long-range mobility. The 'Long March' transferred Mao's Red army from one end of China to the other, and Tito's partisans achieved similar migrations after similar defeats. And wherever the guerrilla army goes, it will apply the essential principles of guerrilla war which are, almost by definition, inapplicable by orthodox forces: (*a*) To pay for everything supplied by the local population ; (*b*) not to rape the local women ; (*c*) to bring land, justice and schools wherever they go ; and (*d*) never to live better than, or otherwise than, the local inhabitants.

Such forces, operating as part of a nationwide political movement and under conditions of popular support, have proved themselves extraordinarily formidable. At their best they simply cannot be defeated by orthodox military operations. Even when less successful, they can be defeated, according to the calculations of British counter-insurgency experts in Malaya and elsewhere, only by a *minimum* of ten men on the ground for every single guerrilla ; that is to say, in South Vietnam by a *minimum* of something like a million Americans and puppet Vietnamese. (In fact, the 8,000 Malayan guerrillas immobilized 140,000 soldiers and policemen.) As the United States is now discovering, orthodox military methods are quite beside the point ; bombs don't work unless there is something other than paddies to make craters in. The 'official' or foreign forces soon realize that the only way to fight guerrillas is by attacking their base, i.e. the civilian population. Various ways of doing this have been proposed, from the old-fashioned Nazi method of treating all civilians as potential guerrillas, through more selective massacre and torture, to the presently popular device of kidnapping entire populations and concentrating them in fortified village compounds, in the hope of depriving the guerrillas of their indispensable source of supplies and intelligence. The American forces, with their usual taste for solving social problems by technological means, appear to have a preference for destroying everything over large areas, presumably in the hope either that all guerrillas in the area will be killed along with the rest of the human, animal and vegetable life, or that somehow all those trees and underbrush will be vaporized, leaving the guerrillas standing up and visible, where they can be bombed like real soldiers. Barry Goldwater's plan to defoliate the Vietnamese forests by nuclear bombs was no more grotesque than what is actually being attempted along these lines.

The difficulty with such methods is that they merely confirm the local population in their support of the guerrillas, and provide the latter with a constant supply of recruits. Hence the anti-guerrillas devise plans to cut the ground from under the enemy's feet by improving the economic and social conditions of the local population, rather in the manner of King Frederick William I of Prussia who is reported to have run after his subjects in Berlin, beating them with his stick and shouting : 'I want you to love me.' But it is not easy to convince people that their conditions are being improved while their wives and children are being drenched in burning oil, especially when the people doing the drenching live (by Vietnamese standards) like princes.

Anti-guerrilla governments are more likely to talk about, say, giving peasants the land, than actually doing it, but even when they carry out a series of such reforms they do not necessarily gain the gratitude of the peasants. Oppressed peoples do not want economic improvement alone. The most formidable insurrectionary movements (including very notably the Vietnamese) are those that combine national and social elements. A people who want bread and *also* independence cannot be conciliated merely by a more generous distribution of bread. The British met the revolutionary agitation of the Irish under Parnell and Davitt in the 1880s by a combination of coercion and economic reform, and not without success – but this did not forestall the Irish revolutionary movement which threw them out in 1916–22.

Nevertheless, there are limitations to a guerrilla army's ability to win a war, though it usually has effective means to avoid losing one. In the first place, guerrilla strategy is by no means applicable everywhere on a national scale, and that is why it has failed, or partly failed, in a number of countries, e.g. Malaya and Burma. Internal divisions and hostilities – racial, religious, etc. – within a country or a region may limit the guerrilla base to one part of the people, while automatically providing a potential base for anti-guerrilla action in another. To take an obvious case ; the Irish revolution of 1916–22, essentially a guerrilla operation, succeeded in the twenty-six counties but not in Northern Ireland, despite a common frontier and active or passive help from the south. (The British government, by the way, never made this sympathy an excuse to drop bombs on the Shannon barrage in order to force the Dublin government to cease its aggression against the free world.)

Again, there may be peoples so inexperienced or so lacking in effective cadres as to allow large-scale and wide-based guerrilla insurrections to be suppressed, at least for some time. That is perhaps the case in Angola. Or the geography of a country may facilitate local guerrilla action, but make coordinated guerrilla warfare remarkably difficult (as perhaps in some Latin American countries). Or a people may be simply too small to win independence by direct action without major outside aid against a combination of occupying countries determined to suppress them. This may be the case with the Kurds, superb and persistent guerrilla fighters of the traditional kind, but who have never achieved their independence.

Beyond these obstacles which vary from country to country, there is the problem of cities. However great the support for the movement in the cities, however urban the origin of its leaders, cities and especially capital cities are the last place a guerrilla army will capture or, unless very badly advised, tackle. The Chinese Communists' road to Shanghai and Canton ran via Yenan. The Italian and French resistance movements timed their urban insurrections (Paris, 1944; Milan and Turin, 1945) for the very last moments before the arrival of Allied armies, and the Poles who did not (Warsaw, 1943) were wiped out. The power of modern industry, transport and administration can be neutralized for a significant length of time only where it lies thin on the ground. Small-scale harassment, such as the cutting of one or two roads and rail tracks, can disrupt military movement and administration in difficult rural terrain, but not in the big city. Guerrilla action or its equivalent is entirely possible in the city – after all, how many bank robbers are ever caught in London – and there have been some recent examples of it, for instance in Barcelona in the late 1940s, and various cities in Latin America. But it has little more than nuisance value, and merely serves to create a general atmosphere of lack of confidence in the efficiency of the regime, or to tie down armed forces and police which might be better used elsewhere.

Finally, the most crucial limitation of guerrilla warfare is that it cannot win until it becomes *regular* warfare, in which case it must meet its enemies on their strongest ground. It is comparatively easy for a widely backed guerrilla movement to eliminate official power from the countryside, except for the strong points actually physically occupied by armed forces, and to leave in government or occupation control no more than the isolated cities and garrisons, linked by a few main roads or railroads (and that only by daylight), and by air or radio. The real problem is to get beyond that point. Textbooks devote a good deal of attention to this ultimate phase of guerrilla war, which the Chinese and Vietnamese handled with brilliant success against Chiang Kai-shek and the French. However, those successes should not include mistaken generalizations. The real strength of guerrilla armies lies not in their ability to turn themselves into regular armies capable of expelling other conventional forces but in their political strength. The total withdrawal of popular support may produce the collapse of local governments often – as in China and Vietnam – heralded by mass desertions to the guerrillas; a crucial military success by the guerrillas may bring this collapse into the open. Fidel Castro's rebel army did not win Havana; when it had demonstrated that it could not only hold the Sierra Maestra but also take the provincial capital of Santiago, the government apparatus of Batista collapsed.

Foreign occupying forces are likely to be less vulnerable and less inefficient. However, even they may be convinced that they are in a war they cannot win, that even their tenuous hold can be maintained only at quite disproportionate cost. The decision to call off the wasting game is naturally humiliating, and there are always good reasons for postponing it, because it will rarely happen that the foreign forces have been decisively defeated, even in local actions like Dienbienphu. The Americans are still in Saigon, apparently drinking their bourbon peacefully, except perhaps for an occasional bomb in a cafe. Their columns still criss-cross the country apparently at will, and their losses are not much greater than those from traffic accidents at home. Their aircraft are dropping bombs wherever they like, and there is still somebody who can be called the prime minister of 'free' Vietnam, though it may be hard to forecast from one day to the next who he will be.

Thus, it can always be argued that just one more effort will tip the balance: more troops, more bombs, more massacres and torture, more 'social missions'. The history of the Algerian war anticipates the one in Vietnam in this respect. By the time it was over, half a million Frenchmen were in uniform there (against a total Moslem population of nine million, or one soldier to every eighteen inhabitants, not counting the pro-French local white population), and the army was still asking for more including the destruction of the French Republic.

It is hard, in such circumstances, to cut one's losses, but there are occasions when no other decision makes sense. Some governments may take it earlier than others. The British evacuated Ireland and Israel well before their military position had become untenable. The French hung on for nine years in Vietnam and for seven years in Algeria, but went in the end. For what is the alternative ? The old style of local or marginal guerrilla actions, like border raiding by tribesmen, could be isolated or contained by various relatively cheap devices which did not interfere with the ordinary life of a country or its occupiers. A few squadrons of aircraft could occasionally bomb villages (a favourite British device in the Middle East between the wars), a military frontier zone could be established (as on the old north-west frontier of India), and in extreme cases government tacitly left some remote and disturbed region to its own devices for a while, merely seeing to it that the trouble did not spread. In a situation like that of Vietnam today or of Algeria in the later 1950s, this will simply not work. If a people does not want to be ruled in the old way any more, there is nothing much that can be done. Of course, if elections had been held in South Vietnam in 1956, as was provided by the Geneva agreements, the views of its people might have been discovered at considerably less cost.

Where does this leave the anti-insurrectionaries ? It would be foolish to pretend that guerrilla war is an invariable recipe for successful revolution or that its hopes, as of now, are realistic in more than a limited number of relatively underdeveloped countries. The theorists of 'counter-insurgency' can therefore take comfort in the thought that they need not *always* lose. But that is not the point. When, for one reason or another, a guerrilla war has become genuinely national and nationwide, and has expelled the official administration from wide stretches of the countryside, the chances of defeating it are zero. That the Mau Mau were defeated in Kenya is no help to the Americans in Vietnam ; all the less help when we remember that Kenya is now independent, and the Mau Mau regarded as pioneers and heroes of the national struggle. That the Burmese government has never been overthrown by guerrillas was no help to the French in Algeria. The problem of President Johnson is Vietnam, not the Phillipines, and the situation in Vietnam is lost.

What remain in such a situation are illusions and terror. The rationalizations of today's Washington policy were all anticipated in Algeria. We were told by French official spokesmen that the ordinary Algerian was on the side of France, or if not actually pro-French, that he wanted only peace and quiet but was terrorized by the FLN. We were told, practically once a week, that the situation had improved, that it was now stabilized, that another month should see the forces of order regain the initiative, that all they needed was another few thousand soldiers and another few million francs. We were told that the rebellion would soon die down, once it was deprived of its foreign sanctuary and source of supplies. That sanctuary (Tunisia) was bombed and the border hermetically sealed. We were told that if only the great centre of Moslem subversion in Cairo could be eliminated, everything would be all right. The French therefore made war on Egypt. In the last stages we were told that there might just conceivably be some people who *really* wanted to get rid of the French, but since the FLN obviously did not represent the Algerian people, but only a gang of ideological infiltrators, it would be grossly unfair to the Algerians to negotiate with them. We were told about the minorities which had to be protected against terror. The only thing we were not told was that France would if necessary use nuclear weapons, because the French didn't then have any. What was the result ? Algeria is today governed by the FLN.

The means by which the illusions are to come true is terror, mostly – in the nature of things – against noncombatants. There is the old-fashioned terror against civilians by frightened soldiers, demoralized by the fact that in this kind of war any civilian may be an enemy fighter, and culminating in the infamous mass reprisals – the razing of villages, such as the Nazis' Lidice and Oradour. Intelligent anti-guerrillas will discourage this, since it is apt to make the local population totally hostile. Still, such terror and reprisals will happen. Furthermore, there will be the more selective torturing of prisoners for information. In the past there may have been some moral limitation on such torture, but not, alas, in our time. In fact, we have so far forgotten the elementary reflexes of humanity that in Vietnam we photograph torturers and victims and release the pictures to the press.

A second kind of terror is that which is at the base of all modern warfare, whose targets nowadays are essentially the civilians rather than the combatants. (Nobody would ever have developed nuclear weapons for any other purpose.) In orthodox warfare the purpose of indiscriminate mass destruction is to break the morale of population and government, and to destroy the industrial and administrative base on which any orthodox war effort must rest. Neither task is as easy in guerrilla war, because there are hardly any cities, factories, communications or other installations to destroy, and nothing like the vulnerable central administration machine of an advanced state. On the other hand, more modest success may pay off. If terror convinces even a single area to withhold support from the guerrillas, and thus to drive them elsewhere, this is a net gain for the anti-guerrillas. So the temptation to go on bombing and burning at random is irresistible, especially for countries like the United States which could strip the entire surface of South Vietnam of life without dipping too deeply into its supply of armaments or money.

Lastly, there is that most hopeless and desperate form of terror, which the United States is at present applying : the threat to extend the war to other nations unless they can somehow get the guerrillas to stop. This has no rational justification at all. If the Vietnamese war were really what the State Department pretends, namely an 'indirect' foreign aggression without 'a spontaneous and local rebellion', then no bombing of North Vietnam would be necessary. The Vietcong would be of no more importance in history than the attempts to set up guerrilla warfare in Spain after 1945, which faded away, leaving few traces except some local newspaper stories and a few publications by Spanish policemen. Conversely, if the people of South Vietnam really were on the side of whatever general at present claims to be their government, or merely wanted to be left in peace, there would be no more trouble in that country than in neighbouring Cambodia or Burma, both of which had or still have guerrilla movements.

But it is clear by now, and should always have been clear, that the Vietcong will not go away quietly, and no miracle will transform South Vietnam into a stable anti-communist republic within the foreseeable future. As most governments in the world know (though one or two, like the British, are too dependent on Washington to say so) there can be no military solution in Vietnam without at least a major conventional land war in the Far East, which would probably escalate into a world war when, sooner or later, the United States discovered that it could not win such a conventional war either. And it would be fought by several hundreds of thousands of American troops, because the allies of the United States, though doubtless willing to send a token battalion or ambulance unit, are not fools enough to involve themselves seriously in a conflict of this kind. The pressure to escalate a little further will mount, and so will the Pentagon belief in the most suicidal of all the many Vietnamese illusions – that in the last showdown the North Vietnamese and Chinese can be terrorized by the prospect of nuclear war into defeat or withdrawal.

They cannot, for three reasons. First, because (whatever the computers say) nobody believes that a United States government, which is genuinely interested in a stable and peaceful world, will actually start a nuclear war over Vietnam. South Vietnam is a question of vital importance for Hanoi and Peking, just as Soviet missiles off Florida were regarded as a vital issue in Washington; whereas the Vietcong are merely a matter of saving face for the United States as Cuban missile bases were of marginal urgency for Khruschev. The Russians backed down over Cuba because to them it was not worth any kind of world war, nuclear or conventional. For the same reason the United States can be expected to back down in South Vietnam, provided it is interested in world peace, and provided, presumably, some sort of face-saving formula can be found.

Second, and on the supposition that the United States really is not prepared for any realistic settlement in South Vietnam, its nuclear threat will not work in the long run because North Vietnam, China (and quite a few other countries) will conclude that nothing is to be expected from concession except further United States demands. There is so much talk about 'Munich' in Washington these days that it is often forgotten how much like Munich the situation must look to the other side. A government which regards itself as free to bomb a country with which it is not at war can hardly be surprised if China and North Vietnam refuse to believe that this is the last concession they will be asked to make. There are, as the United States government is aware, situations today in which countries are willing to face the risks of world war, even nuclear war. For China and North Vietnam, South Vietnam is one such situation and the Chinese have already made that clear. It is dangerous daydreaming to think otherwise.

Third and last, the threat of nuclear war against China and North

Vietnam is relatively ineffective, because it is more appropriately a threat made against *industrialized* belligerents. It assumes that in modern warfare there comes a moment when a country or a people must give up because its back is broken. That is a certain outcome of nuclear war for small and medium-sized industrial states and a probable one for large ones (including the United States), but it is *not* the necessary outcome for a relatively undeveloped state, especially one as gigantic as China. It is certainly true that China (without the USSR) has no chance of defeating the United States. The strength of its position is that neither can it be defeated in any realistic sense. Its token nuclear bombs can be destroyed, and so can its industries, cities and many millions of its 700 million citizens. But all that would merely put the country back to where it was at the time of the Korean war. There are simply not enough Americans to conquer and occupy the country.

It is important for American generals (and for anyone else calculating war on assumptions derived from industrial societies) to realize that a nuclear threat will be regarded by the Chinese either as incredible, or as inevitable but not decisive. It will therefore not work *as a threat*, though doubtless the Chinese will not rush lightly into a major war, especially a nuclear one, even when they believe it cannot be avoided. As in Korea, they are not likely to enter it until directly attacked or threatened. The dilemma of American policy therefore remains. Having three times as many nuclear bombs as the rest of the world is very impressive, but it will not stop people from making revolutions of which Mr McGeorge Bundy disapproves. Nuclear bombs cannot win guerrilla wars such as the Vietnamese are now fighting, and without such weapons it is improbable that even conventional wars can be won in that region. (The Korean war was at best a draw.) Nuclear bombs cannot be used as a *threat* to win a little war that is lost, or even a medium-sized war, for though the populace can be massacred, the enemy cannot be brought to surrender. If the United States can come to terms with the realities of south-east Asia, it will find itself very much where it was before – the most formidable power in the world, whose position and influence nobody wants to challenge, if only because nobody can, but which, like all other powers, past and present, must live in a world it does not altogether like. If it cannot come to such terms, sooner or later it will blast off those missiles. The risk is that the United States, suffering from the well-known disease of infant great powers – a touch of omnipotence – will slide into nuclear war rather than face reality.[1]

(1965)

[1] Though the situation has altered since this article was written, shortly after the United States decision to escalate the Vietnam war in 1965, I have preferred to reprint it unchanged, partly because the general arguments remain valid, but partly also for the pleasure of recording accurate prediction.

18

CIVILIANS VERSUS MILITARY IN TWENTIETH-CENTURY POLITICS

Ever since the French Revolution all modern governments have faced the problem of the relations between civilian governments and the military. Most of them have feared a potential military takeover from time to time, and indeed Napoleon Bonaparte provided the first modern example of this phenomenon and, for a very long time, its characteristic brand-name, Bonapartism. Of course governments had problems with their soldiers before then. Guards officers were proverbial king-makers, or rather emperor-assassinators in eighteenth-century Russia, as janissaries had been in the Ottoman Empire. But, taking central and west European feudal and absolutist states, the armed forces were rarely separable from the nobility and gentry which provided their officers. In extreme cases, no conflict between civilians and military in politics could arise, because the same people, e.g. feudal nobles and country gentry, were both. Or rather, conflict might arise, but only as it were about demarcation lines. It was almost impossible for the armed (i.e. noble) rebels to conceive of any government other than that of the legitimate hereditary dynasty, or of someone who at least pretended to belong to it. They might challenge one particular member of it, or quarrel with particular arrangements within the kingdom, but constitutionally they did not set up an alternative. In fact, as the Meiji Restoration in Japan shows very well, in the last analysis even the most inactive and nominal legitimate king or emperor had for this reason amazing reserves of political power against the most powerful nobles who ruled in his name, if he chose to exercise them.

But we are not considering traditional aristocratic and absoluti societies but modern ones, in which the armed forces are a specia sub-department of public power, different in their personnel an generally in the social recruitment of their officers from other par of it, and not necessarily owing the civilian part a traditiona almost ritual, loyalty. We do sometimes find survivals of the olde relationship, as in nineteenth-century Prussia and imperia Germany, where the corps of army officers (but not the nava ones) consisted largely of junkers, who would have found rebellio against the king, who was the very keystone of their class, hardl conceivable ; at least as long as he behaved as they thought a kin ought to. In a more attenuated form we find it even in Hitler' Germany, where the fact of having sworn a personal oath o loyalty to the chief of state undoubtedly meant much to officers But such phenomena are increasingly marginal to modern states which have increasingly tended to be republics, where loyalty i formally due not to a dynasty or even a person, but to a concep ('the people', 'the republic', 'the constitution', etc.), and t particular groups of individuals such as governments only in so fa as they represent these concepts. It is quite easy to decide that on is loyal to the republic, people or (if vaguely enough defined constitution, whereas the government is not. Plenty of soldier have decided in this manner, and in a number of countries notably the Iberian and Latin American ones from the early nineteenth century, soldiers have claimed a permanent right t make coups by virtue of being the *ex-officio* guardians of people republic, constitution and the basic ideological or other values o the state.

Now virtually all modern states have taken the view, at leas since Napoleon, that the ideal relation between civilian governments and the military is the subordination of the latter to the former. A great deal of thought has been expended in some countries to ensuring this subordination, and nowhere more sc than in the states deriving most directly from the revolutionary tradition, those under the government of communist parties. Their problem was always particularly acute, since revolutionary governments deriving from insurrection and armed struggle are vulnerable to the men who wage it. As the debates of the 1920s in Soviet Russia bear witness, they were extremely sensitive to the possible dangers of 'Bonapartism'. Their determination that army must be subservient to party has been unqualified, and even the Chinese, who during the 'Great Cultural Revolution', appeared to diverge from this tradition, seemed to return to it in 1971. Until now communist regimes have been remarkably successful in maintaining civilian supremacy – we need not venture in prophecy – though it may be argued that in concentrating on the dangers of a military takeover they somewhat neglected another danger, at least until 1956. This was the risk of a *de facto* takeover by the police, open or secret, against which the history of the French revolution provided no warning example. The term 'police' is here used not of the traditional and relatively modest apparatus of public order and internal espionage, but of the phenomenon, for which the nineteenth century provides little precedent, of large and increasingly powerful parallel centres of armed force, administration and power, such as the German SS. Still, by and large communist-governed states have been passionately civilian-minded, as even acknowledged heroes of the nation like Marshal Zhukov were to discover.

Western parliamentary democracies have not, on the whole, denied themselves the publicity value of military glory. It was not only the Weimar Republic which elected its most eminent general to the presidency. Marshall MacMahon and General de Gaulle in France, the Duke of Wellington in Britain, and a remarkably long list of presidential generals in the United States ending (for the present) with Eisenhower, testify to the political appeal of a highly decorated uniform. And, incidentally, to the self-denial of communist governments. In general, however, the typical western states – the term is sufficiently understood not to require pedantic definition – have not had much of a problem of militant takeover. Soldiers have sometimes been very influential in them, and have changed governments or provided the conditions under which governments could change – but – and this is not widely recognized – they rarely governed *themselves* or regarded themselves as possible rivals to civilian government, or its controllers.

Their political analogue was rather the civil service, a body of persons obliged, whatever their private views, to carry out the wishes of any government which had formal sovereignty and the responsibility for taking political decisions. This did not mean that civil services could not drag their feet, indulge in gentle sabotage, in backstairs lobbying for their policies, or interpret such policies in ways congenial to them. It meant that formally they were and are *arms* of government, not government itself. The late A.B.Cobban pointed out this analogy for the French army. Indeed, it is to a great extent true, in spite of the various interventions of that army in politics, and in spite of the fact that for long periods the social origins of its officers, their ideology and their political views (Catholic and Royalist) conflicted almost head-on with those of their political masters. The first Napoleon was the great exception – but only until he seized power. After that he was a normal ruler who happened to go off from time to time to win battles. The army was no more important in his regime than in any other which wages war. Napoleon III was not even a soldier, and his rise to power owes little to the military; if they supported him in 1851 it was because he was *already* the effective government. The army which raised Marshall Petain to power was German and not French. As for General de Gaulle he freed himself of the military conspirators who brought him to power as soon as he could, and subordinated the army to civilian control in the usual way, and with little trouble. He called on it again in 1968, but evidently (until the present) without reviving its political ambitions.

Conversely in such countries (France) the attempts of the army to coerce the politicians were, on the whole, remarkably unsuccessful. When the French army did not accept the existing and operational government as the legitimate one, whatever it happened to be – and it changed loyalties without a tremor in 1830, 1848, 1851 and 1870 – it proved itself weaker than the government. During the Third Republic, when army confronted civilian rulers, as during the Boulanger and Dreyfus crises, the civilians won. I think one can safely say that the threatened refusal of the British army to operate Irish Home Rule in 1914 was the result not of its own determination, but of the chicken-livered hesitations of the liberal government. It did not give firm orders, and an army established on the principles of obeying such orders, had none to obey. Truman was never seriously threatened by Macarthur. In the most extreme case of a self-conscious dissident army opposing the established government, the revolt of the German army leaders against Hitler, the outcome was clear. The real way in which armies in western countries have intervened in government is by playing politics, and the most successful generals in this respect were not those who mobilized their support among brother officers, but in courts or the lobbies of Parliaments. Indeed, one of the reasons for General de Gaulle's strength was his rare combination of the gifts of the army commander and the remarkably subtle, not to say devious, politician. This is a combination which one and a half centuries have taught any French general who wishes to get anywhere, but few have been competent to learn the lessons.

All this suggests that armies are politically neutral, serving any regime with equal obedience, though not equal loyalty. This is the situation of many policemen, and some of them have been known to take pride in their Hobbesian readiness to serve any Leviathan that is likely to come along, though revolutionaries who find themselves interrogated under both capitalist and communist regimes by the same official, have appreciated the virtues of this political theory less. However, though both are disciplined, hierarchical, largely uniformed and armed forces designed to execute and not to make policy, armed forces and police forces are quite different in their political behaviour. As for armies, there appear to be limits to their loyalty. Will they accept social-revolutionary regimes ? The answer is : probably not, though the subject is as usual surrounded by myth. (We do not, for instance, know adequately how many of the armed forces of Spain remained loyal to the republic in 1936 – probably more than is commonly realized – or how large a proportion of tsarist officers loyally served, or would have loyally served, the Soviet government.) Since most revolutions are victorious because the armies which ought to suppress them are no longer reliable instruments of order, and therefore arise on the (perhaps temporary) ruins of the former armed forces, few have doubted that armies are fundamentally against social revolution. Still, they probably are. By and large the evidence shows that army officers in western countries are socially conservative, and so, very often, are the ranks of career soldiers, as distinct from those of conscripts.

That the Reichswehr between the wars was prepared to be loyal to the Weimar Republic and Hitler, both regimes with which its generals had no sympathy, does not prove that they would have been equally loyal to a communist regime. Pretty certainly, they would not have been. Armies refusing obedience to such social-revolutionary regimes might well justify their failure on the grounds that these represented not any kind of order, but disorder and anarchy, or that they were not real regimes, since their power and authority was contested (as might well be the case), but whatever the reasons, they would be following the inclinations of their officers. Conversely, social-revolutionary governments have felt little confidence in the armies of the old regime. Those which have, like the German social democrats of 1918, can by this criterion alone be safely classified as not really revolutionary.

In developed countries which do not happen to be undergoing social revolution (and few of them have) armies therefore intervene in politics only under very exceptional conditions, and then – so far – invariably on the political right. Under what conditions? A breakdown of the normal processes of politics normally seems necessary, the classical example being the conflict between the formal pattern of the system and political or social realities which cannot be absorbed into it: a small, oligarchic party system which threatens to be swamped by mass forces outside it (as seems to have been the case in Japan in the 1920s and 1930s), an organized block of voters whom the electoral system must admit, but the dominant party structure refuses to, thus producing permanent instability. In Argentina, France and Italy, for instance, no stable government can be based both on free elections, the sovereignty of the elected assembly, and the exclusion of the Peronists or Communists respectively from the process of forming governmental alliances. Military rule (as in Argentina), the imposition (by military coup) of a new presidential constitution which devalues the assembly (as in France), the fear of military coups (as in Italy since the middle 1960s) are the consequence. However, one hopes that the Italian example proves that, while necessary, the breakdown of the political system is not a sufficient cause of military intervention. On the other hand the injection into such an endemic crisis of some political issue about which the army, as a corporate professional or even political interest feels very strongly, undoubtedly makes the situation much more explosive. A controversial war, for which the army feels it is not getting sufficient moral support and material resources, may make the temptation to sweep away the hesitant or traitorous civilians irresistible. Still, armies might even so prefer to substitute a 'good' or 'efficient' civilian government for a 'bad' or 'ineffective' one, since in developed countries they are profoundly imbued with the sense of being not political 'masters', but a 'service', and in any case acutely aware of their lack of qualifications for politics. The Reichswehr in Weimar Germany sought any solution rather than that of taking over power itself, and thought it had found a satisfactory one in the strong right-wing Nazi-Nationalist coalition of 1933.

The term 'army' in this context refers for practical purposes exclusively to the officer corps. Among its members the generals are in theory best capable of action, since their numbers are small, they generally know each other and can therefore concert policy more easily, and above all, because they can actually order large bodies of troops about. In practice they are less likely to act (as distinct from permitting action), partly because of the notorious jealousies and ambitions of senior officers, to which the literature of military autobiography bears witness, partly because their personal fortunes are directly dependent on the civilian government, i.e. on playing orthodox politics. They have much to gain within the existing system, and more to lose by abandoning it. Less eminent officers have more to gain, but find it hard to concert action outside the limited field of the regiment, the garrison or the small expeditionary force, though being members of some old-boy network helps to extend their range. On the whole, in developed countries coups not organized, or at any rate covered, by generals, seem unlikely. The most dangerous situation is likely to be one in which the less senior officers are politically mobilized and organized, e.g. in secret nationalist societies, and take the initiative in attempting coups or mutinies, which, even though abortive, force the generals into showing solidarity with movements which are in any case more congenial to them than the discredited civilians. We need hardly discuss the problem of the special role of certain elite corps and units designed for rapid action, such as parachutists and commandos. By and large, in developed countries one may guess that the colonels, halfway between their seniors and juniors, are likely to be politically the most dangerous ranks.

As for the rest coups by non-commissioned officers are rare even in underdeveloped countries with armed forces of any size, and practically negligible in developed ones. If the rank and file of any army plays politics, it is no longer military politics. They intervene in politics because they act as civilians. Their most powerful weapon is analogous to that of the civilian workers' strike, namely the refusal to obey orders. At crucial moments this may decide the fate of governments. The most recent example is perhaps the refusal of the French conscripts in Algeria to follow their officers into a putsch against de Gaulle. To this extent conscript armies have a certain built-in resistance to military coups, but one would not speculate how far this resistance alone would take them. Probably not too far.

So much for western and communist countries. However, there remains the very large part of the world in which military politics play a much more prominent role, especially in times of crisis. This comprises the bulk of the so-called 'Third World' or 'underdeveloped world', i.e. the Iberian and Latin American states, the Islamic states, Africa south of the Sahara and large parts of Asia. The case of Japan belongs more to the 'developed' world, in the sense that military politics there appear as a temporary interim rather than as a permanent probability. However, I know too little about this country to speak with confidence about it.

Throughout this vast area military government has often been the rule and always implied by the very existence of an army, so that its elimination has often seemed to require that of the armed forces themselves.[1] This vulnerability to military politics has been demonstrated more than 150 years in Latin America, the only sector of the Third World which has enjoyed political independence under republics for so long a period, and became evident within a few years of the establishment of political independence in most of the rest of the underdeveloped countries. It is quite easy to draw up a list of western countries which have never been under military rule in the past 150 years, even though sometimes, like Britain and Belgium, engaged in major wars. There are very few countries of the Third World at present under civilian administration, in which the chances of maintaining it over the next twenty years are as good as even. Admittedly the recent drift towards military government has been by no means entirely spontaneous.

[1] This is not as impracticable as it might seem. Though only one state (Costa Rica) has actually abolished the army, Mexico has quietly reduced its armed forces to something like seventy thousand – for a country of perhaps fifty millions – with the result that it has not suffered from military coups since the 1930s.

Why this is so is a question which cannot be answered simply by an analysis of the social composition or corporate interests of the armed forces. Their corporate interests are plainly not negligible, since military expenditure may receive 20 per cent or more of all funds expended by their governments in a given year, to cite one estimate for Latin America in the early 1960s, and the pressure to maintain this disproportionate share of budgets clearly involves armed forces (among whom armies are generally by far the largest group) in national politics. Their social composition itself is not adequately illuminating either. The officer corps is rarely drawn predominantly from a traditional landed aristocracy and gentry, like the Prussian junkers, or from that sector of it which has long family connections with the military life. Either such strata do not exist, or they have been swamped by officers of different social origin, as in Argentina, where only 23 per cent of senior army and air force commanders come from 'traditional' families. Leaving aside the special cases where large sections of the armed forces are recruited from particular minority nationalities, tribes or other groups (such as the 'martial races' which were so conveniently used by former colonialist governments and have sometimes survived into independence), the bulk of officers in the underdeveloped world can be described in one way or another as 'middle class'. But this classification in itself means very little.

'Middle class' may mean that officers are recruited from the established strata exercising economic and political power, as in Argentina, where 73 per cent of army and air force generals come from the 'comfortable bourgeoisie'.[2] In this case their politics, leaving aside corporate interests and the special patterns of military life, are likely to be similiar to those of their class, i.e. on the conservative side. Or, more typically, they may come from the lower middle class or modest provincial bourgeoisie, in which case the army is one of the more promising careers for social promotion open to the sons of this stratum. Officer corps composed largely of aspiring and rising members of a military middle class, increasingly professionalized and technically trained, are less likely to identify with an established upper class, where such a one exists. They may be politically more radical (or 'modernizing') in the civilian sense (e.g., in the nineteenth century, 'Liberal'), or in some specific military sense (as in twentieth-century, 'Nasserism').

[2] José Luis Imaz, *Los Que Mandan*, Buenos Aires, 1968, p. 58.

7—R * *

There are, of course, also the genuinely self-made military leaders who have risen from the ranks. They are common in and after revolutions, and during long periods of political disorder, as in nineteenth-century Latin America, where the *caudillo* was sometimes a grass-roots fighting man who had worked his way up to the point where he commanded a sufficiently large force to surround the nearest presidential palace. Today such self-made, and usually self-promoted chiefs are probably common only in ex-colonies which, before independence, possessed either no native armed units specifically associated with the territory of the subsequent independent state, or at least no significant body of native officers. This is the case in most of sub-Saharan Africa.

Whatever the social composition of such officer corps, the tendency to military rule reflects not so much their character as the absence of a stable political structure. Why is it less common in communist states, some of which were equally 'backward' before the revolution? Essentially because genuine social revolutions set up both a convincing legitimation of civilian power – the movement of the masses itself and the organizations (parties, etc.) which claim to speak in its name – and also because they immediately set about constructing a machine of government which reaches down to the grass roots. The army which emerges from them therefore tends to be not the creator but the creation of the regime or the party, and it is merely one among several institutions created by it. More; it has two primary functions within it, both of which keep it busy: defence and mass education. This does not entirely eliminate the danger. There are special cases such as Algeria where the 'movement' was not primary, or rather where the 'army' coexisted with it independently for long periods before independence, or in Bolivia, where the 'movement', which had largely destroyed the old army in the revolution of 1952, could not retain control of its own army, perhaps chiefly because both came to depend largely on the United States. But on the whole – and this applies to regimes like the Mexican which, though non-communist, are the outcome of genuine social revolution – the army is or becomes subordinate to the party or the civilian organization.[3]

[3] The Mexican case is particularly interesting because the revolution was largely dominated by virtually independent insurrectionary generals, who were only eliminated as a serious political force in the course of perhaps twenty years,

Most of the Third World, however, has not achieved political independence by means of mass movements or social revolutions, Much of it did not even contain the initial bases for a modern state, and indeed, as in so much of Africa, the main function of the new state apparatus was as a mechanism for the production of a national bourgeoisie or ruling class, which previously barely existed. In such countries the legitimation of the state is uncertain. In nineteenth-century Latin America as in mid-twentieth century Africa it may not even be clear what territory the state should occupy, its frontiers being determined by historical accident, such as the administrative divisions of former colonial rule, former imperial rivalry, or economic accidents such as the distribution of large estates. Only military power is real, because the least efficient and experienced of armies is efficient enough to surround the presidential palace and occupy radio station and airport without calling upon any other force, and there is rarely another force to call on, or if there is, the government may hesitate to call upon it. Even that power is often not very real. As the failed coups in parts of former British and French Africa show, a very small European force can often neutralize it. (Conversely, many a putsch has been due in recent years to the official or unofficial encouragement by outside powers.) But broadly speaking the Third World is putschist, because it has had no real revolutions, and today more putschist than ever because both local forces and outside powers wish to avoid revolutions. The much rarer case where soldiers take over because there is a basis for revolution, but no adequate civilian force to carry it out, will be considered below.

Military politics, in advanced countries as in the Third World, is therefore not a special kind of politics, but something that fills the vacuum left by the absence of ordinary politics. It may establish or re-establish ordinary politics when, for one reason or another, these have broken down. At worst they prevent social revolution without putting anything in its place except the hope that sooner or later an alternative solution to it will turn up. This is the case of so many Latin American military regimes – the

---

incidentally giving Mexico the benefit of a military budget of less than 1 per cent of the country's GDP in the 1960s – a lower percentage even than that of Uruguay.

Argentinian and Brazilian, or of the Polish 'colonels' between the wars, and the Greek one at present. If the army coups are lucky, the wheels of the economy will turn, the mills of administration will grind on, and the successful generals can retire to the sidelines or sit out their prolonged term as presidents, benefactors or liberators of their country. If they are less lucky, there may be a slump in primary commodity prices and the wheels of the economy stop, i.e. the taxes stop coming in, the debt cannot be serviced. This has put paid to quite a few military rulers in their time, as in the mid-1950s. If the soldiers are even less lucky, and there is no economy or institutional apparatus behind them, even military government will have no stability. It will last until the next colonel sees his chance to speculate on the big race. The most backward and dependent countries have had the most persistent history of short-lived military regimes.

One reason for this rather negative character of military politics is, that army officers rarely wish to govern themselves, or are competent at any activity except soldiering, and sometimes not even at that. The increasing professionalization and technification of modern armed forces has not substantially changed this. Their qualification and training as a group are wrong for government. A glance at the mess the Brazilian officers made after 1964 when they actually set about administering or purging the administration, is sufficient to prove the point. The normal course of military politics is therefore to decide who is to be the government and then find some civilians to actually carry it on, reserving the right to throw them out when they cease to give satisfaction while perhaps – indeed probably – making the leader of the military coup president or premier. But there may be situations when a more positive role is forced upon them.

These are comparatively rare. 'Nasserism' – i.e. military coups which genuinely function as revolutions, or at least as major movements of fundamental social reform, must not be confused with the frequent sympathy of young officers in backward countries for movements of the left – radical, nationalist, anti-imperialist, anti-capitalist, anti-landlord, etc., or even with their readiness to make political alliances with various sections of the left. The view, widely held in the United States in recent decades, that soldiers are more reliable as well as stable governments of satellite states from an imperial point of view than civilians, is based partly on the belief, taken from western experience, that they are a conservative group, partly on the belief that foreign military advisers and training provide not only technical education but effective political indoctrination, but chiefly perhaps on the capacity of imperial states to bribe them with supplies of the kind of modern equipment and know-how which satisfies the self-esteem of armed forces. In fact it is far from justified. Some of the more revolutionary elements in local armed forces have actually emerged, in Latin America, from among the local military elite trained (e.g. as counter-insurgent Rangers) by the North Americans, as in Guatemala in the middle 1960s.[4] In so far as the military is a force for 'modernization' and social renovation, it is pro-western only so long as the western model appears likely to solve their countries' problems, and this now appears increasingly unlikely in most countries.

Nevertheless, the converse belief, which relatively weak left-wing movements have sometimes held (e.g. at times in Brazil and Venezuela) that the army, or sections of it, can be relied on to bring them to power, is equally ill-advised. Revolutions are rarely successful (unless the result of protracted guerrilla wars) without the breakdown, abstention or partial support of the armed forces, but revolutionary movements which rely on army coups to bring them to power are likely to be disappointed.

We are still left with a few cases of genuinely innovatory soldiers' regimes – Nasser's Egypt, Peru since 1960, perhaps Ataturk's Turkey. We may surmise that they occur in countries in which the necessity of social revolution is evident, where several of the objective conditions of it are present, but also where the social bases or institutions of civilian life are too feeble to carry it out. The armed forces, being in some cases the only available force with the capacity to take and carry out decisions, may have to take the place of the absent civilian forces, even to the point of turning their officers into administrators. They will of course think of doing so only if the officer corps consists of young radical or 'modernizing' members of a discontented middle stratum, and if these contain a sufficiently large number of literate and technically qualified men. There are even today armed forces which would be as incompetent to run the affairs of a modern state (which is different from ruling over those who do)

[4] Turcios Lima, the military chief of the CP guerrillas in that country, began his career as a Ranger officer.

as the Ostrogothic warriors were to run those of the Roman Empire. Still, though the case is rare, armed forces which attempt to function as revolutionaries are not unknown. It does not follow that civilian revolutionaries will welcome their efforts. And though the net results of their efforts may be substantial – it is virtually impossible to think of Egypt, Peru and Turkey as returning to their respective old regimes – they are unlikely to be as radical as the results of the genuine social revolutions. Army radicalism remains a second-best choice ; acceptable only because it is better to fill a political vacuum than to leave it. There is, moreover, at present no evidence to show that it can establish a permanent political solution.

To sum up, military intervention in politics is a symptom of social or political failure. In the developed countries it is a symptom of the breakdown – temporary in the most favourable cases – of the normal process of politics, or a sign that the *status quo* can no longer contain disruptive or revolutionary pressures. If it were to occur in communist countries, it would also be a sign of analogous crises, but there is too little evidence to gauge how well the political structure of such countries could resist it. In the Third World it is a fairly safe symptom of an incomplete or aborted revolution.

There are two possible qualifications of this negative judgment. It is possible in non-revolutionary countries for military intervention to gain time, allowing an otherwise efficient economy and administration to proceed without disruption by political crisis. In underdeveloped countries it is possible for the military to replace, at least temporarily, the revolutionary party or movement. However, if it does so successfully it must sooner or later cease to be a military force and form itself or part of itself into a party, a movement, an administration. Both these cases are rare. In all other cases the political achievements of the military are negative. It can stop revolutions and overthrow governments, without putting anything in their place; not even – in spite of much talk among technocratic officers, 'modernization' and 'economic development'. It can establish order, but contrary to the Brazilian motto which has inspired many generations, 'order' in this sense is generally incompatible with 'progress'. It may not even outlast the general or the consortium of officers, which has restored it, for what one conspiracy of officers has achieved may tempt a succession of others.

The tragedy of the underdeveloped world in the 1950s and 1960s was that the United States and its allies, when it came to the point, preferred 'order' to 'progress' – Mobutu to Lumumba, Ky or Thieu to Ho-Chi-Minh, any Latin general to Fidel Castro. It is possible that the limitations of this policy have now become obvious, though one can hardly say that it has ceased to tempt governments which fear communism above all else. But in the meantime a large part of the globe has been turned into the contemporary equivalent of the old banana republics of Latin America, and is likely to remain in this unhappy situation for a considerable time to come.

(1967)

19
COUP D'ÉTAT

Ever since Machiavelli intelligent observers have exploited one of the most effective stylistic devices of nonfiction, the contrast between the official versions and the realities of politics. It is an effective device for three reasons : because it is easy (all one has to do is use one's eyes), because political reality is notoriously at variance with the moral, constitutional or legalistic claptrap which surrounds political actions, and because, more surprisingly, the public can still be readily shocked by pointing this out. Mr Luttwack is obviously an intelligent and excellently informed observer.[1] One suspects that, like Machiavelli himself, he enjoys truth not only because it is true but also because it shocks the naïve. He has therefore laid out his very able little book on the coup d'état as a manual for potential putschists.

In a way this is a pity, for it both diverts attention from the real interest of the work and somewhat biases his argument. Though it will no doubt be recommended reading in courses organized by the CIA or other bodies with an interest in the quick and efficient overthrow of inconvenient governments, it will not tell experts in the field – and in many countries these include every army and police officer from lieutenant upwards – much that they do not already know and practise, except perhaps to apply some economic rationality to post-coup repression (see the useful Appendix A). Plotters with a literary turn of mind may also benefit from the author's concise, devastating, and very funny analysis of the different types of communiqué announcing that the country is about to be saved. But on the whole Luttwack's information, which has shock value in London or Washington, is common knowledge in Buenos Aires, Damascus, or even Paris, where people's reaction to the appearance of armoured cars at street corners is based on experience.

[1] Edward Luttwack, *Coup d' État, a Practical Handbook*, London, 1968

Those who are most likely to make coups patently do not need Mr Luttwack to tell them how.

Who are they ? *Coup d'État* makes it clear, and its author knows, that they belong to a rather restricted group, since coups are made by armed forces and practically never by anyone else. This imposes both political and technical limitations which exclude most of us. In spite of Mr Luttwack's suggestion to the contrary, coups are not politically neutral. Though officers – and therefore coups – can occasionally favour the left, the circumstances when they do so are comparatively rare, and not by any means universal even in the underdeveloped world. Unfortunately the author omits to discuss these conditions. The general bias of both officers and coups is in the opposite direction. 'Bonapartism' normally tends to be a political move to the conservative side, or at best a corporative self-assertion of the armed forces as a special economic and professional pressure group within the *status quo*.

Social revolutionary regimes, keenly aware of this ever since the days of Napoleon I, have therefore always (at any rate up to Mao Tse-tung) been the firmest supporters of civilian revolutions and civilian supremacy in politics ; even to the point of sacrificing the powerful publicity value of successful generals, to which presidential elections in the United States and elsewhere have long borne witness. The ideal role of the army in classical social revolutions is negative : it ought at the crucial moment to refuse to obey the old regime and after that preferably disintegrate. The left which puts its trust in progressive soldiers (as in Cuba in the days of the young Batista, and up to 1964 in Brazil) has been more often than not disappointed. Even genuinely red armies are traditionally viewed with caution. When revolutionary regimes need marshals, they have in the past preferred to put civilian party leaders into uniform.

The technical limitation on prospective organizers of coups is, that relatively few people are in a position to subvert the required group of officers. (Noncoms are less promising, and the subversion of troops produces not coups but revolutions.) About the only civilians who can do so are already in government – the country's own or that of some dominant or influential foreign power, or that of some vast international corporation which can occupy an analogous position in relation to a poor and backward state. Such people can organize a coup comparatively simply and rather effectively, and perhaps for this reason the process is too uninteresting to detain Mr Luttwack, though it has probably produced more actual coups than any other. Also, of course, it offers little scope for the native self-made coup leader unless he has first got to the top in his country's politics.

Anyone else who tries must, as the author shows convincingly, be on such terms of powerful solidarity with his potential recruits as to be able to rely on their discretion even if they refuse to join him. The best way to get on such terms with them is (*a*) to be an officer and (*b*) to share with the other potential plotters some strong emotional bond such as belonging to the same family, tribe, sect (generally a minority sect), ritual brotherhood, etc. or the comradeship of a regiment, military academy, club or even of ideology. Of course in countries with a long tradition of coups all officers will consider plans for one as potentially successful, and will therefore hesitate to disclose them. Once, as in the classical Iberian *pronunciamento*, the tacit convention has been established that men on the losing side will not be seriously penalized (after all, they might be on the winning side some day), the risks of committing oneself to an uncertain adventure are further diminished.

Still, the number of those in any country who can set out to plan a coup with any hope of success is almost as limited as the number of those who can become important bankers. The rest of us had better stick to different kinds of political activity.

But if we can dismiss *Coup d'État* as a manual for plotters, we can appreciate it as a contribution to the study of the structure of political power. A coup is a game with three players (we omit the dominant foreign power or corporation which may hold an effective veto – or the trump cards). These are the armed forces which can make it, the politicians and bureaucracy whose readiness to accept it makes it possible, and the political forces, official or unofficial, which can check or checkmate it. For the success of a coup depends essentially on the passivity of the existing state apparatus and the people. If either or both resist it may still win, but not as a coup. The Franco regime failed as a military putsch, but won after a civil war. Mr Luttwack has some very interesting things to say about each of these three.

He is probably at his best on the professional soldiers, members of that curious esoteric world which has so little contact with the civilian world, and works in such different ways. The non-professional soldier, the conscript or temporary officer, or in most cases the policeman, however heavily armed, tends to react much more like the civilians to whom he will return or among whom he operates. Separated from the rest of society by a life consisting (in peacetime) of fancy dress, instruction and practice, games and boredom, organized on the assumption that their members at all levels are generally rather stupid and always expendable, held together by the increasingly anomalous values of bravery, honour, contempt for and suspicion of civilians, professional armies tend almost by definition to ideological eccentricity.

As Mr Luttwack rightly reminds us, the politics of officers' corps are frequently quite different from those of their civilian masters, generally being both more reactionary and more romantic. They are, moreover, untrained and unaccustomed to cope with unusual situations, and therefore naturally seek to assimilate them to usual ones. As the author does not fail to note, one of the most convenient mechanisms for explaining away unusual situations is to see them as just another example of the mess politicians are always making. The situation of professional officers is indeed paradoxical: it combines collective power and individual unimportance. After thirty-five years Germany has not yet quite recovered from the transfer of a few hundred scientists from German to foreign laboratories and universities. Yet time and again armies have actually had their effectiveness improved by the mass emigration, expulsion or other elimination of their senior officers – so much so that one is tempted to believe that few wars can be won unless the military leadership is first purged. But the political power of scientists is negligible, whereas in the right circumstances a half-dozen colonels can overthrow a government.

Bureaucracies have been more written about, and most of us have more continuous experience of them. So Mr Luttwack's observations on this subject will probably bring the pleasure of recognition rather than that of illumination. Still, two of his points are always worth remembering. The first is that the only methods that have ever been discovered for controlling the Parkinsonian tendency of bureaucracies, public or private, to grow into infinity, are themselves bureaucratic. One such method consists of setting up another department 'which fulfils its instincts by opposing the growth of all other bureaucratic organizations', a role usually played by the financial bureaucracy; another relies on each empire-building department to do its best to keep its potential rivals in check.

The second observation is that bureaucracies are essentially Hobbesian institutions, which cannot be relied on to defend existing regimes once they suspect that the victory of a new regime is probable. This applies to the police as much as to all other parts of the state apparatus, though with some qualifications. However, Mr Luttwack fails to note that this does not make them politically neutral. Neither army nor police opposed any resistance to the overthrow of fascism in Italy, but as recent events in that country demonstrate, the persistence of the apparatus of the fascist era makes the solution of fundamental problems in post-fascist Italy almost impossible. Marx's observations that revolutions cannot simply 'lay hold of the ready-made state machinery and wield it for its own purposes', however anxious it may be to be taken over, makes even more sense today than it did in 1872.

Lastly, Mr Luttwack's comments on political organizations and movements are original and instructive. Essentially, he argues, we must distinguish between movements geared for real action and those which have settled down to symbolic action such as the organization of voting, the ritual of institutionalized bargaining, or verbal political conflict. Faced with a coup d'état the British Labour Party would be certain, the British Trade Union Congress nearly certain, to do nothing, though the National Union of Students might take to the streets, however ineffectively. On the other hand, the major Italian trade union federation, linked with a communist party, with a long tradition of political strikes and, what is more important, of liberation from fascism by direct mass action, could not be relied on to remain passive. Neither could insurrectionary parties, though of course many once insurrectionary organizations have either turned into machines (i.e. distributors of favours and jobs). Or, like some communist parties, they may have allowed long political stability to atrophy their capacity for rapid action. Also, insurrectionary parties have the disadvantages as well as the advantages of centralization : once decapitated, they drastically and very rapidly lose their effectiveness.

So far as the special case of coups d'état is concerned the distinction between political movements which move and those which do not is sufficient. For in the most favourable case a coup can be defeated by *any* sign of organized resistance, which immediately reveals the weaknesses of the bid for power, and may also give time for the rest of the armed and civilian apparatus to decide that there is no cause to change sides. In much less favourable cases it may still confront a weak, uncertain, or patchily established new regime with effective resistance. But the interest of Mr Luttwack's observations is far wider than this. We are living in a period when various forms of direct action in politics are once again becoming significant in the developed countries. In these countries both the official doctrines of politics and the practical know-how of people in public affairs exclude the politics of extra-legal power. The old have forgotten that governments can be overthrown, or dismissed the possibility from their minds, the young merely believe that they can, but have no idea how. In these circumstances any work which realistically discusses the seizure of power as an operation is particularly helpful.

Mr Luttwack's little book should therefore be immensely useful in bringing up-to-date the political education of all age groups. Students of international affairs, and especially the Middle East, about which the author appears to know a great deal, will also appreciate his remarkably good information. He can be read with pleasure, both for his dead-pan style and above all because he demonstrates that big problems can be adequately treated in short books, if the writer uses words to express thoughts rather than as a substitute for them.

(1968)

V
INSURRECTIONARIES AND REVOLUTION

20
HANNAH ARENDT ON REVOLUTION

The phenomenon of social revolution is one with which all of us have to come to terms in a century which has seen more and greater revolutions than any other in recorded history. By the very nature of their impact, however, revolutions are very difficult to analyze satisfactorily, surrounded as they are and must be by a cloud of hope and disillusion, of love, hatred and fear, of their own myths and the myths of counter-propaganda. After all, few historians of the French Revolution who wrote before the 100th anniversary of its outbreak are now read, and the real historiography of the Russian Revolution, in spite of some accumulation of preliminary material, is only just beginning. The scientific study of revolutions does not mean dispassionate study. It is fairly certain that the major achievements in this field will be 'committed' – generally to sympathy with revolutions, if the historiography of the French is any guide. Committed study is not necessarily mere pamphleteering, as Mommsen and Rostovzeff demonstrated. Yet it is natural that in the early stages of the investigation of social revolutions the market tends to be swamped by pamphlets, sometimes simple, sometimes masquerading as serious historical and sociological work, and therefore demanding serious criticism. Their public is normally not that of the experts or the serious student. Thus it is perhaps not without significance that the four encomia printed on the cover of Miss Hannah Arendt's *On Revolution*[1] come not from historians or sociologists, but from literary figures. But of course such works may hold great interest for the specialist nevertheless. The question to be asked about Miss Arendt's book is whether it does.

The answer, so far as the student of the French and most other

[1] Hannah Arendt, *On Revolution*, New York and London, 1963.

modern revolutions is concerned, must be no. I am not able to judge her contribution to the study of the American revolution, though I suspect that it is not great. The book therefore stands or falls not by the author's discoveries or insights into certain specific historical phenomena, but by the interest of her general ideas and interpretations. However, since these are not based on an adequate study of the subject matter they purport to interpret, and indeed appear almost to exclude such a study by their very method, they cannot be firmly grounded. She has merits, and they are not negligible: a lucid style, sometimes carried away by intellectual rhetoric, but always transparent enough to allow us to recognize the genuine passion of the writer, a strong intelligence, wide reading, and the power of occasional piercing insight, though of a sort better suited, it may seem, to the vague terrain which lies between literature, psychology and what, for want of a better word, is best called social prophecy, than to the social sciences as at present constructed. However, even of her insights it is possible to say what Lloyd George observed of Lord Kitchener, namely that their beams occasionally illuminate the horizon, but leave the scene in darkness between their flashes.

The first difficulty encountered by the historian or sociological student of revolutions in Miss Arendt is a certain metaphysical and normative quality of her thought, which goes well with a sometimes quite explicit old-fashioned philosophical idealism.[2] She does not take her revolutions as they come, but constructs herself an ideal type, defining her subject matter accordingly, excluding what does not measure up to her specifications. We may also observe in passing that she excludes everything outside the classical zone of western Europe and the north Atlantic, for her book contains not even a passing reference to – the examples spring to mind – China or Cuba; nor could she have made certain statements if she had given any thought to them.[3] Her 'revolution' is a wholesale political change in which men are conscious of introducing an entirely new epoch in human history, including (but

[2] Cf: 'That there existed men in the Old World to dream of public freedom, that there were men in the New World who had tasted public happiness – these were ultimately the facts which caused the movement ... to develop into a revolution on either side of the Atlantic' (p. 139).

[3] e.g.: 'Revolutions always appear to succeed with amazing ease in their initial stage' (p. 112). In China? In Cuba? In Vietnam? In wartime Yugoslavia?

only, as it were, incidentally) the abolition of poverty and expressed in terms of a secular ideology. Its subject matter is 'the emergence of freedom' as defined by the author.

Part of this definition allows her, after a brief bout of shadow-boxing, to exclude all revolutions and revolutionary movements before 1776 from the discussion, though at the price of making a serious study of the actual phenomenon of revolution impossible. The remainder allows her to proceed to the major part of her subject, an extended comparison between the American and French revolutions, to the great advantage of the former. The latter is taken as the paradigm of all subsequent revolutions, though it seems that Miss Arendt has in mind chiefly the Russian Revolution of 1917. The 'freedom' which revolutions exist to institute is essentially a political concept. Though not too clearly defined – it emerges gradually in the course of the author's discussion – it is quite distinct from the abolition of poverty (the 'solution of the social problem') which Miss Arendt regards as the corrupter of revolution, in whatever form it occurs; which includes the capitalist.[4] We may infer that any revolution in which the social and economic element plays a major role puts itself out of Miss Arendt's court, which more or less eliminates every revolution that the student of the subject might desire to investigate. We may further infer that, with the partial exception of the American revolution which, as she argues, was lucky enough to break out in a country without very poor free inhabitants, no revolution was or could have been able to institute freedom, and even in eighteenth-century America slavery placed it in an insoluble dilemma. The revolution could not 'institute freedom' without abolishing slavery, but – on Miss Arendt's argument – it could not have done so either if it had abolished it. The basic trouble about revolutions in other words – her own – is therefore this: 'Though the whole record of past revolutions demonstrates beyond doubt that every attempt so solve the social question with political means leads into terror, and that it is terror which sends revolutions to their doom, it can hardly be denied that to avoid this fatal mistake is almost impossible when a revolution breaks out under conditions of mass poverty.'

The 'freedom' which revolution exists to institute is more than

[4] 'Since [the United States] was never overwhelmed by poverty, it was "the fatal passion for sudden riches" rather than necessity that stood in the way of the founders of the republic' (p. 134).

the mere absence of restraints upon the person or guarantees of 'civil liberties', for neither of these (as Miss Arendt rightly observes) requires any particular form of government, but only the absence of tyranny and despotism.[5] It appears to consist of the right and possibility of participating actively in the affairs of the commonwealth – of the joys and rewards of public life, as conceived perhaps originally in the Greek polis (pp. 123–4). However – though here the author's argument must be reconstructed rather than followed – 'public freedom' in this sense remains a dream, even though the fathers of the American constitution were wise enough, and untroubled enough by the poor, to institute a government which was reasonably secure against despotism and tyranny. The crux of the genuine revolutionary tradition is that it keeps this dream alive. It has done so by means of a constant tendency to generate spontaneous organs capable of realizing public freedom, namely the local or sectional, elective or direct assemblies and councils (soviets, Räte), which have emerged in the course of revolutions only to be suppressed by the dictatorship of the party. Such councils ought to have a purely *political* function. Government and administration being distinct, the attempt to use them, e.g. for the management of *economic* affairs ('workers' control') is undesirable and doomed to failure, even when it is not part of a plot by the revolutionary party to 'drive [the councils] away from the political realm and back into the factories'. I am unable to discover Miss Arendt's views as to who is to conduct the 'administration of things in the public interest', such as the economy, or how it is to be conducted.

Miss Arendt's argument tells us much about the kind of government which she finds congenial, and even more about her state of mind. Its merits as a general statement about political ideals are not at issue here. On the other hand, it is relevant to observe that the nature of her arguments not merely makes it impossible to use in the analysis of actual revolutions – at least in terms which have meaning for the historian or social scientist – but also eliminates the possibility of meaningful dialogue between her and those interested

[5] However, Miss Arendt appears to forget her distinction when she observes later (p. 111) that 'we also know to our sorrow that freedom has been better preserved in countries where no revolution ever broke out, no matter how outrageous the circumstances of the powers that be, than in those in which revolutions have been victorious'. Here 'freedom' appears to be used in a sense which she has already rejected. The statement is in any case open to question.

in actual revolutions. In so far as Miss Arendt writes about history – about revolutions, as they may be contemporaneously observed, retrospectively surveyed, or prospectively assessed – her connection with it is as incidental as that of medieval theologians and astronomers. Both talked about planets, and both meant, at least in part, the same celestial bodies, but contact did not go much further.

The historian or sociologist, for instance, will be irritated, as the author plainly is not, by a certain lack of interest in mere fact. This cannot be described as inaccuracy or ignorance, for Miss Arendt is learned and scholarly enough to be aware of such inadequacies if she chooses, but rather as a preference for metaphysical construct or poetic feeling over reality. When she observes 'even as an old man, in 1871, Marx was still revolutionary enough to welcome enthusiastically the Paris Commune, although this outbreak contradicted all his theories and predictions' (p. 58), she must be aware that the first part of the sentence is wrong (Marx was, in fact, fifty-three years old), and the second at the very least open to much debate. Her statement is not really a historical one, but rather, as it were, a line in an intellectual drama, which it would be as unfair to judge by historical standards as Schiller's *Don Carlos*. She knows that Lenin's formula for Russian development – 'electrification plus soviets' – was not intended to eliminate the role of the party or the building of socialism, as she argues (p. 60). But her interpretation gives an additional sharpness to her contention that the future of the Soviet revolution ought to have lain along the lines of a politically neutral technology and a grass-roots political system 'outside all parties'. To object 'but this is not what Lenin meant' is to introduce questions belonging to a different order of discourse from hers.

And yet, can such questions be entirely left outside ? In so far as she claims to be discussing not merely the idea of revolution, but also certain identifiable events and institutions, they cannot. Since the spontaneous tendency to generate organs such as soviets is clearly of great moment to Miss Arendt, and provides evidence for her interpretation, one might for instance have expected her to show some interest in the actual forms such popular organs take. In fact, the author is clearly not interested in these. It is even difficult to discover what precisely she has in mind, for she talks in the same breath of politically very different organizations. The ancestors of the soviets (which were assemblies of delegates, mainly from functional groups of people such as factories, regiments, or villages), she holds, were either the Paris sections of the French Revolution (which were essentially direct democracies of all citizens in public assembly) or the political societies (which were voluntary bodies of the familiar type). Possibly sociological analysis might show these to have been similar, but Miss Arendt refrains from it.[6]

Again, it is evidently *not* 'the historical truth of the matter . . . that the party and council systems are almost coeval; both were unknown prior to the revolutions and both are the consequences of the modern and revolutionary tenet that all inhabitants of a given territory are entitled to be admitted to the public, political realm' (p. 275). Even granted that the second half of the statement is tenable (so long as we define the public realm in terms which apply to large modern territorial or nation states, but not to other and historically more widespread forms of political organization), the first half is not. Councils, even in the form of elected delegations, are so obvious a political device in communities above a certain size, that they considerably antedate political parties, which are, at least in the usual sense of the term, far from obvious institutions. Councils as revolutionary institutions are familiar long before 1776, when Miss Arendt's revolutions begin, as for instance in the General Soviet of the New Model Army, in the committees of sixteenth-century France and the Low Countries, or for that matter in medieval city politics. A 'council system' under this name is certainly coeval with, or rather posterior to, the political parties of 1905 Russia, since it was they who recognized the possible implications of the soviets for the revolutionary government of nations; but the idea of decentralized government by autonomous communal organs, perhaps linked by pyramids of higher delegate bodies, is for practical reasons extremely ancient.

Nor indeed have councils 'always been primarily political, with the social and economic claims playing a minor role' (p. 278). They were not, because Russian workers and peasants did not – and

[6] If she did not, she might be less certain that soviet delegates 'were not nominated from above and not supported from below' but 'had selected themselves' (p 282). In peasant soviets they might have been selected institutionally (as by, say, the automatic nomination of the schoolmaster or the heads of certain families), just as in British farm-labourers' union locals, the local railwaymen – independent of farmer and squire – was often the automatic choice as secretary. It is also certain that local class divisions tended *a priori* to favour or inhibit the selection of delegates.

indeed on Miss Arendt's argument could not[7] – make a sharp distinction between politics and economics. Moreover, the original Russian workers' councils, like those of the British and German shop stewards in the first world war or the Trades Councils which sometimes took over quasi-soviet functions in big strikes, were the products of trade union and strike organization; that is, if a distinction can be made, of activities which were economic rather than political.[8] In the third place, she is wrong because the immediate tendency of the effective, that is, urban, soviets in 1917 was to turn themselves into organs of administration, in successful rivalry with municipalities, and as such, quite evidently, to go beyond the field of political deliberation. Indeed, it was this capacity of the soviets to become organs of execution as well as of debate which suggested to political thinkers that they might be the basis for a new political system. But more than this, the suggestion that such demands as 'workers' control' are in some sense a deviation from the spontaneous line of evolution of councils and similar bodies simply will not bear examination. 'The Mine for the Miners', 'The Factory for the Workers' – in other words, the demand for cooperative democractic instead of capitalist production – goes back to the earliest stages of the labour movement. It has remained an important element in spontaneous popular thought ever since, a fact which does not oblige us to consider it as other than utopian. In the history of grass-roots democracy, cooperation in communal units and its apotheosis 'the cooperative commonwealth' (which was the earliest definition of socialism among workers) play a crucial part.

There is thus practically no point at which Miss Arendt's discussion of what she regards as the crucial institution of the revolutionary tradition touches the actual historical phenomena she purports to describe, an institution on the basis of which she generalizes. And the student of revolutions, whether historian, sociologist, or for that matter analyst of political systems and institutions, will be equally baffled by the remainder of her book. Her acute mind sometimes throws light on literature, including the classical literature of political theory. She has considerable perception about the psychological

[7] Since the poor are, in her view primarily determined by 'necessity' rather than 'freedom', i.e. by economic rather than political motives. Actually this is also wrong.

[8] Miss Arendt is misled by the fact that at the peak of a revolutionary crisis all organizations discuss politics for much of the time.

motives and mechanisms of individuals – her discussion of Robespierre, for instance, may be read with profit – and she has occasional flashes of insight, that is to say, she sometimes makes statements which, while not particularly well-founded on evidence or argument, strike the reader as true and illuminating. But that is all. And it is not enough. There are doubtless readers who will find Miss Arendt's book interesting and profitable. The historical or sociological student of revolutions is unlikely to be among them.

(1965)

21
THE RULES OF VIOLENCE

Of all the vogue words of the late 1960s, 'violence' is very nearly the trendiest and the most meaningless. Everybody talks about it, nobody thinks about it. As the just-published report of the US National Commission of the Causes and Prevention of Violence points out, the *International Encyclopedia of the Social Sciences*, published 1968, contains no entry under this heading.

Both the vogue and the vagueness are significant. For most of the people likely to read books with such titles as *The Age of Violence* (as like as not about symbolist poetry) or *Children of Violence* (which is about physically rather tranquil lives) are aware of the world's violence, but their relation to it is unprecedented and enigmatic. Most of them, unless they deliberately seek it out, can pass their adult lives without direct experience of 'behavior designed to inflict physical injury on people or damage to property' (to use the American commission's definition), or even with 'force' defined as 'the actual or threatened use of violence to compel others to do what they might not otherwise do'.

Physical violence normally impinges on them only in one direct and three indirect ways. Directly, it is omnipresent in the form of the traffic accident – casual, unintended, unpredictable and uncontrollable by most of its victims, and about the only peacetime contingency which is likely to bring most people working in homes and offices into actual contact with bleeding or mangled bodies. Indirectly, it is omnipresent in the mass media and entertainment. Probably no day passes in which most viewers and readers do not encounter the image of a corpse, that rarest of sights in real British life. Even more remotely, we are aware both of the existence in our time of vast, concretely unimaginable mass destruction for which convenient symbols are found ('the bomb', 'Auschwitz' and such like), and also of the sectors and situations of society in which physical violence is common and, probably increasing. Tranquillity and violence coexist.

These are curiously unreal experiences, and we therefore find it very difficult to make sense of violence as a historical or social phenomenon, as is shown by the extraordinary devaluation of such terms as 'aggression' in popular psycho-sociological small talk, or of the word 'genocide' in politics. The prevailing ideas of liberalism do not make it any easier, since they assume an entirely unreal dichotomy between 'violence' or 'physical force' (bad and backward) and 'non-violence' or 'moral force' (good and the child of progress). Of course one sympathizes with this, as with other pedagogic simplifications, in so far as it discourages people knocking one another over the head, the avoidance of which all sane and civilized persons approve. Yet as with that other product of liberal morality, the proposition that 'force never solves anything', there comes a point where the encouragement of the good becomes incompatible with understanding reality – i.e. with providing the foundations for encouraging the good.

For the point to grasp about violence, as a social phenomenon, is that it exists only in the plural. There are actions of differing degrees of violence which imply different qualities of violence. All peasant movements are manifestations of sheer physical force, but some are unusually chary of spilling blood, while others develop into massacres, because their character and objects differ. The English farm-labourers of the early nineteenth century regarded violence against property as legitimate, moderate violence against persons as justifiable under certain circumstances, but systematically refrained from killing, but under different circumstances (such as affrays between poachers and gamekeepers) the same men did not hesitate to fight to kill. It is quite useless, except as a legal excuse for repression or a debating point about 'never yielding to force', to treat these various types and degrees of violent action as essentially indistinguishable. Again, actions of the same degree of violence may differ sharply in their legitimacy or justification, at least in the minds of public opinion. The great Calabrian brigand Musolino, when asked to define the word 'bad' or 'evil' said it meant 'killing Christians without a very deep reason'.

Genuinely violent societies are always and acutely aware of these 'rules', just because private violence is essential to their everyday functioning, though we may not be so aware of them, because the normal amount of bloodshed in such societies may seem to us to be so intolerably high. Where, as in the Philippines, the fatal casualties in every election campaign are counted in hundreds, it seems hardly relevant that, by Filipino standards, some of them are more open to condemnation than others. Yet there *are* rules. In the highlands of Sardinia they constitute an actual code of customary law, which has been formally described in legal terms by outside observers.[1] For instance, the theft of a goat is not an 'offence' unless the goat's milk is used by the family of the thieves, or there is a clear intent to 'offend' or spite the victim. In this case revenge is progressively more serious, up to death.

However binding the obligation to kill, members of feuding families engaged in mutual massacre will be genuinely appalled if by some mischance a bystander or outsider is killed. The situations in which violence occurs and the nature of that violence, tend to be clearly denied at least in theory, as in the proverbial Irishman's question : 'Is this a private fight or can anyone join in ?' So the actual risk to outsiders, though no doubt higher than in our societies, is calculable. Probably the only uncontrolled applications of force are those of social superiors to social inferiors (who have, almost by definition, no rights against them) and even here there are probably some rules.

As a matter of fact some such rules of violence are still familiar to us. Why for instance do abolitionists, who presumably believe in the undesirability of all executions, base so much of their campaigning on the argument that the death penalty sometimes kills innocent people ? Because for most of us, including probably most abolitionists, the killing of the 'innocent' evokes a qualitatively different response from that of the 'guilty'.

One of the major dangers of societies in which direct violence no longer plays much part in regulating the everyday relations between peoples and groups, or in which violence has become depersonalized, is that they lose the sense of such distinctions. In doing so they also dismantle certain social mechanisms for controlling the use of physical force. This did not matter so much in the days when traditional kinds of violence in social relations, or at least the more dangerous among them, were diminishing visibly and fast. But today they may be once more on the increase, while new forms of social violence are becoming more important.

[1] See A.Pigliaru, *La vendetta barbaricina come ordinamento giuridico*, Milan, 1959.

Older forms of violence may be increasing, because the established systems of maintaining public order, elaborated in the liberal era, are increasingly strained, and such forms of political violence as direct physical action, terrorism, etc. are more common than in the past. The nervousness and disarray of the public authorities, the revival of private-enterprise security guards and neo-vigilante movements, are evidence enough. In one respect they have already led to a certain rediscovery of controlled violence, as in the return by so many police forces to a curious medievalism – helmets, shields, armour and all – and the developments of various temporarily disabling gases, rubber bullets, etc., all of which reflect the sensible view that there are degrees of necessary or desirable violence within a society, a view which the ancient common law of England has never abandoned.[2] On the other hand the public authorities themselves have become accustomed to use certain horrifying forms of violence, notably torture, which were regarded until a few decades ago as barbaric, and entirely unsuitable to civilized societies, while 'respectable' public opinion calls hysterically for indiscriminate terror.

This is part of a new *kind* of violence which is today emerging. Most traditional violence (including the revived types) assumes that physical force must be used in so far as no other methods are available or effective, and consequently that violent actions normally have a specific and identifiable purpose, the use of force being proportionate to that purpose. But a good deal of contemporary private violence can afford to be and is non-operational, and public violence is consequently tempted into indiscriminate action.

Private violence does not have to or cannot achieve very much against the really big and institutionalized wielders of force, whether or not these hold their violence in reserve. Where it occurs it therefore tends to turn from action into a substitute for action. The badges and iron crosses of the Nazi army had a practical purpose, though one of which we do not approve. The same symbols on the Hell's Angels and similar groups merely have a motive: the desire of otherwise weak and helpless young men to compensate for their

[2] Between the wars the British Royal Air Force resisted any plans to use it to maintain public order on the grounds that its weapons were too indiscriminate, and that it might hence be liable to prosecution under the common law. It did not apply this argument to the bombing of tribal villages in India and the Middle East...

frustration by acts and symbols of violence. Some nominally political forms of violence (such as 'trashing' or some neo-anarchist bombing) are similarly irrational, since under most circumstances their political effect is either negligible or more usually counter-productive.

Blind lashings-out are not necessarily more dangerous to life and limb (statistically speaking) than the violence of traditionally 'lawless' societies, though probably they do more damage to things, or rather to the companies which insure them. On the other hand such acts are, perhaps rightly, more frightening, because they are both more random and cruel, inasmuch as this kind of violence is its own reward. As the Moors murder case showed, the terrible things about dreams of Nazi jackboots, which flicker through various western underworlds and subcultures today, is not simply that they hark back to Himmler and Eichmann, the bureaucrats of an apparatus whose purposes happened to be insane. It is that for the disoriented fringe, for the weak and helpless poor, violence and cruelty – sometimes in the most socially ineffective and personalized sexual form – are the surrogate for private success and social power.

What is scarifying about modern American big cities is the combination of revived old and emerging new violence in situations of social tension and breakdown. And these are the situations with which the conventional wisdom of liberal ideas are quite incapable of coping, even conceptually; hence the tendency to relapse into an instinctive conservative reaction, which is little more than the mirror image of the disorder it seeks to control. To take the simplest example. Liberal toleration and freedom of expression helps to saturate the atmosphere with those images of blood and torture which are so incompatible with the liberal ideal of a society based on consent and moral force.[3]

We are probably once again moving into an era of violence within societies, which must not be confused with the growing destructiveness of conflicts between societies. We had therefore better understand the social uses of violence, learn once again to distinguish between different types of violent activity, and above all construct or reconstruct systematic rules for it. Nothing is more difficult for

[3] The argument that these images cannot be proved to affect anyone's action merely tries to rationalize this contradiction, and cannot stand serious scrutiny. Neither can the arguments that popular culture has always revelled in images of violence, or that its images act as a sort of replacement for the real thing.

people brought up in a liberal culture, with its belief that all violence is worse than non-violence, other things being equal (which they are not). Of course it is, but unfortunately such an abstract moral generalization gives no guidance to the practical problems of violence in our society. What was once a useful principle of social amelioration ('settle conflicts peacefully rather than by fighting', 'self-respect does not require bloodshed', etc.) turns into mere rhetoric and counter-rhetoric. It leaves the growing area of human life in which violence takes place without any rules, and paradoxically, without even any practically applicable moral principles; as witness the universal renascence of torture by the forces of the state. The abolition of torture was one of the relatively few achievements of liberalism which can be praised without any qualification, yet today it is once again almost universally practised and condoned by governments, and propagated by the mass media.

Those who believe that all violence is bad in principle can make no systematic distinction between different kinds of violence in practice, or recognize their effects both on those who suffer and on those who inflict it. They are merely likely to produce, by reaction, men and women who consider all violence good, whether from a conservative or a revolutionary point of view, that is to say who recognize the subjective psychological relief provided by violence without any reference to its effectiveness. In this respect the reactionaries who call for the return of indiscriminate shooting, flogging and execution are similar to those whose sentiments have been systematized by Fanon and others, and for whom action with gun or bomb is *ipso facto* preferable to non-violent action.[4] Liberalism makes no distinction between the teaching of the milder forms of judo and the potentially more murderous forms of karate, whereas Japanese tradition is perfectly aware that these are intended to be learned only by those who have sufficient judgment and moral training to use their power to kill responsibly.

There are signs that such distinctions are once again being slowly

[4] Rational revolutionaries have always measured violence entirely by its purpose and likely achievement. When Lenin was told in 1916 that the secretary of the Austrian social democrats had assassinated the Austrian prime minister as a gesture of protest against the war, he merely wondered why a man in his position had not taken the less dramatic but more effective step of circulating the party activists with an anti-war appeal. It was evident to him that a boring but effective non-violent action was preferable to a romantic but ineffective one. This did not stop him from recommending armed insurrection when necessary.

and empirically learned, but in a general atmosphere of disorientation and hysteria which makes the rational and limited use of violence difficult. It is time that we put this process of learning on a more systematic basis by understanding the social uses of violence. We may think that all violence is worse than non-violence, other things being equal. But the worst kind is the violence which gets out of anyone's control.

(1969)

22
REVOLUTION AND SEX

The late Che Guevara would have been very surprised and acutely irritated by the discovery that his picture is now on the cover of *Evergreen Review*, his personality the subject of an article in *Vogue*, and his name the ostensible excuse for some homosexual exhibitionism in a New York theatre (see *Oberserver*, 8 May 1969). We can leave *Vogue* aside. Its business is to tell women what it is fashionable to wear, to know and to talk about ; its interest in Che Guevara has no more political implications than the editor's of *Who's Who*. The other two jokes, however, reflect a widespread belief that there is some sort of connection between social revolutionary movements and permissiveness in public sexual or other personal behaviour. It is about time someone pointed out that there are no good grounds for this belief.

In the first place, it ought now to be evident that conventions about what sexual behaviour is permissible in public have no specific connection with systems of political rule or social and economic exploitation. (An exception is the rule of men over women, and the exploitation of women by men which, at a guess, imply more or less strict limitations on the public behaviour of the inferior sex.) Sexual 'liberation' has only indirect relations with any other kind of liberation. Systems of class rule and exploitation may impose strict conventions of personal (for example, sexual) behaviour in public or private or they may not. Hindu society was not in any sense more free or egalitarian than the Welsh nonconformist community, because the one used temples to demonstrate a vast variety of sexual activities in the most tempting manner, whereas the other imposed rigid restrictions on its members, at any rate in theory. All we can deduce from this particular cultural difference is that pious Hindus who wanted to vary their sexual routine could learn to do so much more easily than pious Welshmen.

Indeed, if a rough generalization about the relation between class rule and sexual freedom is possible, it is that rulers find it convenient to encourage sexual permissiveness or laxity among their subjects if only to keep their minds off their subjection. Nobody ever imposed sexual puritanism on slaves ; quite the contrary. The sort of societies in which the poor are strictly kept in their place are quite familiar with regular institutionalized mass outbursts of free sex, such as carnivals. In fact, since sex is the cheapest form of enjoyment as well as the most intense (as the Neapolitans say, bed is the poor man's grand opera), it is politically very advantageous, other things being equal, to get them to practise it as much as possible.

In other words, there is no necessary connection between social or political censorship and moral censorship, though it is often assumed that there is. To demand the transfer of some kinds of behaviour from the impermissible to the publicly permitted is a political act only if it implies changing political relations. Winning the right for white and black to make love in South Africa would be a political act, not because it widens the range of what is sexually allowed but because it attacks racial subjection. Winning the right to publish *Lady Chatterly* has no such implications, though it may be welcomed on other grounds.

This should be abundantly clear from our own experience. Within the last few years the official or conventional prohibitions on what can be said, heard, done and shown about sex in public – or for that matter in private – have been virtually abolished in several western countries. The belief that a narrow sexual morality is an essential bulwark of the capitalist system is no longer tenable. Nor, indeed, is the belief that the fight against such a morality is very urgent. There are still a few outdated crusaders who may think of themselves as storming a puritan fortress, but in fact its walls have been virtually razed.

No doubt there are still things that cannot be printed or shown but they are progressively harder to find and to get indignant about. The abolition of censorship is a one-dimensional activity, like the movement of women's necklines and skirts, and if that movement goes on too long in a single direction, the returns in revolutionary satisfaction of the crusaders diminish sharply. The right of actors to fuck each other on stage is palpably a less important advance even of personal liberation than the right of Victorian girls to ride bicycles was. It is today becoming quite hard even to mobilize those prosecutions of obscenity on which publishers and producers have so long relied for free publicity.

For practical purposes the battle for public sex has been won. Has this brought social revolution any nearer, or indeed any change outside the bed, the printed page, and public entertainment (which may or may not be desirable) ? There is no sign of it. All it has obviously brought is a lot more public sex in an otherwise unchanged social order.

But though there is no intrinsic connection between sexual permissiveness and social organization, there is, I am bound to note with a little regret, a persistent affinity between revolution and puritanism. I can think of no well-established organized revolutionary movement or regime which has not developed marked puritanical tendencies. Including marxist ones, whose founders' doctrine was quite unpuritanical (or in Engels's case actively anti-puritanical). Including those in countries like Cuba, whose native tradition is the opposite of puritan. Including the most officially anarchist-libertarian ones. Anyone who believes that the morality of the old anarchist militants was free and easy does not know what he or she is talking about. Free love (in which they believed passionately) meant no drink, no drugs and monogamy without a formal marriage.

The libertarian, or more exactly antinomian, component of revolutionary movements, though sometimes strong and even dominant at the actual moment of liberation, have never been able to resist the puritan. The Robespierres always win out over the Dantons. Those revolutionaries for whom sexual, or for that matter cultural, libertarianism are really central issues of the revolution, are sooner or later edged aside by it. Wilhelm Reich, the apostle of the orgasm, did indeed start out, as the New Left reminds us, as a revolutionary marxist-cum-freudian and a very able one, to judge by his *Mass Psychology of Fascism* (which was subtitled *The sexual economy of political reaction and proletarian sexual policy*). But can we be really surprised that such a man ended by concentrating his interest on orgasm rather than organization ? Neither stalinists nor Trotskyites felt any enthusiasm for the revolutionary surrealists who hammered at their gates asking to be admitted. Those who survived in politics did not do so as surrealists.

Why this is so is an important and obscure question, which cannot be answered here. Whether it is necessarily so is an even more important question – at all events for revolutionaries who think the official puritanism of revolutionary regimes excessive and often beside the point. But that the great revolutions of our century have not been devoted to sexual permissiveness can hardly be denied. They have advanced sexual freedom (and fundamentally) not by abolishing sexual prohibitions, but by a major act of social emancipation: the liberation of women from their oppression. And that revolutionary movements have found personal libertarianism a nuisance is also beyond question. Among the rebellious young, those closest to the spirit and ambitions of old-fashioned social revolution, also tend to be the most hostile to the taking of drugs, advertised indiscriminate sex, or other styles and symbols of personal dissidence: the Maoists, Trotskyites and communists. The reasons given are often that 'the workers' neither understand nor sympathize with such behaviour. Whether or not this is so, it can hardly be denied that it consumes time and energy and is hardly compatible with organization and efficiency.

The whole business is really part of a much wider question, What is the role in revolution or any social change of that cultural rebellion which is today so visible a part of the 'new left', and in certain countries such as the United States the predominant aspect of it. There is no great social revolution which is not combined, at least peripherally, with such cultural dissidence. Perhaps today in the west where, 'alienation' rather than poverty is the crucial motive force of rebellion, no movement which does not also attack the system of personal relations and private satisfactions can be revolutionary. But, taken by themselves, cultural revolt and cultural dissidence are symptoms, not revolutionary forces. Politically they are not very important.

The Russian revolution of 1917 reduced the contemporary *avant garde* and cultural rebels, many of whom sympathized with it, to their proper social and political proportions. When the French went on general strike in May 1968, the happenings in the Odeon Theatre and those splendid graffiti ('It is forbidden to forbid', 'When I make revolution it makes me feel like making love', etc.) could be seen to be forms of minor literature and theatre, marginal to the main events. The more prominent such phenomena are, the more confident can we be that the big things are not happening. Shocking the bourgeois is, alas, easier than overthrowing him.

(1969)

23
CITIES AND INSURRECTIONS

Whatever else a city may be, it is at the same time a place inhabited by a concentration of poor people and, in most cases, the locus of political power which affects their lives. Historically, one of the things city populations have done about this is to demonstrate, make riots or insurrections, or otherwise exert direct pressure on the authorities who happen to operate within their range. It does not much matter to the ordinary townsman that city power is sometimes only local, whereas at other times it may also be regional, national or even global. However, it does affect the calculations both of the authorities and of political movements designed to overthrow governments, whether or not the cities are capitals (or what amounts to the same thing, independent city states) or the headquarters of giant national or international corporations, for if they are, urban riots and insurrections can obviously have much wider implications than if the city authority is purely local.

The subject of this paper is, how the structure of cities has affected popular movement of this sort, and conversely, what effect the fear of such movements has had on urban structure. The first point is of much more general significance than the second. Popular riot, insurrection or demonstration is an almost universal urban phenomenon, and as we now know, it occurs even in the affluent megalopolis of the late-twentieth-century industrial world. On the other hand the fear of such riot is intermittent. It may be taken for granted as a fact of urban existence, as in most pre-industrial cities, or as the kind of unrest which periodically flares up and subsides without producing any major effect on the structure of power. It may be underestimated, because there have not been any riots or insurrections for a long time, or because there are institutional alternatives to them, such as systems of local government by popular election. There are, after all, few continuously riotous cities. Even Palermo, which probably holds the European record with twelve insurrections between 1512 and 1866, has had very long periods when its populace was relatively quiet. On the other hand, once the authorities decide to alter the urban structure because of political nervousness, the results are likely to be substantial and lasting, like the boulevards of Paris.

The effectiveness of riot or insurrection depends on three aspects of urban structure: how easily the poor can be mobilized, how vulnerable the centres of authority are to them, and how easily they may be suppressed. These are determined partly by sociological, partly by urbanistic, partly by technological factors, though the three cannot always be kept apart. For instance, experience shows that among forms of urban transport tramways, whether in Calcutta or Barcelona, are unusually convenient for rioters; partly because the raising of fares, which tends to affect all the poor simultaneously, is a very natural precipitant of trouble, partly because these large and track-bound vehicles, when burned or overturned, can block streets and disrupt traffic very easily. Buses do not seem to have played anything like as important a part in riots, underground railways appear to be entirely irrelevant to them (except for transporting rioters) and cars can at best be used as improvised road blocks or barricades, and, to judge by recent experience in Paris, not very effective ones. Here the difference is purely technological.

On the other hand, universities in the centre of cities are evidently more dangerous centres of potential riot than universities on the outskirts of towns or behind some green belt, a fact which is well known to Latin-American governments. Concentrations of the poor are more dangerous when they occur in or near city centres, like the twentieth-century black ghettoes in many North American cities, than when they occur in some relatively remote suburb, as in nineteenth-century Vienna. Here the difference is urbanistic and depends on the size of the city and the pattern of functional specialization within it. However, a centre of potential student unrest on the outskirts of town, like Nanterre in Paris, is nevertheless far more likely to create trouble in the central city than the Algerian shanty towns in the same suburb, because students are more mobile, their social universe more metropolitan, than immigrant labourers. Here the difference is primarily sociological.

Suppose, then, we construct the ideal city for riot and insurrection. What will it be like? It ought to be densely populated and not too large in area. Essentially it should still be possible to traverse it on foot, though greater experience of rioting in fully motorized societies might modify this judgment. It should perhaps not be divided by a large river, not only because bridges are easily held by the police, but also because it is a familiar fact of geography or social psychology that the two banks of a river look away from each other, as anyone living in south London or on the Paris left bank can verify.

Its poor ought to be relatively homogeneous socially or racially, though of course we must remember that in pre-industrial cities or in the giant sumps of under-employment of the Third World today, what at first sight looks like a very heterogeneous population may have a considerable unity, as witness such familiar terms in history as 'the labouring poor', '*le menu peuple*', or 'the mob'. It ought to be centripetal, that is to say, its various parts ought to be naturally oriented towards the central institutions of the city, the more centralized the better. The medieval city republic which was the system of flows towards and away from the main assembly space, which might also be the main ritual centre (cathedral), the main market and the location of the government, was ideally suited to insurrection for this reason. The pattern of functional specialization and residential segregation ought to be fairly tight. Thus the pre-industrial pattern of suburbs, which was based on the exclusion from a sharply defined city of various undesirables – often necessary to city life – such as non-citizen immigrants, outcast occupations or groups, etc. did not greatly disrupt the cohesion of the urban complex: Triana was entangled with Seville, as Shoreditch was with the City of London.

On the other hand the nineteenth-century pattern of suburbs, which surrounded an urban core with middle-class residential suburbs and industrial quarters, generally developing at opposite ends of town from one another, affects urban cohesion very substantially. 'East End' and 'West End' are both physically and spiritually remote from each other. Those who live west of the Concorde in Paris belong to a different world from those who live east of the Republique. To go a little farther out, the famous 'red belt' of working-class suburbs which surround Paris was politically significant, but had no discernible insurrectionary importance. It simply did not belong to Paris any longer, nor indeed did it form a whole, except for geographers.[1]

All these are considerations affecting the mobilization of the city poor, but not their political effectiveness. This naturally depends on the ease with which rioters and insurrectionaries can get close to the authorities, and how easily they can be dispersed. In the ideal insurrectionary city the authorities – the rich, the aristocracy, the government or local administration – will therefore be as intermingled with the central concentration of the poor as possible. The French king will reside in the Palais Royal or Louvre and not at Versailles, the Austrian emperor in the Hofburg and not at Schoenbrunn. Preferably the authorities will be vulnerable. Rulers who brood over a hostile city from some isolated stronghold, like the fortress-prison of Montjuich over Barcelona, may intensify popular hostility, but are technically designed to withstand it. After all, the Bastille could almost certainly have held out if anyone in July 1789 had really thought that it would be attacked. Civic authorities are of course vulnerable almost by definition, since their political success depends on the belief that they represent the citizens and not some outside government or its agents. Hence perhaps the classical French tradition by which insurrectionaries make for the city hall rather than the royal or imperial palace and, as in 1848 and 1871, proclaim the provisional government there.

Local authorities therefore create relatively few problems for insurrectionaries (at least until they begin to practise town planning). Of course, city development may shift the town hall from a central to a rather more remote location: nowadays it is a long way from the outer neighbourhoods of Brooklyn to New York's City Hall. On the other hand in capital cities the presence of governments, which tends to make riots effective, is offset by the special characteristics of towns in which princes or other self-important rulers are resident, and which have a built-in counter-insurgent bias. This arises both from the needs of state public relations and, perhaps to a lesser extent, of security.

[1] How far such working-class suburbs can be separated from the central city area and still remain a direct factor in insurrections is an interesting question. In Barcelona Sans, the great bastion of anarchism, played no important part in the revolution of 1936, while in Vienna Floridsdorf, an equally solid bastion of socialism, could do little more than hold out in isolation when the rest of the city's insurrections had already been defeated in 1934.

Broadly speaking, in a civic town the role of the inhabitants in public activities is that of participants, in princely or government towns, of an admiring and applauding audience. The wide straight processional ways with their vistas of palace, cathedral or government building, the vast square in front of the official façade, preferably with a suitable balcony from which the multitudes may be blessed or addressed, perhaps the parade ground or arena: these make up the ceremonial furniture of an imperial city. Since the Renaissance major western capitals and residences have been constructed or modified accordingly. The greater the desire of the ruler to impress or the greater his *folie de grandeur*, the wider, straighter, more symmetrical his preferred layout. Few less suitable locations for spontaneous riot can be imagined than New Delhi, Washington, St Petersburg, or for that matter, the Mall and Buckingham Palace. It is not merely the division between a popular east and middle-class and official west which has made the Champs Elysées the place where the official and military parade is held on 14 July, whereas the unofficial mass demonstration belongs to the triangle Bastille-Republique-Nation.

Such ceremonial sites imply a certain separation between rulers and subjects, a confrontation between a remote and awful majesty and pomp on one side, and an applauding public on the other. It is the urban equivalent of the picture-frame stage; or better still, the opera, that characteristic invention of western absolute monarchy. Fortunately, for potential rioters, this is or was not the only relationship between rulers and subjects in capital cities. Often, indeed, it was the capital city itself which demonstrated the ruler's greatness, while its inhabitants, including the poorest, enjoyed a modest share of the benefits of his and its majesty. Rulers and ruled lived in a sort of symbiosis. In such circumstances the great ceremonial routes led through the middle of the towns as in Edinburgh or Prague. Palaces had no need to cut themselves off from slums. The Vienna Hofburg, which presents a wide ceremonial space to the outside world, including the Viennese suburbs, has barely a yard or two of urban street or square between it and the older Inner City, to which it visibly belongs.

This kind of town, combining as it did the patterns of civic and princely cities, was a standing invitation to riot, for here palaces and town houses of great nobles, markets, cathedrals, public squares and slums were intermingled, the rulers at the mercy of the mob. In time of trouble they could withdraw into their country residences, but that was all. Their only safeguard was to mobilize the respectable poor against the unrespectable after a successful insurrection, e.g. the artisans guilds against the 'mob', or the National Guard against the propertyless. Their one comfort was the knowledge that uncontrolled riot and insurrection rarely lasted long, and were even more rarely directed against the structure of established wealth and power. Still this was a substantial comfort. The King of Naples or the Duchess of Parma, not to mention the Pope, knew that if their subjects rioted, it was because they were unduly hungry and as a reminder to prince and nobility to do their duty, i.e. to provide enough food at fair prices on the market, enough jobs, handouts and public entertainment for their excessively modest needs. Their loyalty and piety scarcely wavered, and indeed when they made genuine revolutions (as in Naples in 1799) they were more likely to be in defence of Church and King against foreigners and the godless middle classes. . . .

Hence the crucial importance in the history of urban public order, of the French Revolution of 1789–99, which established the modern equation between insurrection and social revolution. Any government naturally prefers to avoid riot and insurrection, as it prefers to keep the murder rate down, but in the absence of genuine revolutionary danger the authorities are not likely to lose their cool about it. Eighteenth-century England was a notoriously riotous nation, with a notoriously sketchy apparatus for maintaining public order. Not only smaller cities like Liverpool and Newcastle, but large parts of London itself might be in the hands of the riotous populace for days on end. Since nothing was at stake in such disorders except a certain amount of property, which a wealthy country could well afford to replace, the general view among the upper classes was phlegmatic, and even satisfied. Whig noblemen took pride in the state of liberty which deprived potential tyrants of the troops with which to suppress their subjects and the police with which to harry them. It was not until the French Revolution that a taste for multiplying barracks in towns developed, and not until the Radicals and Chartists of the first half of the nineteenth century that the virtues of a police force outweighed those of English freedom. (Since grass-roots democracy could not always be relied on, the Metropolitan Police was put directly under the Home Office, where it still remains.)

Indeed, three main administrative methods of countering riot and insurrection suggested themselves: systematic arrangements for deploying troops, the development of police forces (which barely existed in the modern form before the nineteenth century), and the rebuilding of cities in such ways as to minimize the chances of revolt. The first two of these had no major influence on the actual shape and structure of cities, though a study of the building and location of urban barracks in the nineteenth century might provide some interesting results, and so might a study of the distribution of police stations in urban neighbourhoods. The third affected the townscape very fundamentally, as in Paris and Vienna, cities in which it is known that the needs of counter-insurgency influenced urban reconstruction after the 1848 revolutions. In Paris the main military aim of this reconstruction seems to have been to open wide and straight boulevards along which artillery could fire, and troops advance, while at the same time – presumably – breaking up the main concentrations of potential insurgents in the popular quarters. In Vienna the reconstruction took the form mainly of two wide concentric ring roads, the inner ring (broadened by a belt of open spaces, parks and widely spaced public buildings) isolated the old city and palace from the (mainly middle-class) inner suburbs, the outer ring isolating both from the (increasingly working-class) outer suburbs.

Such reconstructions may or may not have made military sense. We do not know, since the kind of revolutions they were intended to dominate virtually died out in western Europe after 1848. (Still, it is a fact that the main centres of popular resistance and barricade fighting in the Paris Commune of 1871, Montmartre-north-east Paris and the Left Bank, were isolated from each other and the rest of the town.) However, they certainly affected the calculations of potential insurrectionaries. In the socialist discussions of the 1880s the consensus of the military experts among revolutionaries, led by Engels, was that the old type of uprising now stood little chance, though there was some argument among them about the value of new technological devices such as the then rapidly developing high explosives (dynamite, etc.). At all events, barricades which had dominated insurrectionary tactics from 1830 and 1871 (they had not been seriously used in the great French Revolution of 1789–99), were now less fancied. Conversely, bombs of one kind or another became the favourite device of revolutionaries, though not marxist ones, and not for genuinely insurrectionary purposes.

Urban reconstruction, however, had another and probably unintended effect on potential rebellions, for the new and wide avenues provided an ideal location for what became an increasingly important aspect of popular movements, the mass demonstration, or rather procession. The more systematic these rings and cartwheels of boulevards, the more effectively isolated these were from the surrounding inhabited area, the easier it became to turn such assemblies into ritual marches rather than preliminaries to riot. London, which lacked them, has always had difficulty in avoiding incidental trouble during the concentration, or more usually the dispersal, of mass meetings held in Trafalgar Square. It is too near sensitive spots like Downing Street, or symbols of wealth and power like the Pall Mall clubs, whose windows the unemployed demonstrators smashed in the 1880s.

One can, of course, make too much of such primarily military factors in urban renewal. In any case they cannot be sharply distinguished from other changes in the nineteenth- and twentieth-century city which sharply diminished its riot potential. Three of them are particularly relevant.

The first is sheer size, which reduces the city to an administrative abstraction, and a conglomerate of separate communities or districts. It became simply too big to riot as a unit. London, which still lacks so obvious a symbol of civic unity as the figure of a mayor (the Lord Mayor of the City of London is a ceremonial figure who has about as much relation to London as a town as has the Lord Chancellor), is an excellent example. It ceased to be a riotous city roughly between the time it grew from a million to two million inhabitants, i.e. in the first half of the nineteenth century. London Chartism, for instance, barely existed as a genuinely metropolitan phenomenon for more than a day or two on end. Its real strength lay in the 'localities' in which it was organized, i.e. in communities and neighbourhoods like Lambeth, Woolwich or Marylebone, whose relations with each other were at the most loosely federal. Similarly, the radicals and activists of the late nineteenth century were essentially locally based. Their most characteristic organization was the Metropolitan Radical Federation, essentially an alliance of working men's clubs of purely local importance, in such neighbourhoods as had a tradition of radicalism – Chelsea, Hackney, Clerkenwell, Woolwich, etc. The familiar London tendency to build low, and therefore to sprawl, made distances between such centres of trouble too great for the spontaneous propagation of riots. How much contact would Battersea or Chelsea (then still a working-class area electing left-wing MPs) have with the turbulent East End of the 1889 dock striker ? How much contact, for that matter, would there be between Whitechapel and Canning Town ? In the nature of things the shapeless built-up areas which grew either out of the expansion of a big city or the merging of larger and smaller growing communities, and for which artificial names have had to be invented ('conurbation', 'Greater' London, Berlin or Tokyo) were not towns in the old sense, even when administratively unified from time to time.

The second is the growing pattern of functional segregation in the nineteenth- and twentieth-century city, that is to say, on the one hand, the development of specialized industrial, business, government and other centres or open spaces, on the other, the geographical separation of classes. Here again London was the pioneer, being a combination of three separate units – the government centre of Westminster, the merchant city of London, and the popular Southwark across the river. Up to a point the growth of this composite metropolis encouraged potential rioters. The northern and eastern edges of the City of London and Southwark where the merchant community bordered on districts of workers, artisans and the port – all in their way equally disposed to riot, like the Spitalfield weavers or the Clerkenwell radicals – formed natural flash-points. These were the areas where several of the great eighteenth-century riots broke out. Westminster had its own population of artisans and miscellaneous poor, whom the proximity of king and Parliament and the accident of an unusually democratic franchise in this constituency, turned into a formidable pressure group for several decades of the late eighteenth and nineteenth centuries. The area between the City and Westminster, which was filled by an unusually dense accumulation of slums, inhabited by labourers, immigrants and the socially marginal (Drury Lane, Covent Garden, St Giles, Holborn), added to the ebullience of metropolitan public life.

However, as time went on the pattern simplified itself. The nineteenth-century City ceased to be residential, and became increasingly a pure business district, while the port moved downstream, the city middle and lower-middle classes into more or less remote suburbs, leaving the East End an increasingly homogeneous zone of the poor. The northern and western borders of Westminster became increasingly upper- and middle-class settlements largely designed as such by landowners and speculative builders, thus pressing the centres of artisans, labourers and others inclined to radicalism and riot (Chelsea, Notting Hill, Paddington, Marylebone) on to a periphery increasingly remote from the rest of radical London. The slums between the two cities survived longest but by the early twentieth century they had also been broken into small patches by the urban renewal which has given London some of its gloomiest thoroughfares (Shaftesbury Avenue, Rosebery Avenue) as well as some of its most pompous ones (Kingsway, Aldwych), and an impressive accumulation of barrack-like tenements purporting to increase the happiness of the Drury Lane and Saffron Hill proletariat. Covent Garden and Soho (which elected communist local councillors in 1945) are perhaps the last relic of old-fashioned metropolitan turbulence in the centre of the town. By the late nineteenth century the potentially riotous London had already been broken up into peripheral segments of varying size (the huge and amorphous East End being the largest), surrounding a non-residential City and West End and a solid block of middle-class districts, and surrounded in turn by middle- and lower-middle-class outer suburbs.

Such patterns of segregation developed in most large and growing western cities from the early nineteenth century, though the parts of their historic centres which were not transformed into business or institutional districts, sometimes retained traces of their old structure, which may still be observed in the red-light quarters, as in Amsterdam. Twentieth-century working-class rehousing and planning for motor transport further disintegrated the city as a potential riot centre. (The nineteenth-century planning for railways had, if anything, the opposite effect, often creating socially mixed and marginal quarters around the new terminals.) The recent tendency to shift major urban services such as central markets from the centres to the outskirts of cities will no doubt disintegrate it further.

Is the urban riot and insurrection therefore doomed to disappear? Evidently not, for we have in recent years seen a marked recrudescence of this phenomenon in some of the most modern cities, though also a decline in some of the more traditional centres of such activities. The reasons are mainly social and political, but it may be worth looking briefly at the characteristics of modern urbanism which encourage it.

Modern mass transportation is one. Motor transport has so far contributed chiefly to the mobilization of that normally un-riotous group, the middle class, though such devices as the motorized demonstration (Frenchmen and Algerians still remember the massed horns of reaction hooting *Al-gé-rie française*) and that natural device of sabotage and passion, the traffic jam. However, cars have been used by activists in North American riots, and disrupt police action when on the move, while forming temporary barricades when stationary. Moreover, motor transport distributes the news of riots beyond the immediate area affected since both private cars and buses have to be extensively re-routed.

Public transport, and especially underground railways, which are once again being built in several big cities on a large scale, is more directly relevant. There is no better means of transport for moving large numbers of potential rioters rapidly over long distances than trains running at frequent intervals. This is one reason why the West Berlin students are a rather effective body of rioters : the underground links the Free University set among the remote and spectacularly middle-class villas and gardens of Dahlem, with the town centre.

More important than transport are two other factors : the increase in the number of buildings worth rioting against or occupying, and the development in their vicinity of accumulations of potential rioters. For while it is true that the headquarters of central and municipal government are increasingly remote from the riotous quarters, and the rich or noble rarely live in palaces in the town centres (apartments are both less vulnerable and more anonymous), sensitive institutions of other kinds have multiplied. There are the communications centres (telegraph, telephone, radio, television). The least experienced organizer of a military coup or insurrection knows all about their importance. There are the gigantic newspaper offices, fortunately so often concentrated in the older city centres, and providing admirable incidental material for barricades or cover against fire in the form of delivery trucks, newsprint and packages of papers. They were used for street-fighting purposes as long ago as 1919 in Berlin, though not very much since. There are, as we all know now, the universities. Though the general tendency to move these out of city centres has diminished their riot potential somewhat, there are enough academic precincts left in the middle of big towns to satisfy the activists. Besides, the explosion of higher education has filled the average university to bursting point with thousands, or even tens of thousands, of marchers or fighters. There are, above all, the banks and large corporations, symbols and reality of the power structure, and increasingly concentrated in those massifs of plate glass and concrete by which the traveller recognizes the centres of a proper late-twentieth-century city.

Theoretically these should be individually as much the object of attack by rioters as city halls or capitols, for IBM, Shell or General Motors carry at least as much weight as most governments. Banks have long been aware of their vulnerability, and in some Latin countries – Spain is a good example – their combination of symbolic architectural opulence and heavy fortification provides the nearest thing to those town-citadels in which feudal and feuding noblemen barricaded themselves in the middle ages. To see them under heavy police guard in times of tension is an instructive experience, though, in fact, the only champions of direct action who have been systematically attracted by them are unpolitical robbers and revolutionary 'expropriators'. But if we except such politically and economically negligible symbols of the American way of life as Hilton hotels, and the occasional object of specialized hostility such as Dow Chemicals, riots have rarely aimed directly at any of the buildings of large corporations. Nor are they very vulnerable. It would take more than a few broken plate-glass windows or even the occupation of a few acres of office space, to disrupt the smooth operations of a modern oil company.

On the other hand, collectively 'downtown' is vulnerable. The disruption of traffic, the closing of banks, the office staffs who cannot or will not turn up for work, the businessmen marooned in hotels with overloaded switchboards, or who cannot reach their destinations: all these can interfere very seriously with the activities of a city. Indeed, this came close to happening during the 1967 riots in Detroit. What is more, in cities developing on the North American pattern it is not unlikely to happen, sooner or later. For it is well known that the central areas of town, and their immediate surroundings, are being filled with the coloured poor as the comfortable whites move out. The ghettoes lap round the city centres like dark and turbulent seas. It is this concentration of the most discontented and turbulent in the neighbourhood of a relatively few unusually sensitive urban centres which gives the militants of a smallish minority the political importance which black riots would certainly not have if the 10 or 15 per cent of the US population who are Negroes were more evenly distributed throughout the whole of that vast and complex country.

Still, even this revival of rioting in western cities is comparatively modest. An intelligent and cynical police chief would probably regard all the troubles in western cities during recent years as minor disturbances, magnified by the hesitation or incompetence of the authorities and the effect of excessive publicity. With the exception of the Latin Quarter riots of May 1968 none of them looked as though they could, or were intended to, shake governments. Anyone who wishes to judge what a genuine old-style insurrection of the urban poor, or a serious armed rising, is and can achieve, must still go to the cities of the underdeveloped world: to Naples which rose against the Germans in 1943, to the Algerian Casbah in 1956 (excellent movies have been made about both these insurrections), to Bogota in 1948, perhaps to Caracas, certainly to Santo Domingo in 1965.

The effectiveness of recent western city riots is due not so much to the actual activities of the rioters, as to their political context. In the ghettoes of the United States they have demonstrated that black people are no longer prepared to accept their fate passively, and in doing so they have doubtless accelerated the development of black political consciousness and white fear; but they have never looked like a serious immediate threat to even the local power structure. In Paris they demonstrated the lability of an apparently firm and monolithic regime. (The actual fighting capacity of the insurrectionaries was never in fact tested, though their heroism is not in question: no more than two or three people were actually killed, and those almost certainly by accident.) Elsewhere the demonstrations and riots of students, though very effective inside the universities, have been little more than a routine police problem outside them.

But this, of course, may be true of all urban riots, which is why the study of their relation to different types of towns is a comparatively unimportant exercise. Georgian Dublin does not lend itself easily to insurrection, and its population, which does, has not shown a great inclination to initiate or even to participate in uprisings. The Easter Rising took place there because it was a capital city, where the major national decisions are supposed to be made, and though it failed fairly quickly, it played an important part in the winning of Irish independence, because the nature of the Irish situation in 1917–21 allowed it to. Petrograd, built from scratch on a gigantic and geometrical plan, is singularly ill-suited to barricades or street fighting, but the Russian revolution began and succeeded there. Conversely, the proverbial turbulence of Barcelona, the older parts of which are almost ideally suited to riot, rarely even looked like producing revolution. Catalan anarchism, with all its bomb throwers, *pistoleros*, and enthusiasm for direct action, was until 1936 never more than a normal problem of public order to the authorities, so modest that the historian is amazed to find how few policemen were actually supposed (rather inefficiently) to ensure its protection.

Revolutions arise out of political situations, not because some cities are structurally suited to insurrection. Still, an urban riot or spontaneous uprising may be the starter which sets the engine of revolution going. That starter is more likely to function in cities which encourage or facilitate insurrection. A friend of mine, who happened to have commanded the 1944 insurrection against the Germans in the Latin Quarter of Paris, walked through the area on the morning after the Night of the Barricades in 1968, touched and moved to see that young men who had not been born in 1944 had built several of their barricades in the same places as then. Or, the historian might add, the same places that had seen barricades in 1830, 1848, and 1871. It is not every city that lends itself so naturally to this exercise, or where, consequently, each generation of rebels remembers or rediscovers the battlefields of its predecessors. Thus in May 1968 the most serious confrontation occurred across the barricades of the Rue Gay Lussac and behind the Rue Soufflot. Almost a century earlier, in the Commune of 1871, the heroic Raoul Rigault commanded the barricades in that very area, was taken – in the same month of May – and killed by the Versaillais. Not every city is like Paris. Its peculiarity may no longer be enough to revolutionize France, but the tradition and the environment are still strong enough to precipitate the nearest thing to a revolution in a developed western country.

(1968)

24
MAY 1968

Of all the many unexpected events of the late 1960s, a remarkably bad period for prophets, the movement of May 1968 in France was easily the most surprising, and, for left-wing intellectuals, probably the most exciting. It seemed to demonstrate what practically no radical over the age of twenty-five, including Mao Tse-tung and Fidel Castro, believed, namely that revolution in an advanced industrial country was possible in conditions of peace, prosperity, and apparent political stability. The revolution did not succeed and, as we shall see, there is much argument over whether it was ever more than faintly possible that it should succeed. Nevertheless, the proudest and most self-confident political regime of Europe was brought to within half an inch of collapse. There was a day when almost certainly the majority of de Gaulle's cabinet, and quite possibly the general himself, expected defeat. This was achieved by a grass-roots popular movement, without the help of anyone within the power structure. And it was the students who initiated, inspired, and at crucial moments actually represented that movement.

Probably no other revolutionary movement contained a higher percentage of people reading and writing books, and it is therefore not surprising that the French publishing industry should have rushed in to supply an apparently unlimited demand. By the end of 1968 at least fifty-two books about the May events had appeared, and the flow continues. All of them are rush jobs, some of them no more than brief articles, padded out with reprints of old papers, press interviews, taped speeches, etc.

There is, however, no reason why hasty inquests should not be valuable when conducted by intelligent people, and the Latin Quarter of Paris probably contains more of them per square yard than any other spot on earth. In any case the revolutions and counter-revolutions of France have in their time stimulated some of the most distinguished rush jobs of history, most notably Karl Marx's *Eighteenth Brumaire of Louis Bonaparte*. Moreover, French intellectuals are not merely numerous and articulate, but used to quick and copious writing, a faculty trained by years of moonlighting on reviews and other work for not very generous publishers. Add up the books, reviews, and the newspaper accounts, headed by those in the majestic and indispensable *Le Monde*, and the typical Parisian revolutionary has probably got through the equivalent of several thousand pages about his or her experiences; or at least talks as though he had.

What can we discover from this mass of literature? By far the greater part tries to explain the movement, to analyze its nature and its possible contributions to social change. A fair proportion tries to fit it into one or another of the analytical categories of its sympathizers – who provide the overwhelming majority of the writers – with more or less originality and special pleading. This is natural enough. However, it does not provide us with another *Eighteenth Brumaire* – that is to say, with a study of the politics of May 1968. No doubt the actual events are so vividly engraved on the minds of most French intellectuals that they think they know all about them already. It is no accident that the nearest thing to a coherent analytical narrative of the crisis comes from two British journalists, Seale and McConville. Though not exceptional, it is competent, sympathetic, and invaluable to non-Frenchmen if only because it carefully explains what all the confusing initials of the various ideological groups in the Latin Quarter stand for.

Nevertheless, if May 1968 was a revolution which only just failed to overthrow de Gaulle, the situation which allowed what had been, a few weeks earlier, a squabbling collection of campus sects to make the attempt deserves to be analyzed. And so must the reasons for the failure of these sects. So it may be useful to leave aside the nature and novelty of the revolutionary forces and try to clarify the less exciting question of their initial success and comparatively rapid failure.

There were, it is clear, two stages in the mobilization of the revolutionary forces, both totally unexpected by the government, the official opposition, even by the unofficial but recognized opposition of the important left-wing literary intellectuals in Paris. (The established left-wing intelligentsia played no significant part in the May events; Jean-Paul Sartre, with great tact and intuition, recognized this by effacing himself before Daniel Cohn-Bendit, to whom he acted merely as interviewer.) The first stage, roughly between 3 and 11 May, mobilized the students. Thanks to the government's inattention, complacency, and stupidity, a movement of activists in a suburban campus was transformed into a mass movement of virtually all students in Paris, enjoying vast public support – at this stage 61 per cent of Parisians were pro-student and only 16 per cent definitely hostile – and then into a sort of symbolic insurrection of the Latin Quarter. The government retreated before it, and in so doing spread the movement to the provinces and, especially, to the workers.

The second phase of mobilization, from 14 to 27 May, consisted essentially in the extension of a spontaneous general strike, the largest in the history of France or perhaps of any other country, and culminated with the rejection by the strikers of the deal negotiated on their behalf between the official union leaders and the government. Throughout this period, up to 29 May, the popular movement held the initiative : the government, caught on the wrong foot at the start, was unable to recover itself, and grew progressively demoralized. The same is true of conservative and moderate opinion, which was at this time passive, even paralyzed. The situation changed rapidly when de Gaulle at last took action on 29 May.

The first thing to observe is that only the second phase created revolutionary possibilities (or, to put it another way, it created the need for the government to take counter-revolutionary action). The student movement by itself was a nuisance, but not a political danger. The authorities grossly underrated it, but this was largely because they were thinking about other things, including other university problems and the bureaucratic in-fighting between various government departments, which seemed to them more important. Touraine, the author of the most illuminating of the books published in the immediate aftermath of May, rightly says that what was wrong with the French system was not that it was too Napoleonic, but that it was too much like the regime of Louis-Philippe, whose government was caught equally on the wrong footing by the riots of 1848, which consequently turned into a revolution.

Yet, paradoxically, the very lack of importance of the student movement made it a most effective detonator of the workers' mobilization. Having underestimated and neglected it, the government tried to disperse it by force. When the students refused to go home, the only choice was between shooting and a public, humiliating retreat. But how could they have chosen to shoot ? Massacre is one of the last resorts of the government in stable industrial societies, since (unless directed against outsiders of one kind or another) it destroys the impression of popular consent on which they rest. Once the velvet glove has been put on the iron fist, it is politically very risky to take it off. Massacring students, the children of the respectable middle class, not to mention ministers, is even less attractive politically than killing workers and peasants. Just because the students were only a bunch of unarmed kids who did not put the regime at risk, the government had little choice but to retreat before them. But in doing so it created the very situation it wished to avoid. It appeared to show its impotence and gave the students a cheap victory. The Paris chief of police, an intelligent man, had more or less told his minister to avoid a bluff which virtually had to be called. That the students did not believe it to be a bluff does not change the reality of the situation.

Conversely, the workers' mobilization did put the regime in a risky position, which is why de Gaulle was finally prepared to use the ultimate weapon, civil war, by calling on the army. This was not because insurrection was the serious object of anyone, for neither the students, who may have wanted it, nor the workers, who certainly did not, thought or acted in such political terms. It was because the progressive crumbling of government authority left a void, and because the only practicable alternative government was a popular front inevitably dominated by the Communist Party. The revolutionary students may not have considered this a particularly significant political change, and most Frenchmen would almost certainly have accepted it more or less willingly.

Indeed, there was a moment when even those two Hobbesian institutions, the French police and the army, long accustomed to assess the moment when old regimes ought to be abandoned and new ones accepted, allowed it to be understood that they would not regard a legally constituted popular front government as an insurrection which they were obliged to combat. It would not in itself have been revolutionary – except in its coming to power – and it would not have been regarded as such. On the other hand, it is hard to think of any other positive political outcome of the crisis which even revolutionaries could have expected.

But the Popular Front was not ready to occupy the vacuum left by the disintegration of Gaullism. The non-communists in the alliance dragged their feet, since the crisis demonstrated that they represented nobody except a few politicians, while the Communist Party, through its control of the strongest union federation, was for the time being the only civilian force of real significance, and would therefore have inevitably dominated the new government. The crisis eliminated the sham politics of electoral calculation and left visible only the real politics of power. But the Communists in turn had no means of forcing the date of their shotgun wedding with the other opposition groups. For they had themselves been playing the electoral game. They had not mobilized the masses whose action pushed them to the verge of power, and they had not thought of using that action to force their allies' hand. On the contrary, if Philippe Alexandre is to be believed, they seem to have regarded the strike as something that might stop them from concentrating on the really important job of keeping their allies in line.

De Gaulle, a notoriously brilliant politician, recognized both the moment when his opponents lost their momentum, and the chance of regaining his own initiative. With an apparently imminent communist-led popular front, a conservative regime could at last play its trump card: the fear of revolution. It was, tactically speaking, a beautifully judged performance. De Gaulle did not even have to shoot. Indeed, not the least curious aspect of the entire May crisis is that the trial of strength was symbolic throughout, rather like the manoeuvres of the proverbial Chinese generals of ancient times. Nobody seriously tried to kill anybody. Perhaps five people in all actually were killed, though a considerable number were beaten up.

Whatever happened, both Gaullists and revolutionaries united in blaming the French Communist Party, either for planning revolution or for sabotaging it. Neither line of argument is very significant except as an indication of the crucial role of the CP in May. It was clearly the only civilian organization, and certainly the only part of the political opposition, which kept both its influence and its head. This is not really surprising unless we assume that the workers were revolutionary in the same way as the students or that they were as disgusted with the CP.

But though the workers were certainly far more advanced than their leaders, e.g. in their readiness to raise questions of social control in industry which the General Labour Federation was simply not thinking about, the divergencies between leaders and followers in May were potential rather than actual. The political proposals of the CP almost certainly reflected what most workers wanted, and quite certainly reflected the traditional mode of thinking of the French left ('defence of the republic', 'union of all on the left', 'a popular government', 'down with one-man rule', etc.). As for the general strike, the unions had taken it over almost immediately. Their leaders were negotiating with government and the bosses, and until they came back with unsatisfactory terms, there was no reason at all to expect a major revolt against them. In brief, while the students started their revolt in a spirit of equal hostility to de Gaulle and the CP (from which most of their leaders had seceded or been expelled), the workers did not.

The Communist Party was therefore in a position to act. Its leadership met daily to assess the situation. It thought it knew what to do. But what was it doing? It was certainly not trying to preserve Gaullism, for reasons of Soviet foreign policy or any other. As soon as the overthrow of de Gaulle began to look possible, i.e. between three and four days after the spontaneous sit-ins started to spread, it formally staked its own and the Popular Front's immediate claim to power. On the other hand it consistently refused to have anything to do with advocating insurrection, on the grounds that this would be playing into de Gaulle's hands.

In this it was correct. The May crisis was not a classical revolutionary situation, though the conditions for such a situation might have developed very rapidly as a result of a sudden, unexpected break in a regime which turned out to be much more fragile than anyone had anticipated. The forces of government and its widespread political support were in no sense divided and disintegrated, but merely disoriented and temporarily paralyzed. The forces of revolution were weak, except in holding the initiative. Apart from the students, the organized workers, and some sympathizers among the college-educated professional strata, their support consisted not so much in allies as in the readiness of a large mass of uncommitted or even hostile opinion to give up hope in Gaullism and accept quietly the only available alternative. As the crisis advanced, public opinion in Paris became much less favourable to Gaullism, somewhat more favourable to the old left, but no clear preponderance emerges from the public opinion surveys. Had the Popular Front come, it would certainly have won the subsequent election, just as de Gaulle won his – but victory is a great decider of loyalties.

The best chance of overthrowing Gaullism was therefore to let it beat itself. At one point – between 27 and 29 May – its credibility would have crumbled so much that even its officials and followers might have given it up for lost. The worst policy would have been to give Gaullism the chance of rallying its supporters, the state apparatus, and the uncommitted against a clearly defined, and militarily ineffective, minority of workers and students. Unwilling to expel the striking workers from the factories by force, the army and police were entirely reliable against an insurrection. They said so. And, indeed, de Gaulle recovered precisely because he turned the situation into a defence of 'order' against 'red revolution'. That the CP was not interested in 'red revolution' is another matter. Its general strategy was right for anyone, including revolutionaries, who unexpectedly discovered a chance of overthrowing the regime in a basically non-revolutionary situation. Assuming, of course, that they wanted to take power.

The communists' real faults were different. The test of a revolutionary movement is not its willingness to raise barricades at every opportunity, but its readiness to recognize when the normal conditions of routine politics cease to operate, and to adapt its behaviour accordingly. The French CP failed both these tests, and in consequence failed not only to overthrow capitalism (which it did not want to do just then) but to install the Popular Front (which it certainly did). As Touraine has sarcastically observed, its real failure was not as a revolutionary but even as a reformist party. It consistently trailed behind the masses, failing to recognize the seriousness of the student movement until the barricades were up, the readiness of the workers for an unlimited general strike until the spontaneous sit-ins forced the hands of its union leaders, taken by surprise once again when the workers rejected the terms of trike settlement.

Unlike the non-communist left it was not pushed aside, since it had both organization and mass support from the grass roots. Like them, it continued to play the game of routine politics and routine labour unionism. It exploited a situation not of its own making, but it neither led nor even understood it, except perhaps as a threat to its own position within the labour movement by the bitterly hostile ultra-left. Had the CP recognized the existence and scope of the popular movement and acted accordingly, it might just have gained sufficient momentum to force its reluctant allies on the old left into line. One cannot say much more than this, for the chances of overthrowing Gaullism, though real for a few days, never amounted to more than a reasonable possibility. As it was it condemned itself, during those crucial days of 27 to 29 May, to waiting and issuing appeals. But at such times waiting is fatal. Those who lose the initiative lose the game.

The chances of overthrowing the regime were diminished not only by the failure of the Communists, but by the character of the mass movement. It had no political aims itself, though it used political phraseology. Without profound social and cultural discontents, ready to emerge at a relatively slight impetus, there can be no major social revolutions. But without a certain concentration on specific targets, however peripheral to their main purpose, the force of such revolutionary energies is dispersed. A given political or economic crisis, a given situation, may provide such precise enemies and objectives automatically; a war which must be ended, a foreign occupier who must be expelled, a crack in the political structure imposing specific and limited options, such as whether or not to support the Spanish government of 1936 against the generals' insurrection. The French situation provided no such automatic targets of concentration.

On the contrary, the very profundity of the critique of society implied or formulated by the popular movement left it without specific targets. Its enemy was 'the system'. To quote Touraine: 'The enemy is no longer a person of a social category, the monarch or the bourgeoisie. He is the totality of the depersonalized, "rationalized", bureaucratized modes of action of socio-economic power. . . .' The enemy is by definition faceless, not even a thing or an institution, but a programme of human relations, a process of depersonalization; not exploitation which implies exploiters, but alienation. It is typical that most of the students themselves (unlike the less revolutionary workers) were not bothered about de Gaulle, except in so far as the real objective, society, was obscured by the purely political phenomenon of Gaullism. The popular movement was therefore either sub-political or anti-political. In the long run this does not diminish its historic importance or influence. In the short run it was fatal. As Touraine says, May 1968 is less important even in the history of revolutions than the Paris Commune. It proved not that revolutions can succeed in western countries today, but only that they can break out.

Several of the books about the May events may be briefly dismissed. However, Alain Touraine's book is in a class apart.[1] The author is an industrial sociologist of marxist provenance, the teacher of Daniel Cohn-Bendit at Nanterre, the original flash-point of the student revolt; he was deeply involved in its early stages. His analysis reflects all this to some extent. Its value lies not so much in its originality – where so much has been written, most ideas have already been suggested and contested somewhere – as in the author's lucidity and historical sense, his lack of illusions, his knowledge of labour movements, as well as the incidental contribution of his having first-hand experience. He has, for instance, written the best analysis of the general strike, a grossly under-reported and under-analyzed phenomenon when compared to the quantity of literature about the Latin Quarter. (We know practically nothing of what happened in all those plants and offices, which, after all, produced ten million strikers, most of whom were out of contact with students and reporters.) For foreign readers he has the additional advantage of first-hand acquaintance with other parts of the world, notably the United States and Latin America, which helps to correct the inborn provincialism of the French.

Touraine's argument is elaborate and complex, but a few of the points may be noted. What is happening today is the 'great mutation' from an older bourgeois to a new technocratic society, and this, as the May movement shows, creates conflict and dissidence not only at its margins but at its centre. The dividing line of 'class struggle' it reveals runs down the middle of the 'middle classes', between the 'techno-bureaucrats' on the one side and the 'professionals' on the other side. The latter, though in no sense obvious victims of oppression, represent in the modern technological economy something like the elite of skilled labour in an earlier industrial epoch, and for analogous reasons crystallize the new phase of class consciousness:

> The main actor in the May movement was not the working class but the totality of those whom we may call the professionals . . . and among them the most active were those most independent of the great organizations for

[1] Alain Touraine, *Le mouvement de mai ou le communisme utopique*, Paris, 1969.

which, directly or indirectly, such people work: students, radio and television people, technicians in planning offices, research workers in both the private and public sector, teachers, etc.

They and not the old working-class collectivities of miners, longshoremen, railroads, gave the general strike its specific character. Its core incidentally lay in the new industries: the Automotive-Electronic-Chemical complex.

According to Touraine, a new social movement suited to the new economy is emerging, but it is a curiously contradictory one. In one sense it is a primitive rebellion of men who depend on older experiences to cope with a new situation. It may produce a revival of patterns of militancy or, among the new recruits to the social movement who have no such militant experience, something analogous to populist movements in underdeveloped countries, or more precisely to the labour movement of the early nineteenth century. Such a movement is important not for the fight it is now carrying on along old political lines, but for what it reveals of the future: for its vision rather than its necessarily feeble achievement. For the strength of that vision, the 'utopian communism' which it created in 1968 as the young proletariat created it before 1848, depends upon its practical impotence. On the other hand this social movement also includes or implies an up-to-date kind of reformism, a force which may serve to modify rigid and obsolescent structures of society – the educational system, industrial relations, management, government. The future dilemmas of revolutionaries lie here.

Was this new social movement 'revolutionary' in May – apart from its 'revolutionary' formulation of a 'counter-utopia' of libertarian communism to meet the 'dominant Utopia' of the academic sociologists and political scientists? In France, Touraine argues, the new movement produced a genuine revolutionary crisis, though one unlikely to achieve revolution, because, for historical reasons, the social struggle, politics, and a 'cultural revolution' against all forms of manipulation and integration of individual behaviour were combined. There can be no social movement today which does not combine these three elements, because of the 'progressive disappearance of the separation between state and civil society'. But at the same time this makes the concentration of the struggle, and the development of effective devices for action, such as parties of the bolshevik type, increasingly difficult.

In the United States, by contrast – perhaps because of the absence of state centralization or a tradition of proletarian revolution to focus it – there has been no such combination of forces. The phenomena of cultural revolt, which are symptomatic rather than operational, are the most visible. 'While in France', Touraine writes, 'the social struggle was at the centre of the movement and the cultural revolt was, one might almost say, a byproduct of a crisis of social change, in the United States cultural revolt is central.' This is a symptom of weakness.

Touraine's purpose is not so much to make judgments or prophecies – and in so far as he does so he will be criticized – as to establish that the May movement was neither an episode nor a simple continuation of older social movements. It demonstrated that 'a new period in social history' is beginning or has begun, but also that the analysis of its character cannot be derived from words of the revolutionaries of May themselves. He is probably right on both counts.

(1969)

25
INTELLECTUALS AND THE CLASS STRUGGLE

The characteristic revolutionary person today is a student or (generally young) intellectual, the word being understood to mean anyone who earns or looks forward to earning his living in an occupation which is chiefly recruited from those who have passed a certificate of some kind of academic education or its equivalent. In backward or underdeveloped countries this may include anyone with secondary or even in some areas primary schooling; in developed countries it increasingly tends to mean anyone with a post-secondary education, but not necessarily those whose education, at whatever level, has been primarily vocational, such as accountants, engineers, business executives and artists. One might say that the intellectual is a person holding a job for which the qualification is one which does not teach anything about holding specific jobs. In this sense the definition used here converges with the more familiar conception of the intellectual as someone using his or her intellect in a way which is sometimes defined in a circular fashion and not often very clearly. However, it is preferable to stress the occupational aspect. It is not the fact of thinking, independently or otherwise, which gives intellectuals certain political characteristics, but a particular social situation in which they think.

That revolutionary persons are today characteristically intellectuals (which does not mean that intellectuals are characteristically revolutionaries), can be verified by analyzing the membership of the organizations or groups, generally quite small, which today claim to be committed to revolution in its most literal sense, to insurrection or the total rejection of the *status quo*. It would presumably not be true of countries undergoing revolution or in revolutionary, insurrectionary and semi-insurrectionary situations, but it is certainly true not only of developed 'western' countries, but also of countries in which the situation of the labouring masses is such that one would expect them to be revolutionary.[1] Even there we often find, as among the Peruvian guerrillas of the 1960s or the Indian Naxalites, that intellectuals predominate. So, though the following discussion will deal primarily with 'developed' countries, some of it may also be relevant to others, if perhaps only marginally.

To say that most revolutionary persons today are intellectuals is not to say that they will make the revolution. Who will make revolution, if at all, is a more complicated question, as is the rather more superficial problem who, other than the advocates of immediate insurrection or armed struggle who claim a monopoly of the term, is entitled to call himself revolutionary. For the purpose of the present paper it is not essential to answer either, since its concern is not so much with the objective as with the subjective element in making revolutions. Those who reject or resent any involvement in the *status quo*, and indeed any activity not directly and exclusively designed to 'confront' capitalism with a head-on challenge, are certainly revolutionaries in the most literal sense, and for the purposes of my argument it does not matter that others can also claim to be, perhaps more effectively at times. The point is that most of these all-out revolutionaries are intellectuals, which raises interesting problems both about intellectuals and about 'being revolutionary'.

Of course it may be claimed that intellectuals cannot be revolutionaries without this subjective consciousness, whereas some other social strata can. When Marx spoke of the workers as a revolutionary class, he meant not simply one which 'revolts against individual conditions of a hitherto existing society', but 'against the very "life-production" hitherto existing, the "whole of the activity" on which it is based'. He did not imply that this rejection must be explicit, though he assumed that at a certain stage of historical development it would become so. For him the proletariat was such a class because of the nature of its social existence, and not (except at a rather lower level of the analysis of

[1] Such countries are not necessarily in revolutionary situations, as defined by Lenin or anyone else. Tsarist Russia cried out for social revolution during a long period, but was in revolutionary situations only infrequently.

concrete historical situations) because of its consciousness of this aim. 'It cannot abolish its own conditions of life without abolishing *all* the inhuman conditions of the life of present-day society which are concentrated in its situation. It is not a matter of what this or that proletarian or even the whole poletariat *imagines* at one time or another to be its goal. It is a matter of *what it is*, and what in accordance with this *being* it will be historically forced to do.'[2] Intellectuals as a stratum are not of this kind. They are revolutionary only in so far as their members individually feel that they ought to or must be. So we must begin by considering what makes people feel this way. Naturally, this discussion cannot be confined merely to intellectuals.

Why do men and women become revolutionaries? In the first instance mostly because they believe that what they want subjectively from life cannot be got without a fundamental change in all society. There is of course that permanent substratum of idealism, or if we prefer the term, utopianism, which is part of all human life and it can become the dominant part for individuals at certain times, as during adolescence and romantic love, and for societies at the occasional historical moments which correspond to falling and being in love, namely the great moments of liberation and revolution. All men, however cynical, can conceive of a personal life or society which would not be imperfect. All would agree that this would be wonderful. Most men at some time of their lives think that such a life and society are *possible*, and quite a number think that we ought to bring them about. During the great liberations and revolutions most men actually think, briefly or only momentarily, that perfection is being achieved, that the New Jerusalem is being built, the earthly paradise within reach. But most people for most of their adult lives, and most social groups for most of their history, live at a less exalted level of expectation.

It is when the relatively modest expectations of everyday life look as though they cannot be achieved without revolutions, that individuals become revolutionaries. Peace is a modest and negative objective, but during the first world war it was this elementary demand which turned ordinary people objectively and later subjectively into persons dedicated to the immediate overthrow of society, since peace seemed unrealizable without it. Such

[2] *The Holy Family*, MEGA, 1/3, pp. 206–7.

an assessment of the situation may be mistaken. For instance, it may turn out that British workers can, on the whole, enjoy full employment at a high standard of life for quite a long time without first overthrowing capitalism, a prospect which looked hardly credible forty years ago.[3] But that is another matter. The modest expectations of everyday life are not, of course, purely material. They include all kinds of demands which we make for ourselves or the communities of which we consider ourselves members : respect and self-respect, certain rights, just treatment, and so on. But even these are not utopian demands for a new, different and perfect life, but envisage the ordinary life we see around us. The demands which make North American blacks into revolutionaries are elementary enough, and most whites can take their fulfilment for granted.

Here again, what forces people towards conscious revolutionism is not the ambition of their objective, but the apparent failure of all alternative ways of attaining it, the closing of all doors against them. If we are locked out of our house, there are normally several possibilities of getting back in, though some imply a hopeful patience. It is only when none of these appear realistic that we think of battering in the door. However, it is worth observing that even so we are unlikely to batter in the door unless we feel that it will give way. Becoming a revolutionary implies not only a measure of despair, but also some hope. The typical alternation of passivity and activism among some notoriously oppressed classes or peoples is thus explained.[4]

Commitment to revolution thus depends on a mixture of motives : the desire for the ordinary life, behind which, waiting to emerge, is the dream of the really good life ; the sense of all gates closing against us, but at the same time the sense of the possibility of bursting them open ; the sense of *urgency*, without which appeals to patience and reform or piecemeal improvement do not lose their force. Such motives, mixed in different proportions, may arise in a

[3] The function of a revolutionary ideology such as socialism in mass movements is to liberate their members from dependence on such fluctuations in their personal expectations.

[4] This may be illustrated from the history of South American Indian peasants over the past centuries. Inactive whenever the power structure above them seemed stable and firm, they immediately begin to occupy the communal lands which they never ceased to claim as their own, whenever it seemed to show signs of cracking.

variety of historic situations, among which we may single out two. There is the relatively specialized case of particular groups within a society, like the Negroes in the United States, for which the gates appear to be shut, whereas they are open, or at least capable of opening, for the rest. There is also the more general and significant case of societies in crisis, which appear incapable of satisfying the demands of most of their people, whatever they may do, so that – with relatively small exceptions – all groups feel disoriented, frustrated and convinced of the necessity of some fundamental change, not necessarily of the same kind. Tsarist Russia is a classical example: a society in whose future few believed. Most developed countries of the western world normally belonged, for more than a century after 1848, to the first type, but it is possible that since the 1960s several of them may be transferring to the second.

It is worth repeating that I am talking about what makes revolutionaries, not what makes revolutions. Revolutions can be made without many revolutionaries in the sense I am using the word. At the start of the French revolution of 1789, probably few were to be found outside the ranks of the marginal literary *bohême* and (very much more inactively) of educated middle-class intellectuals. There was discontent, militancy, popular ferment, and in the context of an economic and political crisis of the regime this actually led to revolution, whereas otherwise it might have produced no more than considerable but temporary public disorder. But by and large French revolutionaries were made during, by and in the revolution. They did not initially make it.

Let me briefly make another point. Contrary to a view once fashionable among American sociologists and political scientists, people do not normally become revolutionaries because they are individually alienated or deviant, though revolutionary activities undoubtedly attract a lunatic fringe and some of them – especially the less organized and disciplined – may attract personal misfits. The analysis of the membership of communist parties, and even more that of their supporters, show clearly that their members are typically not of this kind, even in quite small parties. It is of course true that certain kinds of people find it easier or more attractive to join revolutionary movements than do others; e.g. the young as distinct from the old, or people transferred out of their traditional environment, as by emigration; or members of some socially marginal groups. However, these are social categories, not collections of maladjusted individuals. Young Jews who became revolutionary marxists were no more alienated and deviant than other Jews, whether in Zamosc, Wilna or Brooklyn. (It is, by the way, neither established nor even very probable that they were more likely to become revolutionary socialists in emigration than in the old country.) They simply made one choice of several which, for people in their position, was normal.

In my lifetime there have been two periods when numerous intellectuals became revolutionaries, the interwar years and the years since the late 1950s, and more especially since the middle 1960s. I would like to look at both, and attempt to contrast and compare them.

It may be simplest to approach the problem of my own generation through introspection, or if you prefer, autobiography.

A middle-aged and moderate well-established academic can hardly claim to be a revolutionary in any realistic sense, but someone who has regarded himself as a communist for about forty years has at least a long memory to contribute to the discussion. I belong, perhaps as one of its youngest surviving members, to a milieu which is now virtually extinct, the Jewish middle-class culture of central Europe after the first world war. This milieu lived under the triple impact of the collapse of the bourgeois world in 1914, the October revolution and anti-semitism. For most of my older Austrian relatives ordinary life had ended with the assassination in Sarajevo. When they said 'in peacetime' they meant before 1914, when the lives of 'people like us' had stretched before them like a wide straight road, predictable even in its unpredictabilities, comfortably certain, boring, from birth through the vicissitudes of school, career, visits to the opera, summer holidays and family life, to a grave in the Vienna Central Cemetery. After 1914 there was nothing but catastrophe and problematic survival. We lived on borrowed time and knew it. To make long-term plans seemed senseless for people whose world had already crashed twice within ten years (first in the war, later in the Great Inflation). We knew about the October revolution: I speak here of my Austrian relatives, though as a second-generation English citizen I stood at a slight angle to them. It proved that capitalism could and indeed must end, whether we liked it or not. This, you recall, is the mood of that notable and very central European work, Schumpeter's

Capitalism, Socialism and Democracy. We could hardly not know about anti-semitism, any more than the most assimilated middle-class blacks can fail to know about racism.

The first political conversation I ever recall took place when I was six in an Alpine sanatorium, between two Jewish mother-type ladies. It dealt with Trotsky. ('Say what you like, he's a Jewish boy called Bronstein'.) The first political event which made an impact on me as such, at the age of ten, was the great riot of 1927, when the Viennese workers burned down the Palace of Justice. The second political event I recall as such, at the age of thirteen, was the German general election of 1930, when the Nazis won 107 seats. We knew what that meant. Shortly after that we moved to Berlin, where I stayed until 1933. Those were the years of the depression. Marx somewhere says that history repeats itself, occurring first as tragedy, then as farce, but there is a more sinister pattern of repetition: first tragedy, then despair. In 1918–23 the bottom had fallen out of the world of central Europe. For a brief period in the middle 1920s it looked as though some sort of tentative hope was possible, then it fell out again. To say that those who had nothing to lose, the unemployed, the disoriented and demoralized middle classes, were desperate, is insufficient. They were ready for anything. Such were the times in which I became political.

What could young Jewish intellectuals have become under such circumstances? Not liberals of any kind, since the world of liberalism (which included social democracy) was precisely what had collapsed. As Jews we were precluded by definition from supporting parties based on confessional allegiance, or on a nationalism which excluded Jews, and in both cases on anti-semitism. We became either communists or some equivalent form of revolutionary marxists, or if we chose our own version of blood-and-soil nationalism, Zionists. But even the great bulk of young intellectual Zionists saw themselves as some sort of revolutionary marxist nationalists. There was virtually no other choice. We did not make a commitment against bourgeois society and capitalism, since it patently seemed to be on its last legs. We simply chose *a* future rather than *no* future, which meant revolution. But it meant revolution not in a negative but in a positive sense: a new world rather than no world. The great October revolution and Soviet Russia proved to us that such a new world was possible, perhaps that it was already functioning. 'I have seen the future and it works', said Lincoln Steffens. If it was to be the future it *had* to work, so we thought it did.[5]

We thus became revolutionaries not so much because of our own economic problems, though some of us were poor and most of us faced an uncertain future, but because the old society no longer seemed viable. It had no perspectives. This was also clear to young intellectuals in countries in which the social order was not visibly on the point of collapse, such as Britain. The arguments of John Strachey's *The Coming Struggle for Power*, a significant and very influential product of the slump years, also rested on the alternative: if not socialism, then barbarism. The triumph of Hitler seemed to confirm it. (Conversely, Strachey's conversion to the belief that Keynes had shown capitalism an alternative to collapse, backed no doubt by the economic recovery of the late 1930s, turned him back from a revolutionary into a reformist.) Clearly there were also intellectuals who became revolutionaries because they were proletarianized, hungry and desperate, as perhaps in Poland and certainly in our times among the revolutionary petty bourgeoisie of the Bengal cities, but I am not here concerned with them.

Our motives therefore differed in two crucial respects from those of workers who also became revolutionaries in our sense during this period. In the first place, since few of us came from milieux where marxist or other socialist beliefs had been traditional, our break was normally sharper. (This is perhaps not so true of countries like France, where a nominal revolutionism had always been a youthful bourgeois option.) In the second, the sheer economic desperation which drove so many of, say, the German unemployed into the ranks of the Communist Party in 1930–3, was less decisive. But of course we shared with the workers the sense that the old system was breaking down, the sense of urgency, and the belief that the Soviet revolution was the positive alternative.

[5] 'This realization that all attempts to restore capitalism must be wrecked on the rocks of this insoluble contradiction, that the class struggle would end with the common ruin of the contending classes if the revolutionary reconstruction of all society does not succeed, led many a marxist with a knowledge of economics into the camp of the bolsheviks; including myself' (Eugen Varga, *Die wirtschaftspolitischen Probleme der proletarischen Diktatur*, Vienna, 1921, p. 19). This autobiographical passage from the well-known communist economist illustrates the force of the alternative: revolution or ruin, at that time.

Anyone who is today in his or her early twenties has lived an entire life in a period when the old system has never looked like breaking down in this way. On the contrary—until quite recently it has flourished economically as never before. It is plainly no longer the kind of liberal capitalism whose death throes we lived through between the wars, but neither, unfortunately is it socialism, and still less Soviet socialism. It has adjusted itself to the existence of a larger and more powerful socialist sector of the world (but one with far greater internal crises than we anticipated); to global political decolonization; to living permanently with local wars and under the shadow of a nuclear catastrophe. However, until the late 1960s it has been, by and large, a sensational success economically, technologically and – let us make no mistake about this – in the provision of material prosperity (or the hope of it) for the masses. This is the background for the revolutionaries of the 1960s.

This is true even of the revolutionaries in many parts of the Third World. It is true that the intellectual revolutionaries of those countries are like those of my generation inasmuch as they confront problems of mass poverty, oppression and injustice which make any call for patience and gradualism sound almost obscene, and inasmuch as they are convinced that the present system has so solution for the problems of their societies. At all events neo-capitalism and neo-colonialism have not so far solved the problem of underdevelopment, but made it more acute. Nevertheless, if we except some areas where all hope really seems to be running out, such as Bengal, even the poor and underdeveloped countries are today not, on the whole, stagnant or in absolute regression. There may be no hope for them as societies, but there is plenty of hope for their individual members, many of whom, including workers, ex-peasant migrants and even peasants, can now look back on a couple of decades of better living and better prospects. What makes men choose revolution rather than inactivity or reform in the Third World is rarely the immediate or imminent breakdown of the economy or the social order. It is rather (leaving aside such questions as oppression by foreigners or other races) the sheer width of the gap between rich and poor, which is probably growing, and between developed and underdeveloped countries, combined with the demonstrated failure of reformist alternatives. The prospect of medium-term or long-term breakdown also plays a part. Incidentally, the background of change and expansion affects the local intelligentsia personally, in so far as their own individual career prospects are far better than ours were in my generation. The revolutionism of students in many Third World countries, e.g. in parts of Latin America, is remarkably short-lived for this reason. It hardly outlasts graduation.

However, if the Third World in important ways resembles the interwar world, the flourishing neo-capitalism of the West clearly does not. The revolutionism of the western New Left is the product not of capitalist crisis in any economic sense of that word, but of its opposite. In this sense it is comparable to the rebelliousness and revolutionism of the years just before the first world war with which, I have long thought, it has striking affinities. These similarities may extend even further than appears at first sight. For the rebelliousness of an apparently flourishing pre-1914 western world soon became the revolutionism of the crisis of that world. If, as seems likely, we have once again entered a period of general crisis for capitalism, the movements of the late 1960s and early 1970s may seem in retrospect another prelude, like those of 1907–14.

What lies behind the revival of revolutionism in the 1960s is *first*, technological and social transformation of unparalleled rapidity and depth, and *second*, the discovery that the solution by capitalism of the problem of material scarcity reveals, perhaps even creates, new problems (or in marxist terms 'contradictions') which are central to the system and possibly to all industrial society. It is not easy to separate the two aspects and most of the new revolutionaries fail to do so, but both are important. On the one hand we have been living through a phase of economic expansion, techno-scientific revolution and the restructuring of the economy which is without precedent, both in creating material wealth and destroying much of the basis and equilibrium of the social order. But though in the past twenty years certain long-range predictions of the mid-nineteenth century for the first time look as though they might be finally coming true – that capitalism would destroy the European peasantry, traditional religion and the old family structure[6] – we ought not to forget that the more modest social earthquakes of the past were, for those who lived through them, equally without precedent. They adjusted to the new situation, and in the past twenty years the enormous increase in

[6] The crisis of Roman Catholicism is in this respect more significant than that of Protestantism.

wealth, combined with various devices for social management and welfare which were either not available or not used in earlier periods, should have made such adjustment easier. This, at any rate, was the argument of the anti-ideological ideologists of the American 1950s.

On the other hand it has become increasingly clear that we are faced not simply with a problem of human beings adjusting to a particularly dramatic and rapid change within the framework of a functioning system – to something like the problem of mass immigration into the United States between the 1890s and the 1920s – but with central flaws in the system. I am not here concerned with what might be called the macro-economic or macro-political contradictions of the system, which are today being revealed – e.g. the shaky basis of the capitalist international economy or the widening gap between 'developed' and 'underdeveloped' world – nor even with the approaching dangers of an unrestricted technology which is on the verge of actually destroying the fabric of the habitable globe or of precipitating demographic cataclysm. The point to note about 'The Affluent Society' or 'The New Industrial State' (to use the terms of its most eminent liberal critic) is that until the end of the 1960s capitalism functioned splendidly as an economic mechanism; probably better than any alternative at that time. What seemed to 'go wrong' in some profound but not easily specifiable sense was the *society* based on capitalist abundance, and nowhere more obviously than in its chief stronghold, the United States. The uneasiness, the disorientation, the signs of desperation multiplied, to be followed and reinforced by that ominipresent ripple of violence, of more oriented riot and rebellion, of mass dropping-out – symptoms of a socially pathological state, which is what American observers think of when they compare the mood of their country to that of the Weimar Republic. Consequently also the fashionable critique of society ceased for a time to be economic and became sociological: its key terms were not poverty, exploitation, or even crisis, but 'alienation', 'bureaucratization', etc.

Consequently also the new revolutionism in western countries was confined almost entirely to intellectuals and other marginal middle-class strata (e.g. creative artists), or to the middle-class young who took the achievements of the affluent society for granted and concentrated, quite rightly, on its deficiencies. Leaving aside special minorities like the blacks, whose discontents were simpler, the characteristic revolutionary was a middle-class adolescent (usually a student), and he tended to be distinctly to the left of the labour movements, socialist or communist. Even when the two movements appeared to merge, as in France in May 1968 and in Italy in the 'hot autumn' of 1969, it was the students who had written off capitalism, the workers who, however militantly, were still working within it.

I have suggested that this phase of the late 1960s may be temporary, like the years before 1914. At the moment it looks as though the western world has not only entered a new phase of techno-scientific capitalism (sometimes misleadingly called 'post-industrial society'), with a new version of the basic contradictions of capitalism, but more specifically another lengthy period of economic crisis. The revolutionary movements are likely to take place not against a background of 'economic miracles' but against one of economic difficulties. It is too early to assess the amount and kind of political radicalization this may produce, though worth recalling that during the last analogous phase the radical right benefited more than the radical left.[7] So far the most dramatic symptoms of revolutionary agitation in the industrial countries are still those which took place at the height of the boom, i.e. in 1967–9. If one were to venture a prediction, it would merely be that the combination of *social* disintegration and *economic* breakdown is likely to be more explosive than anything that occurred between the wars in industrial countries, with the possible exception of Germany. But also, that social revolution of the traditional sort is by no means its only, or perhaps even its most likely, outcome.

There is, however, one major difference between the new revolutionism and that of my own generation between the wars. We had, perhaps mistakenly, hope and a concrete model of the alternative society: socialism. Today this faith in the great October revolution and the Soviet Union has largely disappeared – I make this as an observation of fact, not as a judgment – and nothing has replaced it. For though the new revolutionaries are looking for possible models and possible centres of loyalty, neither the small and localized revolutionary regimes – Cuba, North Vietnam, North Korea or

[7] A friend, asked by his students, what the political consequences of the great slump of 1929 had been, answered: 'First Hitler came to power. Then we lost the war in Spain. Finally we got the second world war and Hitler ruled most of Europe.'

whatever – nor even China, have provided an equivalent for what the Soviet Union was in my time.[8] What has taken the place of our perspective, is a combination of negative hatred of the existing society and Utopia. Similarly, that immensely powerful form of revolutionary movement, the disciplined mass party, has also lost much of its hold among the new revolutionaries, who appear to operate either in small sects or in unstructured libertarian groups closer to the anarchist than the marxist tradition. All this may be historically inevitable. But it is likely also to produce a much wider gap than in my youth, between revolutionary ferment and effective revolutionary action. I make these points without pleasure, and without the intention of diminishing the new revolutionaries. It is better to have a revolutionary movement than not to have one. This is the one we have got for the moment, and we have to do the best we can with it. The fact remains that it has a great deal to learn or re-learn.

Let me, finally, turn to the question of the role of intellectuals in revolutionary movements, in other words to the questions not why some of them as individuals became revolutionaries, but what their political orientation is likely to be as a stratum of society and what part their activity as such is likely to play. I need hardly say that the two kinds of questions are, or can be, entirely distinct. Marx and Engels were certainly intellectuals, but the number and proportion of German intellectuals who were social democrats was small and probably negligible. My generation of student communists were a small minority of, I would guess, not more than four to five hundred at its maximum out of fifty thousand university students just before the war; in Oxford and Cambridge even the broader socialist clubs were a minority, though not a negligible one. The fact that our tiny minority contained, at times, a remarkably high proportion of the brightest students is not of course insignificant, but does not change the fact that the great majority of west European students before 1939 were not on the left, let alone revolutionary, whereas probably the majority in such countries as Yugoslavia were.

Moreover, even when we can say that intellectuals as a stratum

8 It may be worth noting that this is the first phase of global revolutionary socialism since 1848 which has not so far established an effective international; for the internationals of the small left-wing sects are too restricted to fulfil this function.

are revolutionary (as is often, perhaps generally, the case for young ones in the Third World), we cannot automatically assimilate their attitude or political behaviour to that of other revolutionary forces. To take an obvious example, students played a leading part in the 1848 revolutions. What happened to all of these revolutionary liberals in the Bismarckian era ? Again, students (including secondary students) were extremely prominent in the Russian revolution of 1905, but, so far as one can tell, *not* in that of 1917. This is not inconsistent with the fact that the leadership of the bolsheviks consisted overwhelmingly of intellectuals, as did that of all other popular parties of opposition. To give a third, and perhaps quite local and transitory example. Students as a body in Britain today probably occupy political positions considerably to the left of workers as a body. But at this moment, when there is a greater militancy and readiness for industrial action among the workers than at any time since the General Strike, student mass political activity is at a lower ebb than probably at any time in the past three years. The two groups are evidently not moved in the same way, in the same direction, by the same forces and motives.

What can we say about intellectuals as a social group in industrial countries today ? *First,* that they are today such a social group, which can no longer be simply subsumed as a special variant of the middle classes. They are more numerous, since both the growth of scientific technology and the expansion of the tertiary sector of the economy (including administration and communications) require them in much larger numbers than before. They are technically proletarianized, inasmuch as the bulk of them are no longer 'free professions' or private entrepreneurs but salaried employees ; though this is also true of most of the rest of the middle classes. They are recognizable by specific attitudes, specific consumer demands, specific interests, to which businessmen appeal as such ; e.g. reading the *Guardian* rather than the *Daily Telegraph,* and being relatively impervious to the sales appeal of status symbols as against *Which*-type criteria. Politically, the bulk of this stratum (or at least certain types of occupations within it) is probably today left of centre in the western countries, though perhaps no more than that. In Britain the *Guardian-Observer* type of professional classes are on one side of the political divide, the *Telegraph*-type middle classes on the other. In France during May 1968, the front of the class struggle ran through the centre of the middle classes. In the general strike the research-and-development types, the laboratory and design departments and the communicators tended to come out with the workers, often militantly, whereas the administrators, executives, sales departments, etc. remained on the side of management.

It has been argued, therefore, that the intellectuals are today part of a 'new' working class and in a sense the modern equivalent of that skilled, self-confident, and above all technically indispensable labour aristocracy of 'intelligent artisans' which was so important in nineteenth-century Britain. It has been argued further, that being essentially salaried experts, their economic fortunes as individuals or as a stratum are not bound up with an economy of private enterprise, whose defects they are in any case well able to judge. Indeed, it has been held that since they are at least as intelligent and well educated as those who take decisions in business, and their work gives them at least as much of a general perspective on the policies of the enterprise and the economy, they are less likely to confine their activities to narrow questions of wages and conditions, more likely to envisage changes in management and policy.

Such arguments, put forward chiefly by French sociologists like Alain Touraine and Serge Mallet, have considerable force. However, they are not arguments for regarding the new 'labour aristocracy' any more than the old as a revolutionary force. They rather suggest that it is a very effective reformist force, which is revolutionary only in so far as we envisage a gradual, peaceful but fundamental transformation of society. But whether such a transformation is possible, or if it is, can be regarded as a revolution, is of course a crucial question. To this question the 'new working class' argument suggests what is in effect a neo-Fabian answer, dressed up in marxist terms, which will not be by any means universally acceptable on the left. In the short run, the best thing is to regard them, like their ancestors the labour aristocracy, as moderate reformists. Their professional interests may perhaps incline them slightly more towards a democratic socialism than towards capitalism, so long as such a socialism does not threaten their relatively favourable situation, and their heart may well often be farther to the left than their professional interests, for most of them are likely to have passed through a student phase. But their basic attitude to social change is, and perhaps must be, that a great deal more can be done within the existing system than revolutionary persons, including their children, imagine. And so far as they themselves are concerned, this is undoubtedly true.

Apart from marginal groups such as those middle-class equivalents of the old handloom weavers whose occupations are being made redundant by technological progress – old-fashioned creative artists, writers, etc. – the major group among intellectuals which appears to reject the *status quo* wholesale is that of the young. These consist largely of those being educated for intellectual jobs, though it is by no means clear what the relationship between their rebelliousness and the educational system is.

Young members of the middle strata have a fairly limited experience of society, though probably today a rather wider one than their parents. Most of this experience – and the younger they are the more of it comes to them in this way – is mediated by the experience of family, of school or college, and of peer groups of people from similar backgrounds. (The concept of a general 'youth culture' uniting an entire age group across social distinctions is either superficial or commercial or both. Similar costume, hair-styles, forms of entertainment and social customs do not imply similar political behaviour, as student militants seeking to mobilize young workers have often discovered. How far there is in fact a *single* form of 'youth culture' rather than a complex of such cultures, still remains an open question.) It does not follow that the criticisms of the middle-class young merely reflect a 'generation gap', old or new, a rebellion against their elders, or discontent, justified or not, with their educational institutions. It may reflect, as it often has in the past, a genuine critique of society which is to be taken seriously, however incoherently it may be formulated.

The most serious organized form of youth revolutionism is that of the students (which in a number of countries includes secondary school pupils). It is therefore important to assess the character and possibilities of this student revolutionism. Its political functions are, of course, twofold. It exists both as a movement in its own right, i.e. as one of a group of people selected on grounds of age and/or attendance at educational institutions, and as a recruiting ground for the activists and leaders of the adult political world. The first is at present the more obvious, but the second has been historically the more significant. The political significance of the Ecole Normale Superieure of the Rue d'Ulm at the end of the nineteenth century lies not in the socialist sympathies and Dreyfusard activities of its students at that time, but the subsequent career of *some* of those students, e.g. Jaurès, Léon Blum and Edouard Herriot.[9]

Two general observations can be usefully made about youth/student movements. The first is the platitudinous but nevertheless significant one that such movements are by their nature impermanent and discontinuous. Being young or a student is the prelude to being adult and earning one's living: it is not a career in itself. Unlike celibacy it is not even a programme which could be carried out with personal effort. It can be prolonged somewhat, though the present fashion for regarding anyone past the early twenties as on the verge of middle age tends to curtail it, but sooner or later it must end. Hence a political youth or student movement is not comparable to movements whose members can remain in them all their lives, like those of workers (most of whom go on being workers until they retire), or women and blacks, all of whom belong to their respective category from birth to death. Since there are always young people and students, there is always scope for movements based on them. Since the proportion of both in the population is today high, they are likely to be at least potentially mass movements. But their turnover of membership is *necessarily* 100 per cent within a few years, and the more exclusively such movements define themselves by impermanent criteria, i.e. by how different they are from adults, the harder it is for them to maintain continuity of activity, organization, or perhaps even programme and ideology, as distinct from the continuity of mood or the fact that each new generation faces similar problems. In the past this has rarely been significant for the revolutionary youth, chiefly because their movements have normally regarded themselves as those of adults, often actually refusing to be classified as youth movements, and always aiming at adult status.[10] The present fashion for separate 'youth cultures' may have made such movements potentially larger, but also more fluctuating.

Second, there is the specific historic phenomenon of the past fifteen years or so, which have seen a probably unprecedented expansion of higher education in all countries with three

[9] This is very much more obvious in many underdeveloped countries, where a few numerically quite small student bodies, in domestic or even foreign universities, have provided a very large number of political, including revolutionary, leaders for the adult political world.

[10] The youth sections of left-wing parties have, perhaps for this reason, generally formed relatively small appendages to the much larger adult parties.

consequences: an acute strain on the institutions receiving all these new entrants, unprepared for this influx; a multiplication of first-generation students, i.e. of people entering an entirely new way of life for which no family knowledge or tradition has prepared them; and also, speaking economically, a potential overproduction of intellectuals. For various reasons this virtually uncontrolled expansion is now being slowed down, and the pattern of higher education more or less radically restructured, not least as a result of the explosion of student unrest in the later 1960s. This is also likely to produce various forms of unrest and tension.

The existence of student unrest under these circumstances is not surprising, though the significant fact about it, at least in the industrialized capitalist countries and an important sector of the underdeveloped world, is that it has taken the form of left-wing social-revolutionary (typically anarchizing or marxisant) movements rather than of radical right-wing movements, such as were characteristic of the majority of political students in most of Europe between the wars.[11] It is symptomatic of the crisis of both bourgeois society and the traditional alternatives to it which used to appeal to the disoriented lower middle class (from whom so many of the new students come and to whom they belong) that the characteristic form of student activism should be some kind of ultra-leftism.

This does not, however, guarantee that such student unrest will either remain a serious and permanent, still less an effective revolutionary political force. If the bulk of the new mass of students were to be absorbed into an expanding economy and a stable society, it probably would not. To take an extreme example, the bulk of the sixty thousand or so Peruvian university students (before 1945 there were only some four thousand of them) are the first generation of their families, often provincial Indian or mestizo lower middle class or rich peasants, whose typical ultra-leftism is to some extent a way of coming to terms with a new and disorienting form of life. However, since most of them are still readily absorbed into middle-class jobs, it rarely outlasts graduation. As a current joke has it, they 'do their

[11] It is true that some slogans once characteristic of right-wing movements – such as nationalist ones – have been largely annexed by the marxist revolutionary left, but the hegemony of left-wing ideas in the 1960s student movements is nevertheless most striking.

compulsory revolutionary service' analogous to compulsory military service. It is too early to judge whether they will produce as large a body of adult political leaders as the small body of the students of the 1920s did for the APRA and communist parties, but it seems unlikely.[12]

On the other hand a large body of students either facing unemployment or a much less desirable employment than they have been led to expect from their degree (or other certificate) are likely to form a permanent discontented mass, readily supporting revolutionary movements (or those of the radical right) and providing both with activists. The declassed intellectual or petty bourgeois has formed the basis of such movements in several countries and at several periods. Governments are keenly aware of this prospect, especially in a period of economic difficulties or crises, but the most obvious solution, to cut down the number of students, is impracticable, partly because the political demand for the expansion of higher education is very powerful, partly because the huge student body could not always easily be absorbed into a stagnant economy. In the United States, for instance, cutting it down drastically might mean little more than transferring some hundreds of thousands, perhaps millions, from colleges to an already overstocked labour market. In a sense the system which maintains vast numbers of young people for a few more years outside employment is a modern middle-class equivalent of the Old Poor Law of the early nineteenth century: a concealed system of outdoor relief. Two solutions appear to commend themselves to many governments: to sidetrack the bulk of the 'surplus' students into various institutions in which they can kill time more or less profitably, reserving the serious business of training the cadres of the economy which actually require higher scientific, technical, vocational, etc. qualifications for separate establishments; and to isolate students from the rest of the possibly dissident population. In this latter task they are not impeded by the bulk of student political activists.

The future of the student movement as a revolutionary force therefore depends largely on the prospects of the capitalist economy. If it were to return to the expansion and prosperity of the 1950s and 1960s, it would probably turn out to be a temporary phenomenon, or perhaps its intermittent manifestations would sooner or later become

12 Out of the eight secretaries of the (Maoist) student federation of the main Peruvian university of San Marcos, since 1960, whose whereabouts could be established, not a single one continued to be active on the left in 1971.

an accepted part of the social scene, like the non-political forms of juvenile high spirits – boat race night, Guy Fawkes' day, rag days, panty-raids, *canulars*, etc. – in the era of bourgeois stability. If it were to enter a period of long-term difficulties, it might continue to be, at least occasionally, an explosive political force as the past few years have shown – from time to time intervene decisively, if momentarily, in national politics, as in May 1968. In either case, if the proportion of the age group which undergoes some form of higher education is likely to remain much greater than before the 1960s, students as a group will continue to be politically more significant and (especially where the voting age has been lowered to eighteen) more effective than in the past.

We cannot therefore take it for granted that intellectuals, young or old, will be a significant revolutionary force in the developed countries, though we can predict that they will be a significant political force, very probably more or less on the left. But even if they were to be revolutionary *en masse*, they would clearly not be decisive by themselves. Hence we may conclude this essay with a brief discussion of the relations between the movements of intellectuals and those of workers, peasants or other discontented strata.

In most countries the orthodoxy of the left assumes today that the two converge or even merge, formally or informally, in some sort of socialist labour movement. In many cases this is probably so. Both the British Labour Party, the United States Democratic Party (which is socially rather similar in composition) and many socialist and communist parties elsewhere are in effect alliances of workers and intellectuals, plus special discontented groups such as national or other minorities which do not happen to have developed their own separatist movements. This was not always so. Moreover, there are today signs of divergence, which should not be underestimated. On the one hand the ultra-left, largely composed of intellectuals, is often tempted to secede from the mass working-class parties of its countries which it blames for being too moderate or reformist. On the other, the anti-intellectualism of working-class movements, always latent and sometimes overt, has tended to become more intense. Recent studies of Labour Party local organization suggest that as the party branches have increasingly fallen into the hands of devoted militants from the professional strata, the rank-and-file working-class supporters and militants have drifted into political inactivity. Whether the one phenomenon is the cause or consequence of the other, both reinforce one another. Similarly, relations between students and workers are poor in most industrialized countries, and may be deteriorating.

We cannot therefore take it for granted that a radicalization of workers and students, supposing it were to occur, would automatically produce a single united left movement. It might produce parallel movements, poorly coordinated or even at loggerheads. For the truth is that the analogy between the intellectuals and professionals of today and the 'labour aristocracy' of the past is valid only up to a point. The old labour aristocrats were manual workers, the new ones are not. The gap between blue collar and white collar is wide, and probably growing wider. The old socialist and labour movements of the developed countries were built on the hegemony of the manual workers. Some of their leaders might be intellectuals, and they might attract large numbers of intellectuals, but on the whole the terms on which these joined were, that they subordinated themselves to the workers. These terms were realistic, because on the whole the intellectual and professional stratum was not socialist, or too small numerically to form a major part of the labour movement. Today it is large, economically important, active and effective. Indeed it forms the most rapidly growing sector of the trade union movement, at least in Britain. There is both more tension and, from the side of the workers, more resentment.

Where the two wings of the movement converge or merge, as in France in 1968 or perhaps in Italy in 1969, its power is immense. But it can no longer be taken for granted that their confluence is automatic, nor that it will occur spontaneously. Under what circumstances will it occur, if at all ? Can this be predicted ? Can it be brought about ? These are crucial questions, which can merely be raised here. What the role of intellectuals in the class struggle is to be depends largely on the answers. But if such a junction does not take place, the movement of the intellectuals may settle down as one or both of two things : as a powerful and effective reformist pressure group of the new professional strata, of which consumer agitations and environmentalist campaigns are good examples, and as a fluctuating radical youth and student movement, oscillating between brief brush fires and relapses into passivity by the majority, while a small activist minority indulges in frenzied ultra-left gestures. This is the pattern of the student movements since the middle 1960s.

On the other hand it is also unlikely that the workers will make a successful revolution without the intellectuals, still less against them. They may relapse into a narrow movement of those who work with their hands, militant and powerful within the limits of 'economism', but incapable of going much beyond the confines of rank-and-file activism. Or they may achieve what seems to be the highest point of 'spontaneous' proletarian movements, a sort of syndicalism which certainly envisages and seeks to build a new society, but is incapable of achieving its aims. It does not much matter that the isolated impotence of workers or other masses of the labouring poor is of a different kind from that of intellectuals, since the working people by themselves are capable of overthrowing a social order, whereas the intellectuals by themselves are not. If a human society worthy of the name is to be built, both need each other.

(1971)

INDEX

Abyssinian War, 37, 40 and n
Agrarian Reform and Peasant Revolution in Spain (Malefakis), 79n
Albania, 16
Alexandre, Philippe, 238
Algeria, 27, 118, 230; role of military in, 186; Casbah insurrection, 232
Algerian War, 30, 135, 163, 170–1, 172
Alicata, Mario (Italian communist), 38
alienation, 131–2, 141, 144, 158, 219, 249, 250
Alier, J. Martinez, 88n
Althusser, L., 112n, 114–15, 145–52
American Revolution, 202, 203–4
anarchism, anarcho-syndicalism, vii, 16, 37, 38, 47, 122; relations between bolsheviks and, 57–70; in Spain, 59, 65, 68–9, 71–81, 153, 156, 159, 233; today's revival of interest in, 82–7; contribution to socialist theory, 87–91 and to revolutionary strategy and tactics, 89–91; sexual morality and, 218
Angola, 169
Aragon (Spain), 75, 76, 77, 166
Aragon, Louis, 28, 29, 30
d'Aragona, Ludovico, 66
Arendt, Hannah, 201–8
Argentina, 65n, 182, 185, 188
'aristocracy of labour', 121–9, 259, 265
armed forces, army (the military), in Spain, 73, 74–5, 178, 181; guerrilla warfare and, 163–76; relations between civilian government and, 177–91; coups d'état, 192–7; French, 237
Asiatic mode of production, Marx's, 116–17, 149
Asturias, miners' strike in, 84
Atatürk, Kemal, 189
Auschwitz concentration camp, 6
Austria, 19, 61, 147, 223, 250; *see also* Vienna
Austrian Communist Party, 22, 53
Automotive-Electronic-Chemical complex, 243
Avanguardia group, 63

Bakunin, Mikhail, Bakuninists, 46, 57, 58, 75, 78, 79, 85, 88, 89, 100
Balibar, Etienne, 145n, 149
Barbato, Nicola, 37
Barcelona, 73, 74, 84; urban insurrection and, 221, 223 and n, 233
Barontini, Ilio, 40n
Bastille, storming of, 223
Batista, Fulgencio, 170, 193
Bauer, Otto, 132
Belgium, 71, 184
Bell, Daniel, 132, 136
Belloc, Hilaire, 29
'Belmonte de los Caballeros' (Spain), 75
Bernstein, Eduard, Bernsteinian revisionism, 98, 107, 122–3, 130–1, 132, 133
'Birmingham Alliances', 123, 127
Bismarck, Count Otto von, 60

Blanqui, Louis-Auguste, Blanquism, 18, 21, 86
Bloc National (France), 27
Bloch, Ernst, 132, 136–41
Blum, Léon, 21, 261
Boehme, Jacob, 140
Bogota, 232
Boldrini, Arrigo, 41n
Bolivia, 186
bolsheviks, bolshevism, 3, 4, 6, 13, 17, 21, 47, 111, 143, 144, 155, 156, 160, 258; relations between anarchists and, 57–70; *see also* Russian Revolution, Soviet Union
Bolte, Friedrich, 100
Bonapartism, 177, 178, 193
Bordiga, Amedeo, Bordighism, 63, 64
Borodin, Mikhail, 9
Boulanger crisis, 180
Brandler, Heinrich (German communist), 50
Brazil, 65n, 75, 117, 188, 189, 190, 193
Brazilian Communist Party, 64, 65n
Brecht, Bertolt, 28, 151, 155
Brenan, Gerald, 84
Britain, 19, 30, 117, 163, 187, 248; students and intellectuals in, 113, 252, 257, 258; and anarchists, 60; Spanish Civil War and, 72; Marx's attitude to and influence on labour movement in, 96–108; marxist dialogue in, 110, 113, 116, 119, 120; labour aristocracy in, 121–9; Malayan guerrillas defeated by, 166, 167; Irish revolutionary agitation against, 168–9, 171, 180; Israel evacuated by, 171; role of military in, 179, 180, 184; *see also* London
British Communist Party, 22, 33, 48, 105; loyalty to Soviet Union of, 5–6, 7, 49; problems facing historian, 7–10; social composition of, 11–12; and revolutionary element in, 13–15; YCL leaders, 50; post-1956 resignation of marxist intellectuals from, 113
British Independent Labour Party (ILP), 63, 105
The British Labour Movement in 1912 (Lenin), 122
British Labour Party, 7, 8, 12, 14, 104; parliamentary left-wing, 105; non-active role of, 196; relations between intellectuals and workers in, 264–5
British Social Democrats, 105, 106
British Socialist Labour Party (SLP), 105, 106
British Socialist Party, 13
Bruno, Giordano, 138
Bukharin Nikolay, 69, 132
Bulgaria, 16, 133
Bunday, McGeorge, 175
bureaucracy, 60, 61, 118, 195–6
Burma, guerrillas in, 168, 171, 173
Burns, John, 105

'Cahiers du Bolchevisme', 64
Cambodia, 173
Campbell, J. R. (British communist), 49
Canovas del Castillo, Antonio, 71
Capital (Marx), 95, 98, 104, 144, 147, 148, 149, 158
Capitalism, Socialism and Democracy (Schumpeter), 250–1
Caracas, 232
Carlists, 74
capitalism, 3, 22, 36, 58, 131; subordinate position of Western labour movement within, 16–17, 54; in Spain, 71, 72, 73, 74, 76; stability of, 86, 95–6; British working class and, 96, 97–9, 103–8 *passim*; marxist case against, 110–11; imperialist phase of, 118; transition from feudalism to, 119; 'aristocracy of labour' under, 121–9; 'law of uneven development' within, 123; revisionist view of, 131–2; structure of, 142–52; Korsch's concentration on problem of, 155; interwar crisis of, 250–2, 253; and Western techno-scientific, 253, 254–6
'Carnet B' (France), 61
Carr, Raymond, 72, 73, 74, 75, 78

Castro, Fidel, Castroites, 145, 170, 191, 234
Catalonia, 73, 76, 77, 83; *see also* Spain
Caute, David, 25–30 *passim*
central European marxist movement, 143–5, 154, 155, 159
Ceylon, 4
CGT, *see* General Confederation of Labour
Chartism, 14, 96–7, 101, 106, 108, 225, 227
Chiang Kai-shek, 170
China, 59
Chinese Communist Party, 79, 117
Chinese Peoples Republic, 134, 257; revolution, 17n; marxism in, 116, 117, 133, 143; manpower of, 163; Vietnam war and, 164, 174; and guerrilla warfare, 167, 169, 170; US threat of nuclear war against, 174–5; subordinate role of army in, 179
Chomsky, Noam, 77
CIA, 4, 192
Cité Universitaire (Paris), 26
cities *see* urban insurrection
civilian government, the military *v.*, 177–91
CNT (Spanish *Confederación Nacional del Trabajo*), 66, 68, 75, 76, 80
Cobban, A. B., 180
Cohn-Bendit, Daniel, 235–6, 242
Colombia, 79, 117
Cominform, 32
Comintern (Third Communist International), vii, 4, 5, 6–7, 9, 14, 17, 21, 44, 51n, 52, 115, 124; Italian Communist Party and, 32, 33, 35–6, 38, 39; Soviet domination of, 23, 35, 48; 'Third Period' of, 33; German Communist Party and, 46, 49–50; anarchists and, 58, 63–4, 66–7, 68–9; Spanish policy, 76–7
The Coming Struggle for Power (Strachey), 252
communism, communists, vii; foreign parties subordination to USSR, 3–5; nationalism *v.* internationalism, 5–7; in Britain, 7–15, 113; in France, 16–24; intellectuals and, 25–30; in Italy, 31–42; and Germany, 43–54; bolshevist-anarchist relations, 57–70; post-Stalin crisis of, 84; non-communist marxists, 113–14, 115; revitalization of theory, 115–16; centralized organization, 117; *see also* individual communist parties
Communism and the French Intellectual (Caute), 25–30
Communist World Congresses, Fourth, 10; Sixth, 65n
Communist Internationals, *see* Comintern (Third); First International; Second International
Communist Manifesto, 146
Comte, Auguste, 75
Congress for Cultural Freedom, 131
Congress of Livorno (1921), 32
Congress of Tours, 18
conventional war, 163, 173–4; *see also* guerrilla war; nuclear war
Cook, A. J., 14
Cooper, Thomas, 97
Coser, Prof., 135
Costa Rica, 184n
councils (soviets), 205–7
Coup d'Etat (Luttwack), 192–7
coups d'état, vii, 187–8, 192–7
CPSU, *see* Soviet Communist Party
CPUSA, *see* US Communist Party
Crisis of Britain (Dutt), 117n
Cuba, 3, 193, 218, 256; anarchists in, 65 and n; independence, 73; role of Communist Party in, 118; missile crisis, 174
cultural revolution, in China, 179; in France and USA, 243–4
Curiel, Eugenio, 40
Czechoslovakia, 85, 116

Darwin, Charles, Darwinism, 140, 144
Davitt, Michael, 168
DDR, *see* East Germany
Deborin, A. M., 132
Debray, Régis, 86
Descartes, René, 140

Detroit, 1967 riots in, 231
Dienbienphu, battle of, 165, 170
Differences in the European Labour Movement (Lenin), 122
Dimitrov, George, 33
Djilas, Milovan, 133
Draft Theses on the Agrarian Question (Lenin), 124, 128
Dreyfus, Dreyfusards, 30, 180, 260–1
Duclos, Jacques, 62
Dutch Communist Party, 62
Durruti, Buenaventura, 76
Dutt, R. Palme, 116n, 117n
Duvignaud, J., 135

East Germany (German Democratic Republic), 43, 51n, 52n, 53, 85, 116, 137
Easter Rising (Dublin), 233
Ecole Normale Supérieure (France), 26, 145, 260–1
Edinburgh, 224
Egypt, 116, 172, 189, 190
Eichmann, Adolf, 213
1844 Manuscripts (Marx), 149, 150
Eighteenth Brumaire of Louis Bonaparte (Marx), 235
Einstein, Albert, 112
Eisenhower, Gen. Dwight, 179
Eisler, Gerhart, 51n
End of Ideology (Bell), 136
English Debates on a Liberal Workers' Policy (Lenin), 122
Engels, Friedrich, 46, 97, 98, 99, 100, 102, 108, 112, 140, 144, 156, 218, 226, 257; attitude to anarchism, 57–8; 'aristocracy of labour' concept, 121, 122
Establet, Roger, 145n
Evergreen Review, 216
Fabians, Fabian socialism, 21, 98, 103–4, 107, 122–3, 131, 133, 154
Fanon, Frantz, 214
fascism, 23, 31, 33–4, 36–42, 61, 85, 86, 110, 156, 196
Fenians, 100
Ferrer, Francisco, 78
Finnish Communist Party, 31, 53
First International, 58, 101
first world war, 18–19, 107, 111, 124, 247, 250
Fischer, Ruth, 48, 50
FLN (Algerian National Liberation Front), 30, 172
Fourier, Charles, 89
France, 135, 145, 169, 187, 252; intellectuals and students in, 25–30, 144, 260–1; Algerian war, 30, 135, 163, 170–1, 172, 184; anarchists in, 59, 61–2, 63, 64, 67–8, 78, 82; and Spanish Civil War, 72; marxist dialogue in, 110, 114–15, 116; Althusser's new approach to marxism, 145–52; Indo-Chinese War, 163, 165, 170, 171; military-civilian relations in, 177, 179, 180, 181, 182, 184; *see also* French Revolutions; Paris
Franco, Francisco, 41, 75, 194
Frankfurt group, 132
Frederick William I, King of Prussia, 168
Free University (West Berlin), 230
freedom, Hannah Arendt's concept of, 203–4
French Communist Party (PCF), communists, 9, 16–30, 31, 116, 146, 150; Comintern supported by, 5–6; as mass workers' party, 17–18, 54; evolution of labour movement, 18–20; bolshevization of, 20–1, 51–2, 61; and problem of non-revolutionary environment, 21–2; intellectuals and, 25–30; leadership, 50 and n; non-revolutionary political acts by, 52; ideological trends within, 64; failure to act in May 1968 uprising, 237–41
French Radical Party, 21
French Revolution (1789), 80, 100, 177, 179, 201–2, 203, 206, 223, 225, 249
French Revolution (1848), 80, 226, 236, 258
French Socialist Party, 19, 21
Freud, Sigmund, 104, 139, 140, 148
Friedman, Prof. Milton, 88

Fruehschriften (Landshut and Mayer), 144

Galbraith, John Kenneth, 107, 255
Gallacher, William, 14
Galli, Giorgio, 134
Garaudy, Roger, 29, 116, 145, 146, 150
Garibaldi Brigades, 34–5
Gaulle, Gen. Charles de, Gaullism, 179, 180, 181; May 1968 uprising and, 234–41 *passim*
Geist der Utopie (Bloch), 137
General Confederation of Labour (French CGT), 19, 90, 239
General Soviet of the New Model Army, 206
General Strike (Britain, 1926), 14, 106, 258-9
General Theory (Keynes), 130
Gerlach, Erich, 153, 157
German Communist Party (KPD), 7, 9, 19, 31, 41, 42, 43–54, 252; founding and early composition of, 44–5; bolshevization of, 46–9; and leadership, 49–51; inability to develop political alternatives, 51–2, 53–4; suppressed by Nazis, 52, 53; and post-1945 failure to revive, 52–3; creation of East Germany and, 53; Korsch expelled from, 156
German Democratic Republic, *see* East Germany
German Federal Republic, *see* West Germany
German Independent Socialists, 44, 45, 50
German Social Democratic Party (SPD), 49, 51, 52 and n, 53, 130–1, 154
Germany, 6, 22, 25, 38, 39, 41, 60, 63, 72, 126, 163; Weimar Republic, 43, 47, 50, 51n, 52 and n, 53, 54, 179, 183; civilian-military relations in, 178, 179, 180, 181, 182, 183; inter-war intellectuals in, 250-2, 256, 257
Geschichte und Klassenbewusstsein (Lukács), 153
Ghana, 118
Giap, vo Nguyen, 165
Giuliano (Sicilian bandit), 37
Giustizia e Liberta, 34 and n, 37, 39, 40
Godelier, Maurice, 149
Goethe, Johann Wolfgang von, 140
Goldmann, Lucien, 135
Goldwater, Barry, 88, 168
Gomulka, Wladislaw, 29, 134
gradualism, *see* revisionism
Gramsci, Antonio, 4, 36, 143, 144, 147, 150
Great Depression, Slump (1929–33), 16, 64–5, 70, 130, 251, 252, 256
Great Soviet Encyclopedia, 26
Greece, 16, 188
Griffith, W., 131
Groot, Paul De (Dutch communist), 262
Grundisse (Marx), 151
Guatemala, 189
guerrillas, guerrilla war, 37, 79, 87, 246; dynamics of, 163–76; *see also* urban insurrection
Guesdism, 18
Guevara, 'Che', 86, 87, 165, 166, 216

Harry Quelch (Lenin), 124
Hegel, Friedrich, Hegelian marxists, 112, 131–2, 138, 140, 143, 144, 145, 146, 149, 150, 154, 155, 156
Hell's Angels, 212–13
Henderson, Arthur, 19
Herder, Johann, 140
Herriot, Edouard, 261
High Tide of Political Messianism (Talmon), 136
Hill, Christopher, 113
Himmler, Heinrich, 213
historical development, determinism, marxist theory of, 149–50, 155, 159
history, of communist movements, 3–10, 115–16; Hannah Arendt's approach to, 204–7
History of Anarchism (Yaroslavsky), 68–9
History of the Communist Party of Great Britain (Klugmann), 8n
Hitler, Adolf, 33, 52, 54, 84, 113, 153, 178, 180, 252, 256n

Ho-Chin-Minh, 191
Hooch, Pieter de, 139
hope, Bloch's principle of, 136–41
Hungary, 9, 116, 131
Husserl, Edmund, 146

Iberian States, 178, 184; *see also* Spain
ILP, *see* British Independent Labour Party
Imaz, José Luis, 185n
imperialism, 5, 110; labour aristocracy and, 124–8; *see also* neo-colonialism
Imperialism (Lenin), 121, 124, 125
Imperialism and the Split (Lenin), 124–5, 126, 127, 128
In England, the Pitiful Results of Opportunism (Lenin), 122
India, 110, 134, 171; Bengal, 252, 253
Indo-China, 27, 163, 165, 170, 171; *see also* Vietnam
Industrial Democracy (Webb), 122–3
Ingrao, Pietro (Italian communist), 38
Inprecorr, 9
insurrection, vii, 80; cities and, 169, 220–33; intellectuals' commitment to, 245–6; *see also* May 1968 uprising
intellectuals and artists, 26, 39, 78, 113; French, 25–30, 144, 234–6; anarchist, 59, 82–3, 84, 87; commitment to revolution of, 245–50; inter-war, 250–2, 256, 257; Third World, 253–4; new Western revolutionism, 254–7; group role in revolutionary movements, 257–60; and students, 260–4; relations with workers and peasants, 264–6
International Brigades (Spanish Civil War), 34, 35
internationalism, *see* Comintern
Introduction to the Critique of Political Economy (Marx), 149
Ireland, Marx's view of, 101; revolutionary agitation in, 168–9, 180; and Dublin Easter Rising, 232–3
Islamic States, 184
Israel, 163, 171; *see also* Jews
Italian Communist Party (PCI), 4, 9, 17, 26, 28, 30, 31–42, 48, 54, 66, 196; 'promotion' of, 31–3; Comintern policy towards, 33, 35–6, 38; anti-Fascist activities, 33–4, 36–8; and Spanish Civil War, 34–5, 38–9; support by youth for, 38, 50; and second world war, 40–1; marxist dialogue in, 115, 118
Italian Socialist Party, 34, 38, 40
Italy, anarchists in, 59, 61, 63, 66, 67, 78, 82; and Spanish Civil War, 72; localism in, 75; and guerrilla action, 165, 169; role of military, 182; 1969 'hot autumn' in, 256, 265; *see also* fascism

Jacobins, 18, 73
Japan, 59, 116, 134, 163, 177, 182, 184, 214
Jaurès, Jean, jauresism, 64, 261
Jews, 250–2
Jogiches, Leo, 44
Johnson, Lyndon B., 171–2
Joyce, James, 116
Jung, Carl Gustav, 139

Kafka, Franz, 116
Kanapa, Jean (French communist), 28
Kant, Immanuel, 132
Karl Marx (Korsch), 153, 158
Kautsky, Karl, Kautskyism, 86, 113, 143, 144, 154, 155, 156
Kendall, Walter, 12, 13–15
Kenya, defeat of guerrillas in, 166, 171
Kepler, Johannes, 140
Kerensky, A. F., 66
Keynes, J. M., 104, 130, 252
Khrushchev, Nikita, 3, 29, 174
Kiernan, V. G., 74
Kinsey, 141
Klugmann, James, 8–10
Kolakovski, L., 132
Korean War, 175
Korsch, Karl, 153–60
KPD, *see* German Communist Party
Krause, Karl, 75
Kriegel, Annie, 17–24 *passim*, 61
Kronstadt rising, 67
Kropotkin, P. A., 83, 88

Kurdish guerrillas, 169
Kuusinen, Otto, *Fundamentals of Marxism-Leninism* by, 117n
Ky, President (of S. Vietnam), 191

Labedz, Leopold, 131n, 134
Labriola, Antoine, 147
Landshut, R. and Mayer, J. P., 144
Lange, Oscar, 116
Langkau, Goetz, 153
Latin America, 133, 248n, 254; anarchists in, 59, 64–5 and n, 82; and guerrilla movements, 87, 169; military politics in, 178, 184–91 *passim*, urban insurrection in, 221
Lawrence, D. H., 139
Lefebvre, Henri, 132, 143, 145
'legal Marxists', 131, 132
Lenin, V. I., vii, 4, 5, 7, 21, 22, 25, 44, 46, 48, 51, 66, 67, 86, 106, 112, 113, 115, 118, 143, 147; attitude to anarchism, 57–8; aristocracy of labour concept, 121–9; Korsch's criticism of, 155–6; his formula for Russian development, 205; and attitude to violence, 214n
leninism, 18, 57, 58, 64, 131, 133, 134, 143, 155–6
Levi, Paul (German communist), 50
Lévi-Strauss, Claude, 149
Lewin, Kurt, 158
litertarian communism, *see* anarchism
Lichtheim, George, 143
Lidice, Nazi razing of, 172
Liebknecht, Karl, 44, 50
Lima, Turcios, 189n
Lire le Capital (Althusser *et al.*), 145, 147, 149, 151
Lloyd George, David, 'Lloyd Georgism', 127, 202
Locke, John, 140
London, urban insurrection and, 222, 224, 225, 227–9
London Congress (of Second International, 1896), 58
Long March (Mao's), 167, 169
Longo, Luigi, 34, 35, 36, 50
Louis-Philippe, King, 236
Lozovsky, A., 68
Lukács, George, 132, 134, 143, 153, 154
Lumumba, Patrice, 191
Lussu, E., 34n
Luttwack, Edward, 192–7
Luxemburg, Rosa, Luxemburgism, 44, 45, 50, 51, 63, 64, 67, 132, 134, 143, 144, 155
Lysenko, T. D., 112

MacArthur, Gen. Douglas, 180
Macherey, Pierre, 145n
MacMahon, Marshall, 179
Madrid, 77, 78
Makhnovshchina (Ukrainian), 83
Malatesta, Errico, 66
Malaya, defeat of guerrillas in, 166, 167, 168
Malefakis, E., 79, 80
Mallet, Serge, 135, 259
Malvy, L. J. (French Minister of Interior), 61
Mann, Tom, 105, 106
Mao Tse-tung, 165, 167, 193, 234
Manuilsky, D., 2, 68n
Maoism, Maoists, 37, 87, 90, 145, 219, 263n
March on Rome (Mussolini's), 33
Marx, Karl, vii, 25, 46, 75, 109, 112, 114, 115, 116, 118, 119, 128, 132, 138, 141, 143, 144, 154, 155, 156, 196, 205, 235, 257; attitude to anarchism, 57–8; anniversary of death of, 95–6; British Labour movement and, 96–108; 'aristocracy of labour' and, 121, 122; stalinist view of, 145, 146; and Althusser analysis, 146–52; political economy as backbone of his theory, 158; his definition of revolutionary proletariat, 246–7
Marx et Engels contre l'anarchisme, 68
Marxism and Revisionism (Lenin), 122
Marxismus und Philosophie (Korsch), 153, 158
marxists, marxism, vii, 4, 16, 18, 21, 89; intellectuals, 25, 109, 113; anarchists *v.*, 57–70, 83; British labour

marxists—*continued*
movement and, 96–108; dialogue on, 109–20; Lenin and the 'aristocracy of labour', 121–9; revisionism, 130–5; the principle of hope, 136–41; post-Stalin rethinking, 142–3; central European left, 143–5, 154, 155, 159; Althusser's approach, 145–52; and Karl Korsch, 153–60; sexual morality and, 218
Marxist-Syndicalists, *see* Avanguardia group
Masaryk, T. G., 133
Maslow, A. (German communist), 48, 50
Maspero, François, 145
Mass Psychology of Fascism (Reich), 218
Materialism and Empiriocriticism (Lenin), 155
Mau Mau (Kenya), 171
Maximalists (Italy), 38, 76
May 1968 uprising (Paris), 87, 90, 91, 219, 232, 233, 234–44, 258, 264, 265
Mazzini, Giuseppe, 37
Mehring, Franz (German communist), 143
mensheviks, 59, 66, 111
Metropolitan Radical Federation, 227–8
Mexico, 65n, 75, 80, 184n, 186 and n
Meyer, Ernst (German communist), 50
Mikoyan, Anastas, 29
the military, *see* armed forces
Mobutu, Joseph, 191
Mommsen, Theodor, 201
Monatte, Pierre, 64, 68n
Le Monde, 150, 235
Monmousseau, Gaston (French communist), 62
monopolies, monopoly capitalism, Lenin's theory of, 122, 125, 127
Moors murder case, 213
Morocco, 27
Le mouvement de mai ou le communisme utopique (Touraine), 242n
Musolino (Calabrian brigand), 210
Mussolini, Benito, 33, 35, 40, 41, 42

Nanterre university (Paris), 221, 242
Naples, insurrection in, 225, 232
Napoleon Bonaparte, 177, 178, 180, 193
Napoleon III, 180
Napoleonic wars, 165
Nasser, Gen. Gamal Abdel, Nasserism, 185, 188, 189
national accounting, marxist technique of, 113
Nationalism Socialism, *see* Nazis
National Union of Students (Britain), 196
nationalism, 5–6, 18, 19, 22, 39–40, 118, 165–6
NATO, 163
Naxalites (India), 246
Nazism, Nazis, 6, 16, 36, 38, 41, 52, 53 and n, 172, 179, 180, 212, 213, 251
Netherlands, 59
neo-colonialism (neo-imperialism), 110, 111, 253; *see also* imperialism
neo-capitalism, 253, 254; *see also* capitalism
Nettl, J. P., 144
New Left, 90, 136, 218, 219, 254
New Delhi, 224
New York City, urban insurrection and, 223
Newton, Isaac, 140
Newton, Kenneth, 11–12
Nietzsche, Friedrich, 86, 148
nonconformist protestantism, 103
North Korea, 256
North Vietnam, 3, 73, 164, 173, 174–5
nuclear weapons, war, 168, 172, 173, 174–6, 253

O'Brien, Bronterre, O'Brienism, 100–1, 103
October Revolution, *see* Russian Revolution
On Revolution (Arendt), 201–8
opportunism, 59, 122, 125, 126, 127, 145
Oradour, Nazi razing of, 172
Origins of French Communism (Kriegel), 17

Ottoman Empire, 177
Owenism, 103

pacifism, 19, 60
Palermo, 221
Paracelsus, 140
Paraguay, 65n
Paris, Commune, 78, 80, 205, 226, 242; May 1968 uprising, 87, 90, 91, 219, 232, 233, 234–44, 258, 265; urban insurrection and, 169, 221, 222–3, 224, 226, 230, 232, 233; *see also* France, French Communist Party, French Revolutions
Parnell, Charles Stewart, 168
Pavlov, Ivan, 112
PCF, *see* French Communist Party
PCI, *see* Italian Communist Party
Pentagon, 165
Peru, 79, 110, 164, 189, 190, 246, 262–3 and n
Pestaña, Angel, 67
Pétain, Marshall, 180
Petrovsky-Bennet, D., 9
phenomenologists, 144
Philippines, 172, 211
Piana degli Albanesi, 37
Pigliaru, A., 211n
Plekhanov, G. V., 113, 132, 147
Po Prostu circle (Poland), 134
Poland, 133, 134, 169, 188, 252
political economy, 147, 158
Pollitt, Harry, 49
popular fronts, 23, 28, 65; failure in May 1968 uprising of, 237–41
Pour Marx (Althusser), 112n, 145, 146, 150, 151
Poverty of Philosophy (Marx), 146
Prague, 224
Primo de Rivera, Gen., 75
Das Prinzip Hoffnung (Bloch), 136–41
professionals, role in revolutionary and labour movements, 242–3, 258–9, 264–5
pronunciamentos, 74; *see also coups d'état*
Proudhon, P-J., Proudhonism, 18, 21, 57, 58, 68n
Prussia, 178, 185
psychoanalysis, psychology, 139, 144, 148, 158
public order, urban insurrection and, 225–6
public transport, urban insurrection and, 221, 230

Radek, Karl, 46
Radicals (in Britain), 11–15, 225, 227–8
Rancière, Jacques, 145n
Red Army, 53
Red International of Labour Unions, 64
reformism, 4, 21, 58–9, 60, 80, 96, 107, 128, 259–60; *see also* revisionism; social-democrats
Reich, Wilhelm, 218
Remmele, Hermann (German communist), 50n
revisionism, 98, 107, 122–3, 130–5, 143, 144, 158–9, 160
Revisionism (Congress of Cultural Freedom symposium), 131, 134–5
The Revolution of 1854 in Spanish History (Kiernan), 74n
The Revolutionary Movement in Britain (Kendall), 13n
Rigault, Raoul, 233
Robespierre, Maximilien de, 21
Rochet, Waldeck, 145
Roman Catholic Church, 26, 27, 29, 254n
Rosicrucianism, 141
Rosmer, A., 64, 68n
Rostow, W. W., 107
Rostovzeff, M., 201
Royal Air Force, 212n
Russia, 177, 246n, 249
Russian Revolution (1905), 258
Russian Revolution (October 1917), 3–4, 17, 18, 19, 22, 45, 57, 64, 66–7, 69, 79, 84, 95, 101, 107, 117, 118, 143, 154, 201, 203, 219, 233, 250, 251–2, 256, 258
Russian Social Democratic Labour Party, 111
Rust, William (British communist), 50

St Petersburg (Petrograd), 224, 233

San Domingo, 232
Sardinia, 211
Sartre, Jean-Paul, 27, 144, 145, 150, 235–6
Schelling, Friedrich, 137, 140
Schönberg, Arnold, 139
Schulze-Gaevernitz, G. v., 121
Schumpeter, Josef, 250–1
SDF, *see* British Social Democrats
Seale and McConville, 235
Secchia, P. (Italian communist), 50
Second International (1889–1914), 3, 17, 58, 63, 124–5, 143, 154; Stuttgart Conference of, 127–8
second world war, 5–6, 9, 40, 256n
SED (German *Sozialistische Einheibpartei Deutschlands*), 43
La Semaine Sainte (Aragon), 30
Semard, Pierre (French communist), 50n
The Session of the International Socialist Bureau (Lenin), 124
Seville, 222
sex, revolution and, 216–19
Shaw, George Bernard, 'Impossibilities of Anarchism' by, 88
Shelley, Percy Bysshe, 82
Short History of the CPSU (Stalin), 68, 112, 132, 142
Sismondi, Jean Charles Simonde de, 128
SLP, *see* British Socialist Labour Party
Smith, Adam, 147
Snowden, Philip, 104
social-chauvinism, 125
social democracy, social democrats, 4, 5, 17, 18, 22–3, 25, 33, 44, 45, 58, 60–1, 64, 66, 67, 68, 86, 106, 107, 111, 119, 120, 123, 133, 144
social organization, sexual permissiveness and, 216–19
socialist realism, 112, 116
The Sociology of British Communism (Newton), 11–12
Sorel, Georges, 86
Sources françaises du socialisme (Garaudy), 146
South Africa, 217
South Vietnam, 163, 167, 170, 171, 173, 174
South Wales Miners' Federation, 14
Soviet Communist Party (CPSU), 3, 4, 22n, 23, 48, 111, 115, 117; Twentieth Congress, 110
Soviet Union, 13, 16, 22, 35, 53, 115, 142, 144, 163, 164, 251; relations with China, 3, 117; foreign communists' loyalty to, 3–7; purges, 27, 35, 53n; German KPD and, 46–50; anarchists in, 59, 66–7; Spanish Civil War, 72; post-Stalin crisis of communism, 84–5; marxist dialogue in, 111, 112, 113, 116, 118–19; economic theory of, 116; Korsch's non-commitment to, 155, 156; Vietnam War and, 164; and Cuban missile crisis, 174; role of army in, 178–9; workers' councils, 205–7; inter-war revolutionaries' faith in, 256–7; *see also* Russian Revolution
soviets, *see* councils
Spain, 27, 41; anarchism in, 59, 65, 68–9, 71–81, 82, 83–4, 88n, 153, 156, 159; guerrilla activity in, 165, 166, 173; and role of army, 178, 181
Spain 1808–1939 (Carr), 72
Spanish Civil War, 31, 34–5, 38–9, 65, 68, 70, 72–3, 76, 77–8, 81, 82, 83–4, 100, 181, 194, 233, 241, 256n
Spanish Communist Party, 31
Spartacus League, 45, 49, 50, 51
SPD, *see* German Social Democratic Party
Spinoza, Baruch, 140
spontaneity, spontaneous revolutionism, 58, 60, 64, 78–9, 87, 89–90, 123, 129, 236
Spriano, Paolo, 9, 32–3, 35, 40n, 50n
Stalin, Josef, 3, 4, 5, 33n, 48, 68, 69, 78n, 84, 112, 114, 115, 119, 149
stalinism, stalinization, 22n, 23, 27, 29, 48, 53n, 85, 111, 115, 132, 134, 142, 144–5, 146, 153, 218
Steffens, Lincoln, 252
Stil, André, 28
Stirner, Max, 86

Storia del Partito Communista Italiano (Spriano), 9n, 32–3, 35, 50n
Strachey, John, 117n, 252
strikes, 14, 18, 20, 40, 84, 87, 106, 258–9; *see also* May 1968 uprising
structuralism, 148, 149
students, communist membership, 26; appeal of anarchism to, 84, 87, 90; May 1968 uprising, 87, 90, 91, 219, 232, 233, 234–44, 256; urban insurrection and, 221, 230–1; revolutionism of, 260–4; *see also* intellectuals
Switzerland, 117
syndicalism, 4, 17, 19, 20, 21, 50, 58–9, 60, 61, 107, 143, 154, 159; *see also* anarchism; trade unionism
Syria, 27

Talmon, Prof. Jacob, 136
Thaelmann, Ernst (German communist), 50 and n, 51n, 52
Thalheimer, August (German communist), 50
Théorie (ed. Althusser), 145
Thieu, Pres. (of South Vietnam), 191
Third World, 222; military politics in, 184–91; intellectual revolutionaries in, 253–4, 258
Thomas Münzer als Theologe der Revolution (Bloch), 137
Thorez, Maurice, 52
Three Internationals (Dutt), 116n
Tito, Josip Broz, 5, 29, 132, 167
Togliatti, Palmiro, 4, 29, 33, 34, 35, 48, 50, 118
Touraine, Alain, 236, 240, 241, 242–4, 259
town planning, urban insurrection and, 223, 226, 227–9
trade unionism, unions, 207; in Britain, 14, 96, 102, 106, 108, 121–9; German, 49; anarchists in, 62–3, 65; in Spain, 74, 76; *see also* syndicalism
Treint, Albert (French communist), 63
Trilisser-Moskvin, M. A., 35
Trotsky, Leon, 36, 46, 48, 112, 132, 251
Trotskyism, 4, 63, 64, 67, 68n, 87, 90, 130, 134, 144, 218, 219
Truman, Harry S., 180
TUC (Britain), 7, 196
Tunisia, 172
Turkey, 189, 190; *see also* Ottoman Empire

UGT (Spanish *Union General del Trabajadores*), 75, 76
Unitarians (Italy), 38
United States, 109, 186, 248, 255; anarchists in, 63; and student revolutionaries, 90, 263; superiority of industrial power, 163; Vietnam War, 163–4, 167–8, 170, 171–2, 173; and threat of nuclear war by, 173–6; Cuban missile crisis, 174; civilian-military relations in, 179, 180; Third World policy of, 188–9, 190–1; Revolution in, 202, 203–4; violence in, 209, 213; and negro question, 221, 231–2, 248, 249; urban insurrections and, 223, 224, 231; and cultural revolt, 243–4
US Communist Party, 63, 135
US Democratic Party, 264
US National Commission of the Causes and Prevention of Violence, 209
universities, *see* students
urban insurrection, 80, 169–70, 220–33; *see also* May 1968 uprising
Uruguay, 187n
USPD (Germany), 49
utopianism, utopian communism, 89, 137–41, 144, 146, 207, 243, 247, 257

Value, Price and Profit (Marx), 104
Varga, Eugen, 252n
Venezuela, 189
Vidali, Vittorio, 34
Vienna, 221, 223 and n, 224, 226, 250, 251; *see also* Austria
Vietcong, 174, 175
Vietnam, guerrilla war in, 163–75 *passim*
Vietnamese Communist Party, 79

Vilar, Pierre, 73
violence, rules of, 209–15
Vogue, 216
Volpe, Galvano della, 147
voluntarism, 86, 87, 144, 154

Die Wandlung des deutschen Kommunismus (Weber), 43–4, 46
Warsaw Pact countries, 163
Washington, 224
Webb, Sidney and Beatrice, 122–3, 127, 150
Weber, Hermann, 43–4, 46–7, 48, 49–50, 54
Webster, Sir C. and Frankland, N., 9
Wellington, Duke of, 179
Wesley, John, 103
West Berlin, 230
West Germany (German Federal Republic), 43, 54, 63, 109, 137, 153, 230
What Is To Be Done? (Lenin), 123, 128
Why you should be a socialist (Strachey), 117n
Wurmser, André, 28

Yaroslavsky, E., 68–9
Yezhov, N., 35
'youth culture', concept of, 260
Yugoslav Communist Party, 30, 79
Yugoslavia, 16 and n, 71, 75, 133, 163, 167, 257

Zhukov, Marshal, 179
'Zimmerwald' current (1915–17), 19
Zinoviev, G. Y., 9, 10, 46, 48, 66, 67
Zionists, 251